Frederick Bracher

THE NOVELS OF James Gould Cozzens

GREENWOOD PRESS, PUBLISHERS
WESTPORT, CONNECTICUT

The Library of Congress has catalogued this publication as follows:

Library of Congress Cataloging in Publication Data

Bracher, Frederick George, 1905-
The novels of James Gould Cozzens.

Bibliography: p.
1. Cozzens, James Gould, 1903-
[PS3505.O99Z57 1972] 813'.5'2 72-6187
ISBN 0-8371-6448-6

Originally published in 1959
by Harcourt, Brace and Company, New York

Reprinted by arrangement
with Harcourt Brace Jovanovich, Inc.

First Greenwood Reprinting 1972

Library of Congress Catalogue Card Number 72-6187

ISBN 0-8371-6448-6

Printed in the United States of America

TO GEORGE BRACHER, M.D.

ACKNOWLEDGMENTS

I wish to thank those who have helped me get together material for this book: Richard M. Ludwig, of Princeton University; Howard T. Young, of Pomona College; Julien Michel, of the Honnold Library; and James B. Meriwether, who generously permitted me to draw upon his James Gould Cozzens check list. To Henry Nash Smith and Henry F. May, of the University of California at Berkeley, I am indebted for the stimulus of argument and for encouragement to pursue this project. I am especially grateful to my colleague Ray Frazer for a thorough and unsparing reading of the manuscript.

A travel grant from the West Coast Committee for the Humanities of the American Council of Learned Societies made possible some of the work incorporated in this book. The editors of *The Pacific Spectator* and *Critique* have kindly permitted me to use material originally printed in their pages. James Gould Cozzens and Brandt and Brandt have given permission to reprint selections from *Cock Pit*, *S.S. San Pedro*, and *Castaway*. To them, and to the publishers listed below, who have granted permissions to reprint copyright material, I am most grateful.

Harcourt, Brace and Company, Inc., and James Gould Cozzens. For permission to quote passages from the following books, all of which are copyrighted by James Gould Cozzens in the respective years shown: *The Last Adam*, copyright, 1933; *Men and Brethren*, copyright, 1936; *Ask Me Tomorrow*, copyright, 1940; *The Just and the Unjust*, copyright, 1942; *Guard of Honor*, copyright, 1948; *By Love Possessed* © 1957.

The Atlantic Monthly. For permission to quote from "Acceptance of the Nobel Prize," by Albert Camus.

Commentary. For permission to quote from "By Cozzens Possessed," by Dwight Macdonald.

Doubleday & Company, Inc. For permission to quote from *The American Novel and Its Tradition*, by Richard Chase.

Harper & Brothers. For permission to quote from *An American Dilemma*, by Gunnar Myrdal, and *An Interpretation of Christian Ethics*, by Reinhold Niebuhr.

William Morrow & Company, Inc. For permission to quote from *The Son of Perdition*, by James Gould Cozzens, copyright, 1929.

The New York Times Book Review. For permission to quote from "When the Angry Men Grow Older," by Stephen Spender, and "The World of Arthur Winner, Jr.," by Malcolm Cowley.

The Princeton University Library Chronicle. For permission to quote from "A Reading of the James Gould Cozzens Manuscripts," by Richard M. Ludwig.

Random House. For permission to quote from *Go Down, Moses and Other Stories*, by William Faulkner, copyright 1941 by William Faulkner.

The Viking Press, Inc. For permission to quote from *The Liberal Imagination*, by Lionel Trilling.

CONTENTS

I

THE NOVELIST

Throughout the 1930's and 1940's James Gould Cozzens was virtually ignored by literary critics and historians. Seven of the eight novels that he now acknowledges were published between 1931 and 1948, but it was not until 1949, after *Guard of Honor* had been awarded the Pulitzer prize, that the first full-length critical article appeared. Stanley Edgar Hyman's pioneering essay, despite its occasional eccentricities, was a remarkably perceptive and comprehensive study which might have been expected to stimulate further criticism. By 1957, however, only three more essays had appeared. For the writer of seven novels comparable to the best produced in America since 1930, this was scanty recognition indeed; and the obscurity to which Cozzens had been relegated by critical neglect was made official in 1948 when the three-volume Spiller-Thorp *Literary History of the United States*, though giving respectful attention to Archie Binns, Kenneth Roberts, and Albert Halper, made no mention whatever of James Gould Cozzens.

His record of continuing achievement proved that he could survive critical neglect, but the publication of *By Love Possessed* raised in acute form the question whether his reputation, by 1957 at least respectable, could withstand a belated sudden blare of acclaim. Critics who ignore a writer are innocuous enough, but who shall save a man from the excesses and exaggerations of his friends? Now that the shouting has died down a little, *By Love Possessed* seems neither so superlatively good as was claimed by reviewers such as Brendan Gill or John Fischer, nor so bad as was charged when the reaction set in. In the course of their violent attacks on the novel, Dwight Macdonald and Irving Howe revealed that a good part of their hostility was directed at the "middlebrow" reviewers who had praised the book excessively and were thought to be using it in defense of middle-class values. It seems probable, too, that the antagonism a few months later of some British reviewers was initially aroused by the jacket of the English edition, which carried excerpts from the most intemperately enthusiastic American reviews.

There is a curious paradox in the bitterness of the critical warfare that followed the publication of this book. For thirty years Cozzens had carefully avoided publicity and the exploitation of his personal life. He had scrupulously refrained from magisterial pronouncements on life and letters and had kept himself apart from the ideological warfare raging among critics and writers in the thirties and forties. During this period he had applied himself with complete dedication to the novelist's main business: defining in character and action his own view of human life and values. The violent attacks that rewarded this exemplary minding of one's own business afford a glimpse of the latent resentments seething behind the dignified front of the world of letters, and the whole episode may provide another demonstration of the ancient truth that, if enough people join in calling Aristides "the just," Aristides is in for trouble, no matter what his actual merits may be.

In any case the concentration of heat, and a little light, on this one book was unfortunate in that it distracted attention from the *body* of Cozzens' work. It is on this body of novels, with their steady growth in technical skill, psychological richness, and moral depth, that the writer's ultimate position in literary history must depend. The eight novels published since 1931 include at least four that are of major importance by any set of standards, and taken as a whole the Cozzens novels constitute a record of continuing achievement matched in our time only by Faulkner and Hemingway. The judgment implicit in such a comparison obviously cannot be proved; it can only be recorded, with a due recognition of the potential fallacy inherent in any attempt to compare unlike things. Fortunately, the precise degree of a writer's excellence is not so important as the nature of his excellence. In the house of art there are many mansions, and while it is certainly essential to decide whether or not a writer is to be admitted, the rough initial evaluation which determines that a writer is good enough to be taken seriously may well be followed by an effort to see precisely what kind of excellence he has. One way of doing this is to examine the limitations imputed to him by critics and reviewers. No novelist can be all kinds of novelist at once, and marking out the boundaries of the field in which Cozzens' excellences appear may be a means of defining also his unique quality.

Perhaps the most serious charge against him, in the eyes of either neo-Marxist or existentialist critics, is his apparent lack of personal commitment. Though full of ideas, the novels present no ideology. At a time when violent social conflicts might seem to force a writer to consider the dynamics and direction of American society and to take a firm stand on one side or another, Cozzens has remained a spectator rather than a partisan. Moreover, his analysis of society—highly intellectual by comparison with that of Hemingway or Faulkner—is not based on the coherent framework of organized abstract doctrine, "general and inclusive," that distinguishes ideology and the political novel. Cozzens' thinking is empirical and eclectic; he follows his sense of experienced reality rather than any abstract pattern of ideas. Accordingly, although he deals with politicians and his books may have political implications, he is not in Irving Howe's sense a political novelist. Instead he belongs to the line of social novelists, headed by Jane Austen, who enjoy "the luxury of being able to take society for granted." Whether any serious novelist can today afford this luxury may be debatable. Cozzens nevertheless does take society for granted, and writes about it as though its gradations were static and permanent. "Social change

—the essential dynamism of American society and one of the central themes of American literature—is seldom more than a vague, troubling background to his stories. Without showing a . . . nostalgia for the old days, he evinces an obvious dislike of the new." His preference for setting his stories in old, established eastern small towns enables him to utilize the historical dimension in picturing modern man, and his protagonists are not confronted with unique contemporary problems, but are shown struggling with the perennial old ones.

To the critic who thinks of literature in terms of its social effect, a consistent ideology is essential in a novelist; the lack of it relegates a writer to the trifling role of entertainer or innocent bystander. But critical attempts to evaluate writers on ideological grounds have not, in the past, been notably successful; it might even be argued that a lack of ideology, in the strict dogmatic sense, is a condition of real literary excellence. There are more things in heaven and earth than are dreamed of in a consistent philosophy. If the chief business of a novelist is to record what he can see of the infinite variety of human experience, it would seem wise to abjure the color filter of abstract doctrine. Cozzens' view of human life is limited by his temperament—"the struck balance of his ruling desires, the worked-out sum of his habitual predispositions"—but he does not further limit it, artificially, by putting on the blinders of ideology.

Nevertheless, by comparison with most of his contemporaries Cozzens is a highly intellectual novelist. One of his special gifts is a talent for subtle, articulate interpretation—as when Arthur Winner, between two remarks in a conversation, runs over in his mind before answering Mrs. Pratt his low-keyed "feelings of mildly exasperating entanglement, of faint distaste, of half-baffled incredulity, of vague consternation." The analysis occupies almost four pages and ranges from a doubt that he may have underestimated his opponent to a consideration of her creed's "emotional murk of mysteries and dreams," to a long meditation on the solace that the Catholic Church offers its converts (including freedom from guilt when the flesh rebels) to a realization of Mrs. Pratt's unconscious pleasure in having aroused—with the best intentions of course—sensuous imaginings in her auditor, to a final description of the dismay with which he becomes aware that Mrs. Pratt is leading around to a discussion of his own sexual experiences. No summary can do justice to the subtlety of the analysis or the articulate richness of its expression. This constant sense of the author's intelligence brooding over his characters, this full intellectual grasp of his material, is Cozzens' outstanding excellence. As Dr. Johnson said of Burke, "His stream of mind is perpetual."

Recognizing this quality, some critics have regarded it as a fault and have deplored Cozzens' lack of emotional involvement with his characters. The charge has some descriptive validity, though it is not at all certain that the aesthetic distance he maintains from his characters is necessarily a fault. He depicts human behavior from the vantage point of Addison's Spectator—a little removed from the follies and misadventures he describes, critical yet sympathetic. Although Cozzens professes an especial admiration for Swift, he seems to have more in common with Addison's endeavor to enliven morality with wit and to temper wit with morality than with Swift's indiscriminate lashing of man's pride.

Cozzens has frequently been described as "conservative," and in some of its senses the term is justified, as John Lydenberg has shown. Prominent in the novels is the assumption that duty and accomplishment are more important than enjoyment or happiness. Moreover, Cozzens' doubts of the possibility of progress, his disbelief in human perfectibility, his preference for liberty and diversity rather than equality and conformity, and his respect for traditional values embodied in a settled, stratified social order are conservative traits. Cozzens distrusts the simplistic habit of mind that resolves social complexity into the elementary stereotypes around which liberal and revolutionary enthusiasms concentrate. He has a high degree of "sensitivity to the institutional side of life," reflected in his sympathetic pictures of the Army, the clergy, and the law; and he displays a "profound respect for the responsible citizens who actually make our civilization work."

In Richard Chase's terms, Cozzens writes "novels" rather than "romances." His work belongs to the tradition of *Middlemarch*, with its "temperate, moralistic rendering of life and thought," rather than to the tradition that exploits, as in *Moby Dick*, "the profound poetry of disorder." In Chase's terms the novel, a product of the English tradition, is "notable for its great practical sanity. . . . absorbing all extremes, all maladjustments and contradictions into a normative view of life." The romance—typically American—has exploited, from Hawthorne to Faulkner, "the aesthetic possibilities of radical forms of alienation, contradiction, and disorder." Like Henry James, Cozzens combines some elements of both traditions, but he inclines markedly toward the normative tradition of the novel.

Stephen Spender in discussing Britain's "angry young men" distinguishes between anger, which "contains within it the seed of reconciliation, when the basis of irritation is removed," and protest. "Protest is based on objections which are not subjective. It derives from values that are rooted in personal relationships, social conscience, and an awareness of the continuity of a past which is critical of almost everything in modern life." Although Cozzens is not in any sense an angry man, he is a stubborn protestant. We do not need Julius Penrose, noting in passing that "this age is cheap, this age is maudlin" and that "sentimentality is now nearly everyone's at least private indulgence," to make explicit Cozzens' protest against modern society. All the novels contribute to a formidable indictment of the cheapness and vulgarity that seem inseparable from mass culture. Cozzens protests against a "liberal" church which substitutes personal adjustment for worship and encourages self-satisfaction instead of humility. He attacks the self-indulgence, product of a weakened sense of personal responsibility, which leads to juvenile delinquency and adult infantilism; the moral complacency which protects the genteel from reality; the failures of discrimination and taste exemplified in the "gilded swill" offered by mass media of entertainment; the dwindling of a sense of honor among people only concerned to get their share. Nevertheless, despite his admiration for Swift, Cozzens does not share Swift's misanthropy; his attack is aimed, not at man, but at the things men do. "The sentence . . . is on the act, not the person."

In his protest against the vulgarizing of sensibility Cozzens resembles Henry James, and there are other similarities. It is remarkable, for example, how closely he observes the precepts set down in James's Prefaces. Relevant here is the concern to make the hero "an eminent instance of our own conscious kind," not "a morbidly special case." Whereas Fitzgerald's heroes strive for the unique, ineffable experience and by the strength of their aspiration sway a reader's sympathy toward the romantic quest for the unobtainable, the central figures of Cozzens' novels lead normal workaday lives and are more apt to renounce even those modest satisfactions sometimes available in ordinary life than to try to pluck bright honor from the pale-faced moon. If they are not precisely common men, they are at least conscious representatives of the modes of life in the classes to which they belong; and their solid, tangible reality gives force to Cozzens' analysis of the upper levels of American society.

In a literary sense, too, Cozzens might be called conservative, or even neoclassic. He is interested in situations rather than processes; his plots, limited by the unities of time, place, and action, define a dramatic present instead of tracing an evolutionary development. Cozzens seems to be one of those writers who find limitations, whether self-imposed or traditional, stimulating rather than stultifying. For the most part his style is lucid and direct; he makes no use of the "system of screens and obstacles" that Harvey Breit attributes to Faulkner—a method which requires that the story be "dredged up, fragment by fragment" out of a welter of jumbled times and places and persons. Cozzens' style is precisely articulate, even in those occasional passages that resound with a deliberate Victorian magniloquence. Such rhetorical flourishes are consciously artificial, and along with the quotations and allusions woven into the texture of the later novels, their ironic contrasts provide incidental commentaries on contemporary life. They also serve, at moments of emotional pressure, as a defensive device, holding the reader off at arm's length. To anyone with Cozzens' avowed distaste for the unbuttonings and letting down of hair so dear to the sentimentalist, the degree of intimacy between writer and reader encouraged by Whitman or Sherwood Anderson would be felt as excessive and unseemly.

The tone of Cozzens' writing is, in Richard Ellmann's words, "detached, . . . cool, disenchanted, a little superior." If at times it seems also a little arrogant, at least it avoids the disdain of the convert, smug and secure in his fanatical commitment to some cause. What appears in Cozzens, rather, is the mild arrogance of self-respect often observable in men who, like Julius Penrose and

Abner Coates, judge themselves by stricter standards than those they tolerate in other people. The tone is appropriate to the principal characters in the novels, who are usually superior in competence to the masses and intelligent enough to recognize the fact, though too sensible to proclaim it in a society that is largely other-directed. The opinion that a man is superior, Colonel Ross reflects, can only be decent when other people hold it, and Abner Coates, in *The Just and the Unjust*, has taken pains to conceal "that moderate yet essentially jealous ambition, that egotism of confidence in one's ability and one's resulting right, which can never be shown safely, since it intrenches on every other man's ego."

But the fact is inescapable that some men are more competent than others. While it may be indecent to proclaim one's own superiority, it would be folly for a novelist to ignore the differences in ability inherent in men. In concerning himself primarily with the more able members of society Cozzens avoids a failing pointed out by Lionel Trilling: "The literature of our liberal democracy pets and dandles its underprivileged characters, and, quite as if it had the right to do so, forgives them what faults they may have." Cozzens seems to feel a good deal of sympathy for the less competent members of society, but compassion does not blind him to the gap separating the highly gifted from the handicapped. Accordingly, though he understands the masses, he never romanticizes them.

Instead of joining uncritically in praise of the American egalitarian ideal, Cozzens makes a serious effort to define and embody the ideal configuration of the gentleman, which E. H. Cady has shown to be a dominant and fruitful theme in American literature. The Cozzens heroes belong to the group of natural aristocrats which Jefferson and John Adams finally agreed in hoping for: men who are fitted for leadership not merely by hereditary position or wealth, but by natural endowment and liberal education. Whether born to privilege and status or not, Cozzens' heroes cultivate what native gifts they may have, and in this respect they continue the Renaissance tradition of the gentleman, derived ultimately from Aristotle and Cicero.

Aristotle's "character" of the magnanimous man, echoed in the courtesy books of four centuries, may repel members of a mass society in an age of sophisters, economists, and calculators, when the art of pleasing others is the chief means of self-advancement. It is, nevertheless, a fairly accurate picture of the Cozzens hero.

> Now, the magnanimous man appears to be he who, being really worthy, estimates his own worth highly. . . . and acts with propriety on subjects of honour and dishonour. . . . In wealth and power, and all good and bad fortune, however it may come to pass, he will behave with moderation: and not be too much delighted at success, nor too much grieved at failure. . . . [The magnanimous man] may have the appearance of superciliousness. . . . : he feels contempt justly, for he forms his opinions truly. . . . [He] neither shuns nor is fond of danger. . . . but when he does run any risk, he is unsparing of his life, thinking that life is not worth having on some terms. . . . Again, it is charac-

teristic of the magnanimous man to ask no favours, or very few, of anybody, but to be willing to serve others; and towards men of rank or fortune to be haughty in his demeanour, but to be moderate towards men of middle rank . . . for to be [haughty] amongst persons of humble rank is bad taste, just like making a show of strength to the weak. . . . He must also necessarily be open in his hatreds and his friendships; for concealment is the part of a man who is afraid. He must care more for truth than for opinion. He does not recollect injuries. . . . but he rather overlooks them. He is apt to possess rather what is honourable and unfruitful, than what is fruitful and useful; for this shows more self-sufficiency. The step of the magnanimous man is slow, his voice deep, and his language stately.

Aristotle's character sketch has no more warmth than the statue of a Roman senator, but the ideal of conduct it implies has a grave nobility which can still excite our admiration. We may not love Arthur Winner or Colonel Ross or Martin Bunting or Ernest Cudlipp, but we respect them. Their sober virtue is not employed as a means to an end; its value is intrinsic. The mild arrogance of self-respect appears in Abner Coates' explanation of why he'd like to do what is right.

"Jesse told me your Senator Perkins said you wouldn't worry so much about what people were thinking of you if you remembered that most of the time they weren't. . . . Does he mean that most of the time there's nobody looking, so you can do what you want? I don't give a damn whether anybody is looking or not. I'm looking. I care whether I look like a louse. Certainly I care what people think of me. They may only do it for ten seconds once in ten years, but I still care."

The tradition of magnanimity is essentially pagan and, despite the high value it places upon personal honor, may well seem coldly selfish to anyone brought up in the moral tradition of Christianity. Certainly it undervalues humility, and in this respect the Cozzens hero departs from the Aristotelian ideal. In the novels the basic magnanimity of the central characters is modified by an increasing humbleness in the face of the contingencies of human existence. One evidence of it is an increasing tolerance in the later novels for contradictory ideas, a practice of balancing alternatives by giving each man's views and values a fair hearing. Cozzens' basically Pyrrhonistic habit of mind appears both in his distrust of absolutes and in his custom of stating both sides of a case without committing himself to a final explicit evaluation. The problems raised in the novels, like those in real life, are usually insoluble if regarded in simple terms of right and wrong. When circumstances force a hero to an overt decision, the result is apt to be some kind of compromise, and the necessity for adapting principle to particular occasions is a common theme of the later novels. But for the most part Cozzens does not try to solve problems; he defines them in all their concrete complexity. In this respect he displays something like the ability to rest "in uncertainties, mysteries, doubts" which Keats called "negative capability"; and while it may seem unsatisfactory to the dogmatic or naïve, this habit of increasing the tension by balancing alternatives is a major source of power in the novels.

It is also the justification for calling Cozzens primarily

a moral writer. Intensely American in his distrust of arbitrary authority, he shares the Protestant reliance on the moral judgment of the individual. He attacks the Communists partly because he does not share their Utopian hopes, but mainly because he dislikes their arrogant dogmatism and finds their methods mechanical and inhuman. Cozzens is not an authoritarian moralist in any sense; he neither accepts unconditionally the morality of the past nor hands down a new set of moral commandments of his own. But throughout the novels he wrestles incessantly with particular problems of right and wrong in all their ambiguous complexity. And during three decades of ideological struggle he has preserved the humanist's equable willingness—having carefully examined the alternatives—to settle for the better rather than the unattainable best. Cozzens' moral posture is suggested by the introductory description of Arthur Winner, his head "at a reflective angle . . . as though he scanned, scrutinous and unhurried, the middle distance." The Hellenism of the attitude, though widely unpopular among contemporary Hebraists, justifies itself at a time when man's ability to give up partisanship and develop habits of tolerance and forbearance seems to be a condition of survival.

In the earliest critical survey of Cozzens, Stanley Edgar Hyman especially stressed "a vivid and pulsing sense of reality" based on the writer's "uncompromising honesty," and this characteristic has been recognized by most subsequent critics. Cozzens is a conscious realist. In a letter written in 1934 he said, "I simply put down, when

I write, what the things I have seen and known look like to me." And in 1949, speaking of his "intense aversion to what seems . . . false and maudlin," he says, "I could not write with pleasure and certainly not with conviction what did not seem to me real or true." Cozzens' novels demonstrate this effort to represent human life as it is rather than as it ought to be, and his heroes join in a common message: Fancy's feasts may gratify the young or the sentimental, but a responsible adult must confront dispassionately and without illusion the factual situation. "The only wisdom worth having," declares a character in the earliest novel, *Confusion*, "is that which the equipped mind derives from experience"; and this Lockean pronouncement, with its dismissal of intuition and the wisdom of the heart, is representative of the epistemology of all the later novels.

Moreover, the experience of the individual is continually shown as being affected by society. A person becomes aware of himself only through his contacts, often bruisingly unpleasant, with other people, and a large part of what happens to him is determined by chains of social cause and effect that he cannot be aware of and hence cannot change or modify. Cozzens does not go to the extremes of the naturalist school. Although he analyzes exhaustively the determining causes of critical events, his characters are not shown as the victims of a strict mechanistic determinism. They act as though they had free will, and their choices seem to them, and to the reader, to be morally significant. Unlike the cross section of life depicted by such a naturalist as Dos Passos, Cozzens' picture of society is selective, and by choosing the *aristoi* as his principal subject matter he tends to increase our awareness of the upper ranges of human possibilities. In this respect the novels share the classical aim of establishing an ideal of human behavior, without ignoring contemporary man's falling away from the ideal.

Despite his radical pessimism, Cozzens' sensibility is moral rather than tragic. Instead of relinquishing themselves to inevitable defeat his heroes are shown exercising their reason in the hope of staving off, to whatever degree is possible, the disasters of life. Cozzens' sense of vicissitude and mortality is poignant, but the feeling that dominates his novels is not tragic acceptance, but regretful "compunction . . . for the human predicament." He has no illusions about the permanence of such happiness as man occasionally achieves; "in Cozzens' world, chaos is always threatening to break out." It may sometimes be controlled by the exercise of reason, but we are continually reminded of two potential, ever-present sources of disorder. One is the inescapable, tangled network of cause and effect, in both the physical and the social worlds, which operates without our knowledge to determine a large part of what will happen to us. The other source is psychological: passions spin the plot and we are betrayed by what is false within. All men are in some sense possessed by love; accordingly, to certain mortality and always potential external disaster must be added the disorders that follow when passion and reason become self-division's cause. But these disorders and disasters do not lead to tragedy; the feeling underlying the novels is moral urgency rather than tragic catharsis. Some of man's ills, Cozzens reiterates, can be avoided or prevented, and one way of avoiding them is to understand their causes: the dark drives of the human spirit and the complexities of an imperfect, and imperfectible, society.

Cozzens' novels represent a serious effort to understand and recreate an important segment of American society. The tone is at once ironic and sympathetic, the structure is perspicuous, and the writing for the most part is lucid and polished. The kind of novel Cozzens writes is, to be sure, only one of many kinds, and the class to which it belongs and the virtues it possesses have not been highly esteemed in the critical contention of our time. The average novel-reader has been discouraged by the lack of romance and sentimental sweetening. More sophisticated readers, misled by the absence of fashionable literary techniques, have often underestimated Cozzens' achievement. To the reader interested in life rather than exhibitions of a writer's exotic sensibility, Cozzens offers a scrupulously honest report of American society as seen by a detached, highly perceptive observer. It is somewhat old-fashioned fare, but nourishing. The best of Cozzens' works are evidence that the traditional social novel, with its high seriousness and moral urgency, is still viable in a period of experiment and disorder.

2

THE EARLY NOVELS

Of Cozzens' twelve published novels only the last eight are listed opposite the title page of *By Love Possessed.* The four earliest novels—*Confusion,* 1924; *Michael Scarlett,* 1925; *Cock Pit,* 1928; and *The Son of Perdition,* 1929—are the kind of youthful experiment for which most writers are fortunate enough not to find a publisher. All four books seem confused in intention and weak in structure, but they show nevertheless a real gift for phrasing and a sharp eye for significant detail. No one of them could be called successful, but taken together they represent a remarkable achievement for a man in his early twenties.

Cozzens' characteristic firm style and achieved purpose appear first in the novelette *S.S. San Pedro* (1931). *The Last Adam* (1933) is transitional; it is the final, best expression of some of the interests and values embodied in the earlier novels, but also the first full-length example of the writer's mature manner and subject matter. *Castaway,* which appeared a year later in 1934, is completely atypical. Its subject matter, the murky heart of darkness in all men, and its experimental, Kafkaesque technique set it apart from all the other books. Many critics would place it among Cozzens' best works, but despite its undeniable brilliance it is a tour de force, exploring a vein which Cozzens chose not to follow further. Accordingly I shall discuss it, at some length, along with the earlier novels.

The five major and characteristic novels are *Men and Brethren*, 1933; *Ask Me Tomorrow*, 1940; *The Just and the Unjust*, 1942; *Guard of Honor*, 1948; and *By Love Possessed*, 1957. All five novels are centered on a professional man's working life, presented in accurate detail and with an abundance of good shoptalk. *Men and Brethren*, an account of a weekday in the life of an Episcopal priest, was praised by clergymen for its realistic picture of clerical life. *Ask Me Tomorrow* is to some degree autobiographical, and its portrait of the writer as a young man is appealingly familiar. Zechariah Chaffee, Jr., reviewing *The Just and the Unjust*, recommended the novel to every beginning law student as an accurate picture of the life of a lawyer. *Guard of Honor* was submitted in manuscript to an Air Force general in order to eliminate errors of fact, and he is said to have found none. *By Love Possessed* accurately recreates the everyday life of professional men in a small Delaware Valley community—a clergyman, a doctor, a judge, and several attorneys.

Underlying all the major novels is a basic moral principle: men must learn to adapt both their desires and their principles to the irresistible forces of circumstance. The principal conflict in the novels is internal and psychological; the problem is to reconcile the discrepancy between the ideal and the possible. The heroes solve the problem in a variety of ways, but a condition of any answer appears to be the reaching of a new stage in the long process of maturing.

Men and Brethren offers as a solution a more or less orthodox Christian belief in the providence of God. *Ask Me Tomorrow*, a curiously negative book, gives a negative answer: pride is an obstacle and overcoming it a necessary, if not sufficient, condition of maturity. *The Just and the Unjust* stresses the importance of a reason which is reasonable enough to recognize both the necessity of an inflexible system of law and the need occasionally to modify it in the interest of justice. *Guard of Honor* stresses the point that inevitable concessions to circumstance do not, as the immature or romantic may imagine, necessarily negate the validity or importance of the ideal; and it builds up the notion of moral responsibility as the source and guard of what honor there is in life. *By Love Possessed*, presenting a variety of conflicts between passion and reason, tries to draw the fine line between the freedom which alone dignifies a man and the necessity which limits him in his choices.

Although primarily concerned with moral problems, Cozzens is not given to outright moralizing. Despite the lengthy comments on the action inherent in the talk and speculations of the principal characters, Cozzens accurately describes his practice in a letter written in 1950;

he rejects "tracts or theses" and insists, "I mean to make what points I can in action." For the intelligent and articulate characters of whom he writes, "action" includes what is thought and what is said. By unobtrusively directing the reader's sympathy toward some of these characters, Cozzens embodies his moral values in the heroes. The novels thus fill the ancient traditional function of providing models of behavior; and they enrich sensibility by showing men not only how to act, but how to feel.

The heroes who reflect Cozzens' moral sensibility have a good many traits in common. In the later novels they are matured, responsible, decent members of the upper middle class, neither romantic rebels against society nor visionaries who believe they can cure the troubles of our proud and angry dust. Their epitome is Colonel Ross in *Guard of Honor*, a mature man in both years and experience, who exercises in a position of authority and responsibility the virtues of good taste, self-control, and rational judgment. But the disciplined man of reason has not always held the center of Cozzens' moral stage. In the early novels the central figures are active rebels, fighting authority in its various forms and protesting against the iniquities of society and the condition of man. A vestigial remnant of the type appears as late as 1933 in Doctor Bull of *The Last Adam*. Gradually the dissatisfied, rebellious hero grows into the controlled, resigned protagonist who first appears in *Men and Brethren*. The process of evolution by which the hot protestant against authority changes into the mature hero who adapts to the unremitting constraint of circumstance can be traced in a survey of the early novels.

The two earliest, *Confusion* (1924) and *Michael Scarlett* (1926), have similar heroes and a common theme: a glittering, accomplished youth, at odds with society, is finally defeated by a world which does not measure up to the standards he demands. These novels are romantic not only in their glorification of the aristocratic rebel, but in their richly sensuous decor and sympathetic picture of romantic love. Both suggest that a major literary influence on Cozzens when he began to write was the Fitzgerald of *This Side of Paradise*.

Cerise d'Atrée, the heroine of *Confusion*, is descended from a noble French family so ancient that their part in the Hundred Years' War is a relatively modern instance of patriotic service going back to the eighth-century struggle against the Moors. She is the perfect exemplification of "good blood well trained"—rich, beautiful, talented, and accomplished. An extended tour of the more glamorous sections of the Mediterranean and, by way of a New England school for girls, the Fitzgerald country from Park Avenue to Long Island, leaves her untouched and dissatisfied. There is no need to trace the improbable series of events that culminates in her death in an auto wreck. What is significant is the initial picture of a girl who has everything: masculine courage, strength, and opportunity; feminine charm and sensitivity; intelligence, wealth, and social position. She reappears, in a minor role, as Lady Ann Shelton of *Michael Scarlett*, and finally as Ruth Micks of *Cock Pit*.

The second novel displays her masculine counterpart, Michael Scarlett, the future Lord Dunbury. Expert in languages and courtesy and formidable in manly accomplishments, Michael is an apotheosis of the Elizabethan perfect gentleman. His adventures at the court of Queen Elizabeth and with the rowdy university wits—Marlowe, Nashe, Ben Jonson, and Donne—make up a loosely organized story which centers on a conflict of loyalties in Michael's heart. Apparently basic in Cozzens' view of life, it is the conflict between law and the human sense of justice, between duty and love, between reason and feeling. As a loyal subject Michael has an obligation to serve the Queen—that is, to support the struggling forces of law and order which Elizabeth was so carefully nurturing. As romantic lover, he has an obligation to serve his lady, who is being used by the Queen in an attempt to separate Michael from his riotous companions. But as friend and patron, Michael feels an intense loyalty—originally inspired by the magnificent Spanish youth he had tried to rescue after the defeat of the Armada—toward the roistering writers who live under his protection at the Golden Asse, especially the surly, talented Marlowe and the ambitious, scheming Nashe. In the end he defies the Queen's orders in an effort to protect his friends and is killed in an heroic fight against great odds.

Though the principal theme of the book is the conflict of responsibilities, a secondary theme recalls Cerise d'Atrée. Michael can find nothing to do worthy of his potential magnanimity. Though a friend of Southampton and Essex, he is too young to be entrusted with a command or diplomatic mission, and he goes through a period of deep frustration in which politics seems to be mere squabbling between rival factions divided by personal dislike instead of significant issues; literature seems either ornate frivolity or a mere political weapon; and even love is reduced to an affair in a summerhouse with the wife of a wealthy merchant. Cerise and Michael, magnificently unprepared for the long littleness of life, are cut off from a vital part in society by their high birth, youth, and sensitivity—a predicament not unlike that of the young writer hero of *Ask Me Tomorrow.*

Although *Confusion* and *Michael Scarlett* are very immature performances, they foreshadow the later novels in several important ways. Both are vivid, carefully researched and documented pictures of a society at a particular time. Cerise's tour of fashionable centers gave the young Cozzens a chance to demonstrate his knowledge of how the rich and well-born lived before and during World War I; and although the account is a little snobbish—ostentatiously filled with the lore of wines, food, dress, and decor—it anticipates the detailed picture of upper middle-class life that distinguishes *By Love Possessed. Michael Scarlett*, despite its unfortunate archaic style, is a vivid recreation of an historical period. By an impressive imaginative effort, the twenty-year-old Cozzens managed to breathe life into his panorama of England at one of its most glittering periods. The scene shifts from a lonely castle on the Yorkshire coast to Cambridge, with its dissipations and town-and-gown riotings, and finally to London, from court to brothel, with lively sketches of the rioting in the theaters, the bustle of Paul's yard, drinking in alehouses, duels, bear-baiting, the terrors of the plague, and the animosity of the Puritans.

Both *Confusion* and *Michael Scarlett* are concerned chiefly with the upper classes, and this interest in the *aristoi*, which runs through all but one of Cozzens' later books, takes a new turn in his next two novels. In the mid-twenties Cozzens lived for a time in central Cuba as tutor to the children of an American executive in a sugar mill. Both *Cock Pit* (1928) and *The Son of Perdition* (1929) make use of Cuban background, and the new type of hero suggests that the brutal, colorful life of the sugar plantations was eye-opening to a youth whose picture of life must have been formed largely by private schools and Harvard. In place of the courtly exquisites of the first two books the Cuban novels glorify the strong, ruthless, durable individual who, unhampered by scruples of taste or conscience, devotes himself with undivided mind to the exercise of power. The fighting cock is a symbol of the unrelenting aggressiveness of American engineers and executives battling in the cock pit of central Cuba, while the natives watch from the side lines. Such men are antisocial in the sense that they fight to preserve their own rights even when serving the Company, and the outstanding example is Lancy Micks, the field engineer in *Cock Pit.*

Micks is a stubborn, crude, violent man, whose honesty and strength Cozzens clearly admired. Like the fighting cock, he is the embodiment of pugnacious, self-sufficient masculinity. He holds out against the great machine that is the Company, and by his insistence on making an honest report defeats some elaborate chicanery planned by his superiors. Micks is a kind of noble savage; his revolt is motivated, not by theory or principle, but by a sense of pride and honor. He reappears, his surly independence and scorn of pretense only slightly toned down, as Doctor George Bull in *The Last Adam.* The fighting-cock type of man also recurs, though not in a sympathetic light, in Benny Carricker of *Guard of Honor* and Warren Winner of *By Love Possessed*—both, significantly, fighter pilots.

Lancy Micks has a daughter who, like Cerise d'Atrée and Lady Ann Shelton, has every gift—beauty, position, intelligence, charm. But she also demonstrates a male hardness and determination of will, which reappear in considerably modified form in later competent, half-masculine heroines such as Clarissa Winner and Bonnie Drummond. In *Cock Pit* Ruth Micks displays masculine competence to an almost alarming degree: she arranges a kidnaping, supervises the torture of the Mexican killer who has been hired to shoot her father, and uses the information he finally divulges to defeat the plans of the great Don Miguel. She is sharply contrasted with the soft and sensitive Cuban gentleman who courts her and with the ineffectual son of Don Miguel. The only fit mate for her is her father, and the hint of incest is made explicit in *The Son of Perdition*, where an important point of the plot turns on an incestuous relation between brother and sister. The sensational subject matter suggests a youthful delight in shocking the reader and may anticipate the violence—rape, abortion, adultery, madness, suicide, and murder—which in the later novels contrasts so sharply with Cozzens' low-keyed method of telling a story.

The two Cuban novels introduce another theme that is prominent in Cozzens' later books: the importance of a man's work. The vast holdings of the United Sugar Company run from the cane fields and mills of the interior to the sea terminal of the railroads at Dosfuegos, and the entire life of the interlocked communities is controlled by the seasonal rhythm of harvesting and processing the crop of sugar cane. In addition to a detailed picture of the operation of a mill—even down to the technical minutiae of tests made by a young American chemist—we are given some understanding of the network of economic control and government corruption which makes the whole operation possible. The overriding loyalty is to the job. The engineers may fight the Company, as Micks does, but no engineer will sabotage the work that is the justification for his existence. When the crop is ripe, it must be got in. "One does not wear one's life out for sixteen years learning the sacred meaning of that word 'crop' and discard its traditions and obligations so easily." The responsibilities of professional skill are stressed in most of the later novels: seamanship in *S.S. San Pedro*, the practice of medicine in *The Last Adam*, the ministry of God in *Men and Brethren*, military duty in *Guard of Honor*, the administration of law and justice in *The Just and the Unjust* and *By Love Possessed*. The expert, set apart from the masses by his competence, has a self-imposed but imperative obligation not to do shoddy work; getting the job done supersedes all other values. For the early Cozzens hero, role is more significant than personality.

The fighting-cock hero reappears in the second Cuban novel, *The Son of Perdition*, but he has changed sides. He is no longer the rebel but has become the godlike man in authority who keeps the whole machine running. Mr. Joel Stellow, Chief of Cuban Operations and Administrator General of the United Sugar Company, shows in his behavior "the strong impersonality and intelligent ruthlessness of which all great men are made." He is a kind of father-image—omniscient, strong, and stern—representing and wielding the enormous power of the far-flung Company. The rebel against his authority is no longer the crude but admirable Lancy Micks. Now he is the "son of perdition," Oliver Findley, a ne'er-do-well remittance man from a good New England family. He represents both Satan and Judas, and wherever he goes death follows. As Judas he betrays those who trust or help him, and in the end Stellow exiles him from Cuba. But before he leaves, his actions have compelled Stellow to violate his imperturbable, inhuman efficiency. Findley's revolt against the Company—"against the whole human world"—has partially restored the humanity of Stellow, who in his years with the Company has lost "the innocence of surprise, the thoughtlessness of anger, the humanness of any appetite" and become a stiff personification of authority. The theological implications of this almost allegorical figure will be considered later. But it is significant that in *The Son of Perdition* the rebel, the individual against society, is no longer an admirable figure, but like the rebels and reformers of the later novels is shown as evil, even though his intransigence has the unexpected effect of humanizing the tired God who had become "a Company instead of a person."

The tired God reappears in *S.S. San Pedro* (1931), no longer the dependable creator of order and source of security, but a victim of the steady attrition of age and mortality. Captain Clendening, master of the ill-fated *San Pedro*, is a kind of inversion of Joel Stellow; his role demands impersonal authority and decisive assurance, but he is sick in body and paralyzed in will, and his infirmities are mirrored in the progressive deterioration of the ship as it lists more and more dangerously to port. Cozzens took the outlines of his story from the accounts of the mysterious sinking of the *Vestris* on November 13, 1928. An investigation by the British Admiralty showed the probable cause of the list that eventually sank the ship to be an open coal door near the water line; but the inaction of the captain, who waited until it was too late before sending an S O S or giving an order to abandon ship, was noted and condemned as causing the needlessly large loss of life. Cozzens interprets the sinking as the result of an implacable, inexplicable fate, personified in Doctor Percival, a somewhat too obvious symbol of death. From the time when Doctor Percival, wearing overcoat and gloves even in the heat of the engine room, raises a doubt as to whether the turbines will always work when needed, it is clear that the ship, like its stricken skipper, is doomed. Discipline, the *tela* of which the Brazilian quartermaster is so proud, slowly disintegrates as the ship breaks up internally from the loose water rolling in her hull. Captain Clendening stubbornly insists on retaining his authority, though he is no longer able to wield it effectively; and the other officers, including the competent Mr. Bradell, cling with desperation to the empty framework of command, which, while it makes for a taut ship in good times, practically insures disaster when initiative and quick action are required.

The novels preceding *S.S. San Pedro* are all concerned in some way with attitudes toward a father-image; the important characters either rebel against authority or exemplify the calm, competent assurance of the man in charge. The scanty biographical detail available strengthens the guess that this early preoccupation with power and revolt reflects the young Cozzens' ambivalent attitude toward Father Sill, the head of Kent School. As "Doctor Holt" in a series of *Saturday Evening Post* stories dealing with "Durham School," the headmaster has two roles. In some of the stories he is the personification of authority against whom the more spirited students rebel, as Lancy Micks rebelled against the authority of the Company. In others, he is a beneficent father-figure whose mature wisdom straightens out every schoolboy problem. *S.S. San Pedro*, by emphasizing the limitations of the captain-father, points the moral that a man must give up his youthful dependence on the image of an omnipotent father, who inevitably turns out to be, not God, but an all-too-fallible human being.

The discovery that a father is only human is the point of a prize-winning short story published in 1936, "Total Stranger." The father in the story is a preliminary study for Judge Coates, Arthur Winner Senior, and Colonel Ross. He was "interested only in proved facts," he "could see no sense in breaking the simple, necessary rules of any organized society," and he "had the habit, half stoical, half insensitive, of making the best of anything there was." When the schoolboy narrator sees his father courting an old flame, met by chance at a country hotel, he sees him for the first time as a human being. "I could see, too, that he really hadn't changed. What he said and did was new to me, but not new to him." The story, in short, portrays a young boy's initiation into an adult attitude toward his parent, although it does not stress the weakness or incompetence of the father.

In the later novels the limitations of the father are increasingly apparent. Judge Coates is crippled by a stroke and relinquishes to his son the necessary, daily task of doing the impossible. Colonel Ross, anticipating a stroke if he does not slow down, has already accepted the secondary though essential role of picking up after his youthful senior officer, General Beal. Arthur Winner is no more able to protect the best interests of his son Warren than are two other frustrated parents, the angry Mr. Moore and the pathetically stupid Mr. Dummer. As the ordinary human fallibility of the father-image becomes increasingly apparent to a young man, the need for fighting it decreases. Rebellion becomes unnecessary, and the few rebels who appear in Cozzens' later books are shown—always in an unflattering light—as either immature and benighted or as the kind of frustrated emotional cripple epitomized in Lieutenant Edsell.

An exception is Doctor Bull of *The Last Adam* (1933), the final admirable exemplar in Cozzens' novels of the fighting-cock hero, likable, despite his faults, for his primitive qualities of independence, strength, and vitality. Doctor Bull resembles his animal namesake in violent, surly self-sufficiency. Unmarried and childless, though by no means chaste, he is the antithesis of the "social" man, temperamentally unfit to live in any group which he cannot dominate. A shrewdness born of long experience serves him as well as intelligence, and he is completely free of neurotic doubts or guilt reactions. He represents what psychologists call the "id": the violent, irrational, primal source of energy in man. Doctor Bull has, in bountiful measure, "something unkillable. Something here when the first men walked erect . . . a good greedy vitality . . . never quite fed full." We see him in a memorable picture sitting in the dark kitchen of a bare old farmhouse, like a caveman taking his ease. He is sixty-seven years old; he has just survived a rattlesnake bite, a typhoid epidemic, and a town meeting called to oust him from office. Now, danger temporarily over, he grunts comfortably in the heat from the fireplace and drinks whiskey with his mistress.

The Last Adam not only marks the final appearance of the early type of Cozzens hero, but introduces what is to be the principal subject matter of the later novels: American society. The village of New Winton, Connecticut, is an organism, a tight, closed system of interrelated energies. It is presented and analyzed in detail: social structure, mores, economy, government. Doctor Bull "belongs" by virtue of ancestry, but he is an outsider at heart, and the plot of the novel turns on his successful struggle against, and continued domination of, the rigid social patterns of a New England village. The rebel is still opposing society, but in *The Last Adam* he shares the center of the stage with the microcosm of New Winton—a society which, despite the virtues of some of its members, is as a whole narrow, selfish, and complacent. In the later novels society, with all its faults, is pictured as nevertheless providing the stability and order essential to any kind of good life, and the admirable men have learned to adapt to it instead of fighting it.

A transitional book in this progression of attitudes toward society is *Castaway* (1934). In this short novel society does not appear at all, but by a picture of one man's helpless inadequacy in solitude the book demonstrates our dependence on other men. *Castaway* is an experiment in allegorical fantasy unlike anything else Cozzens has written, but it is extraordinarily effective and compelling. An ambiguous, richly imaginative psychological ghost story, it leaves the reader with a haunting sense of significances just over the threshold of consciousness. The single character of the book, far from being a competent representative of the *aristoi*, is mediocre in both intelligence and sensibility; the theme developed by his isolated desperation is the alienation of modern man. Critics like Stanley Edgar Hyman and

Richard Ellmann, finding both technique and theme sympathetic, rate it high among Cozzens' works.

The action takes place in an enormous deserted department store, closed and locked. Mr. Lecky, as unexplained as the circumstances in which he finds himself, appears first in the basement of the store, with a ringing in his ears "like the last of a loud detonation or stupendous jar." He is listening, terrified, for sounds of pursuit, but there is only a deep and ominous silence. Noting that his watch shows a quarter past five, Mr. Lecky climbs to the main floor, arms himself with a butcher knife, and makes his way to the eighth floor in search of a gun. Here he builds himself a temporary refuge—a platform on top of the fitting cubicles in the sports clothing section. He notices that his watch, still showing a quarter past five, has stopped.

Next day he makes a fortified camp out of a lavatory on the ninth floor by piling furniture in a semicircle around the door. When he goes back to the grocery department on the sixth floor to bring up more food, he surprises an apelike figure feeding at the counter. The creature, apparently an idiot, advances despite warnings until Mr. Lecky, in desperation, fires his shotgun. There follows a gruesome hunt through the various levels of the store. Mr. Lecky locates his quarry by a naked footprint on the fourth floor, shoots and wounds the idiot, pursues him to the third floor, and after one narrow escape—the idiot almost steals the shotgun—at close range blows off one side of his enemy's face. But though mortally wounded, the idiot drags himself down to the main floor. Mr. Lecky, despairing of helping him and horrified by his suffering, cuts his throat and drags the body into the basement.

Secure now, for the noise of shooting would surely have roused anyone else in the store, Mr. Lecky sets about enjoying the wealth of his private kingdom. But he finds himself uneasy and dissatisfied, and he is terrified by the sporadic, mysterious ringing of a huge electric bell on a pillar on the main floor. His will to choose paralyzed by an embarrassment of riches, he is haunted by the feeling that, time being short, any particular choice he may make among the riches of the store will rule out even more desirable possibilities. Eventually he settles in one of the model bedrooms in the furniture department and finds solace in drunkenness induced by a bottle of witch hazel extract.

Next morning, while an agonizing hangover directs his thoughts to death and dissolution, he hears the terrible bell for the third time—an intolerable and imperative summons. His perfidious body—"it was, as he had always known, his enemy"—conveys him down past sporting goods, house furnishings, groceries, men's clothing, children's wear, and women's apparel to the main floor, where the bell is still ringing. He looks at his watch; it is running again, but still shows quarter after five. Dusk begins to fall, though it is presumably only midday, and Mr. Lecky hears the idiot painfully crawling up from the basement, holding his cut throat together. Studying the uninjured side of the creature's face, Mr. Lecky finds it familiar, but not the face of any man he has ever met.

Suddenly he recognizes it as his own face, and he drops the watch. He knows now "who had been pursued and cruelly killed, who was now dead and would never climb more stairs. He knew why Mr. Lecky could never have for his own the stock of this great store."

That this richly suggestive tale is not to be taken simply as a horror story is evident at once, but what it is intended to mean is impossible to say with certainty. In a fairly obvious sense it is the story of a man who kills his *Doppel-gänger* and thereby kills himself. The alter ego seems to be the body, the brute physical man—Mr. Lecky's "personal Judas." Throughout the story are frequent hints that Mr. Lecky is watching and pursuing himself. The idiot is first discovered feeding on sardines in the same place, position, and manner in which Mr. Lecky had made his first meal in the store. As the tale progresses Mr. Lecky's pallid face and hulking form are described as resembling, increasingly, the appearance of the idiot. A parallel to the shooting is the violent detonation when a can of soup explodes on an improvised stove, scalding one side of Mr. Lecky's face.

The movement of the plot is cyclic, and the stopping of time at quarter after five suggests that all the events taking place in the store are simultaneous. Mr. Lecky finds himself in the basement, climbs upstairs, finds and shoots the idiot, is himself wounded by the exploding can of soup, and is drawn unwillingly back to the main floor by the imperiously strident bell—all at quarter after five, while time stands still. When at the very end of the story the untimely shadows gather and his watch begins to run again, Mr. Lecky hears the idiot's body painfully dragging itself up from the basement. Time begins to move once more, and in the moment of recognition Mr. Lecky, dropping the watch, knows himself to have been murdered.

In this sense the story is a kind of parable of self-destruction through the ignorant terror or primitive jealousy that attributes to any stranger the temper of an adversary or rival. Mr. Lecky is at one point specifically identified with Cain, "his prototype," and his violation of the love one owes a brother man leads to judgment and death. The nine floors of the store which he must descend suggest the circles of the Inferno; and when the idiot, at least partially resurrected, answers the summons of the bell, clanging like the Last Trump, he confronts his betrayer and the slayer of himself. In another sense the story suggests the schizoid modern personality—the guilt-ridden, obsessed neurotic compulsively playing out the role of self-murder assigned him because of his inability to recognize and accept the idiot alter ego within every man. Such interpretations, whether theological or psychological, or both, would center on the sin of solitariness and the ignorant pride that refuses to accept the condition of man, in part bestial even though, potentially, darkly great.

Another, not necessarily alternative, interpretation might begin with the parallels between *Castaway* and *Robinson Crusoe*. The connection is suggested in the title and in the epigraph, which quotes Crusoe's reflection on the goodness of Providence in limiting man's knowledge of the potential dangers around him. Even without the quotation from Defoe the parallels with Crusoe's adventures would be hard to miss. Mr. Lecky (nauseated, like Crusoe vomiting sea water) first appears as a castaway on a presumably uninhabited island—the department store shuttered and locked off from the street. He builds his first temporary shelter above the ground, like Crusoe sleeping in the tree, having first armed himself for fear of wild creatures. Later he moves to a more permanent refuge—the fort built in a half circle around the lavatory-cave. After dreaming of maniacs and cannibals, Mr. Lecky is terrified at the sight of the idiot, whose naked footprint on the polished linoleum leads to his capture and death. Like Crusoe, Mr. Lecky never goes abroad without his shotgun (Crusoe's fowling piece), and he wears in his belt the butcher knife which parallels Crusoe's cutlass. The final throat-cutting recalls Friday's decapitation of the wounded cannibal.

The resemblances do not end with such particular and often minor correlations. The two books have a common theme: man's effort to survive as a solitary castaway. But a marked difference between them affords an ironic comment on modern man. Crusoe, with prudent reasonableness and a blunt, matter-of-fact common sense, overcomes both his terror and his material inadequacies and builds for himself a decent, comfortable, though lonely way of living. Even his loneliness is ameliorated when, by saving the life of a former cannibal, he makes a friend of his man Friday. Mr. Lecky, however, confronts his idiot with the terrified hostility of ignorance and unreason and as a result wounds and then kills his only companion. Moreover, where Crusoe shows admirable adaptability and inventiveness in improvising what he needs, Mr. Lecky, with all the resources of modern civilization piled up at his disposal, leads a very mean and squalid existence. He does not know how to run the elevators, he does not know how to load or fire the gun that is his first, fierce desire—the modern symbol of security. He cannot cook; he can neither read profitably nor fall back on the resources of a well-stocked mind. Wherever he goes in the store he leaves a trail of destruction (shattered mirrors, broken perfume bottles, smashed cabinets), dirt (the empty sardine tins), or death (the corpse in the basement).

If the story is to be taken as a parable of modern man cast away in the prison of a material civilization he can no longer control, and in which every stranger is a potential rival or enemy, there are a number of possible corollaries. Starvation in the mist of plenty was an obsessing paradox during the Depression, when *Castaway* was written; spiritual starvation among unprecedented facilities for the enrichment of life is a painfully common experience of twentieth-century man. The story may be incidentally commenting on the helpless inadaptability of the modern city-dweller, dependent for both moral and physical survival on mechanical gadgets which he does not know how to create, operate, or maintain. To get the gun and pack basket that make his forays after food practicable, Mr. Lecky has to go to the sporting goods department, symbol of lost skills which now barely survive among vacationers. Mr. Lecky is incapable of tying even a simple square knot, and so his primitive device for hoisting treasure up to the ninth floor crashes into the stair well. In this artificial environment, in which synthetic chemistry has produced from coal tar the "perfumes of flowers which might possibly have bloomed but never had, and the strong smelling saps of trees either lost or not yet evolved," even the animals have been perverted and made dependent. The exotic fish in the aquariums will die when Mr. Lecky stops feeding them or a power failure stops the aerators; the birds he tries to release, in the hope that they may forage on their own, refuse to leave their cages.

In still another sense *Castaway* reiterates Cozzens' pervading sense of the differences between the *aristoi* and the masses. Wealth has value only to those qualified by native ability or training to utilize it. Mr. Lecky is just sufficiently endowed to sense that he is not getting the maximum gratification from the material wealth spread invitingly around him. All the riches of civilized society are his for the taking, but he does not know how to make any of it his own. In most of Cozzens' novels the values of a cultivated life are explicitly detailed and the squalid life of the incompetent only implied. In *Castaway* the situation is reversed; by showing the rude poverty of Mr. Lecky's personality, Cozzens calls to mind the kind of person whose self-reliance and control might enable him to live well in the same circumstances. One of Mr. Lecky's most noticeable traits is his lack of control; he either acts on impulse, almost by reflex, or remains apathetic, paralyzed by indecision and uncertainty. His behavior is exactly opposite to the firm decisiveness of Cozzens' typical heroes.

If Doctor Bull represents the culmination of a strain, begun in the Cuban novels, of admiration for the strong, uncomplicated natural man, *Castaway* marks a complete rejection of such sentimental primitivism. Mr. Lecky is a kind of ignoble savage—alternately terrified and dangerous, undecided, unpredictable, and living out, in truth, a life that is nasty, mean, brutish, and short. In any case, although the fertile wealth of implications and the precision of the writing make *Castaway* a richly enigmatic little masterpiece, it is atypical. In writing it Cozzens demonstrated how successfully he could exploit the vein of Kafkaesque fantasy, and having shown it, turned back to the lucidity and fully articulated intention of his later novels. Like Alexander Pope, he might claim for himself that he had not wandered long in Fancy's maze, but had, in his later novels, turned to Truth and moralized his song.

3

STYLE AND STRUCTURE

Until 1957, reviewers and the few critics who wrote of him at all were almost unanimous in praise of the lucid precision of Cozzens' style, and Bernard De Voto after the publication of *Guard of Honor* concluded that the author's reputation would rest largely on his technical achievements as a writer. This prediction seemed reasonably safe until the appearance of *By Love Possessed*, in which the occasional idiosyncrasies of Cozzens' basically classical style were at times exaggerated into the convolutions of the baroque, if not the eccentricities of the rococo. Malcolm Cowley, in a discerning review of the novel, took gentle note of the change: "His style used to be as clear as a mountain brook; now it has become a little weed-grown and murky, like the brook when it wanders through a meadow."

Other critics were more harsh. Deploring "prose of an artificiality and complexity that approaches the impenetrable—indeed often achieves it," Dwight Macdonald quoted excerpts to illustrate a whole gallery of supposed faults. The device is not very impressive to a reader who knows how easily stylistic effects can be distorted when sentences are removed from the field of force generated by their context; and Macdonald's bald lists of examples are certainly unfair. In an attempt to discredit Cozzens without damaging other writers notable for their complex meanderings, he adds,

> James's involutions are (a) necessary to precisely discriminate his meaning; (b) solid parts of the architecture of the sentence; and (c) controlled by a fine ear for euphony. Faulkner does meander, but there is emotional force, descriptive richness behind his wanderings. . . . Their style is complex because they are saying something complicated. . . .

Confronted with such arbitrary condemnation one can only try to make some further distinctions, not so much in the expectation of making converts among those who find Cozzens' latest style antipathetic as with the hope that his style may be seen for what it is, whether anyone likes it or not. The following is the kind of sentence hostile critics like to pin up on the wall as a horrible example:

> Here was Elmer Abbott, an Orcutt, a well-off man (with all that meant in the way of perfect freedom to quit himself like a man) so tame, so pridelessly relieved at the withdrawal of a false charge, at the permission to continue his namby-pamby round, keep his piffling post, his unpaid job's clung-to prerogative of inflicting on a captive audience his mediocre music, that he cried!

This is knotty and mannered, and the alliteration is perhaps excessive. But in context this summarizing sentence is a deliberately rhetorical conclusion to a long passage (six pages) of meditation by Arthur Winner on Elmer Abbott's past. In the passage, Cozzens makes fully articulate the flashes of remembrance or intuition that occur in the mind of a principal character during the course of action or talk. The device is used constantly throughout the novels (it is especially effective in the brilliant scene with Mrs. Pratt in the garden); and if it is unrealistic in the strict sense that thought so fully explicated would take up much more time than a momentary pause in a conversation, the device is obviously intended to be taken with that willing suspension of disbelief which any convention, on the stage or in a novel, requires. Moreover, such meditative interpolations do not lack psychological realism. Cozzens is only articulating in precise detail a pattern of thought which perceptive minds might hit upon in flashes of intuition. The convention that readers are asked to accept is no more than the exposition of the full, coherent content of such intuitions. If the passages are neither euphonious nor simple, it is because they clearly were not meant to be; they are intended to arrest and challenge. In its context the sentence about Elmer Abbott is appropriate and functional in providing a deliberately rhetorical conclusion to the long interpolated meditation.

It should also be noted that the baroque style of *By Love Possessed* is neither completely representative nor entirely new. The eccentricities are exaggerated, to be sure, but they are exaggerations of tendencies already present, though kept under stricter control, in Cozzens' earlier novels. So far as sentence structure is concerned, Cozzens has two characteristic traits: a fondness for elaborate subordination which results in nests of parenthetical comments within subordinate elements, and a habit of appositival coordination in which one expression (noun, verb, modifier) is followed by others that explain and bear the same grammatical construction as the first. These traits, infrequent in dialogue, are common in meditative or descriptive passages.

Though the waking mind clutched at its relief of recognizing the dream as such—not really real, not really happening, not really requiring such an anguished effort to grasp and to explain—the dreaming mind with desperate hypnagogic attachment would not let go, leave off. A running engine of phantasmogenesis, powerfully engaged again, pressed him to dream on; and, little as life, Dunky (could that man be still alive?) angrily, excitedly, confronted him.

The two devices just illustrated are common as early as *Men and Brethren* (1936).

The words returned, of themselves, with unforced deliberation, over and over. Soon he was aware, without the distraction or the interruption of taking an interest in it, of the automatically increasing depth of his breathing, the modulation of his heart beat. Set, by the familiar practice of his will, on the deceptive threshold over which some people stepped to a supposed spiritual apprehension—where the senses, starved of nervous energy, were narcotized, kept no more check on actuality; where reason, deprived of ideas to work with abdicated, impotent; where Grace might very well appear, as Calvin supposed, irresistible—Ernest released himself.

Compare a typical passage from Faulkner which uses the same devices, especially the piling up of appositival absolute constructions.

In the surrey with his cousin and Major de Spain and General Compson he saw the wilderness through a slow drizzle of November rain just above the ice point as it seemed to him later he always saw it or at least always remembered it—the tall and endless wall of dense November woods under the dissolving afternoon and the year's death, sombre, impenetrable (he could not even discern yet how, at what point they could possibly hope to enter it even though he knew that Sam Fathers was waiting there with the wagon), the surrey moving through the skeleton stalks of cotton and corn in the last of open country, the last trace of man's puny gnawing at the immemorial flank, until, dwarfed by that perspective into an almost ridiculous diminishment, the surrey itself seemed to have ceased to move (this too to be completed later, years later, after he had grown to a man and had seen the sea) as a solitary small boat hangs in lonely immobility, merely tossing up and down, in the infinite waste of the ocean while the water and then the apparently impenetrable land which it nears without appreciable progress, swings slowly and opens the widening inlet which is the anchorage.

Cozzens' style is perspicuous, even when twisted and baroque, in the sense that its ornate complications serve to qualify, sharpen, and enrich an approximately specific meaning already established by the basic structure. In Faulkner the interminable increment of absolute phrases is cumulative: the meaning is not defined by an articulated structure but emerges as a kind of essence of the tangle of sentence elements, heaped up like branches on a bonfire—a glow that appears now and then dimly through the smoke and occasionally bursts free in bright flame. Though Cozzens' later style is, in rare instances, smokily obscured, it characteristically gives off a steady, dry light.

This is to say that Cozzens' style, although sensitive and ornate, is not poetic. The surface is dense and in the later novels often forbidding, but it is clear in the sense that the poetry of Pope is clear—the meaning not always easy to grasp on a first reading, but fully articulated and expressed if a reader makes the effort required by the compression and complication of the structure. The prose of Faulkner, on the contrary, even when the structure is relatively simple, is suggestive rather than explicit; and it is ambiguous in the sense that, like poetry, it sometimes manages to express what cannot really be said. The one Cozzens novel that might be called poetic—both in its primary use of image and symbol and in the feeling it gives of being autogenetic, of having been discovered as an organic whole by the writer instead of being deliberately constructed—is *Castaway*. But even here the writing is sharp and precise. Cozzens seems to know, and to be able to say, exactly what he wants to express; as to ornament he would probably agree with Aristotle that "the perfection of style is to be clear without being mean." It is true that Cozzens' later style makes heavy demands on the reader, but it richly rewards those who still cultivate the art of full reading.

In addition to being complex and ornate in its structure, Cozzens' style is "literary" in the sense that the reflective and descriptive passages use a good many uncommon words, similar to the inkhorn terms of Elizabethan writers, and a wealth of half-quotations and allusions. Again, it is ridiculously easy to make fun of this vocabulary by compiling lists of outlandish terms from Cozzens' novels. Out of context they give a false impression of their frequency of appearance and a smack of the pedantic Latinism of Dr. Johnson's *Dictionary*. Actually, since such words are not common in the dialogue that makes up a large part of the novels, their frequency can easily be, and has been, exaggerated. They do not occur on every page but tend to cluster in occasional set pieces of rhetorical fireworks. While some of them—*anfractuosities*, *furibund*, or *succussive*—make no obvious addition to the meaning, many of them (including most of those listed by Dwight Macdonald) make the precise discriminations appropriate to the literate sensibilities of the characters through whom comment on the action is made. Colonel Ross, who constantly quotes Milton and Pope, may be allowed an occasional word like *chicanery*, *senescence*, or *irruptive*, especially when, as in the last example, the word is so effectively used: "that horrid irruptive roar" of airplanes passing close overhead.

Apart from their preciseness of connotation, Cozzens seems often to use exotic words out of an almost Elizabethan exuberance, a simple delight in rich materials. Reminded of the phrase "an old style Princeton Seminary supralapsarian," Ernest Cudlipp interjects "What a marvelous word, by the way!" and rolls on his tongue its opposite, "infralapsarian," which he equates with "a dreary Arminianism, a mess of Methodist pottage." The orotund terms and the veiled allusion, are sharpened by contrast with the Anglo-Saxon earthiness of "Calvin would spit on them!" The rhetorical effect—colloquialism pointing up rhetorical opulence, and vice versa—is a marked characteristic of Cozzens' style, and it can be extraordinarily effective in puncturing a balloon, as in the following passage describing the Catholic Church's facility in dealing with the weakness of the flesh:

> But among the forewarned, forearmed faithful, such escapes were no occasion for panic, nor even for agitation. The strays were the devil's—bad; they worked evil; they spread confusion among pious or sacred thoughts and intentions; but what would you? Evil's energies must flag, too; and when they flagged, means to recapture and recommit the unclean spirits had been appointed. Grace, failing to confine, still enabled contrition; mercy saved the contrite—just keep your shirt on! Meanwhile, nature must take nature's course.

Similarly the studied, self-mocking, defensive artificiality of Julius Penrose's speech achieves an additional incongruity when used to describe some bald fact and gives a mild relish of irony to the style. Cozzens writes for an audience literate enough to enjoy deliberate virtuosity and able to look at the literary equivalent of late Victorian gingerbread architecture, not with Puritan outrage, but with amusement and affection.

These devices—the ornate complexity of sentence structure, the use of literary words, the excess of alliteration—give to parts of Cozzens' later novels their stylistic effect of slightly old-fashioned magniloquence. Cozzens is said to admire Macaulay, and he justifies his own style, by implication at least, when Arthur Winner contemplates the florid Victorian inscription in the lobby of the Union League Club:

> That epigraph embodied a seriousness of purpose still respectable. Were people really the better for not talking like that any more? Was there any actual advantage of honesty when high-sounding terms went out? Had facts of life as life is lived been given any more practical recognition?

The bare, plain style recommended by Bishop Sprat for use by the Royal Society in the late seventeenth century is not the only possible style, and those who insist on its use in the novel seem to fall into the Puritan fallacy of assuming that all ornament is bad. Even at its most rhetorical, Cozzens' style in *By Love Possessed* is rich, sonorous, and masculine. The sentences are architectural in their feeling for rich materials and their concern for an explicitness of structure which baroque embellishment may cover but does not conceal. If the decoration is occasionally so literary as to approach the grotesque, at least it is determinate and perspicuous, sharp in the sunlight with no blurred, fuzzy edges. Its rhetorical opulence is a pleasant surprise in a day when the concept of unembellished functionalism has been so widely and unconsciously accepted that Renaissance splendor (as revealed, say, in a film like *The Titan*) comes as a shock to the average American.

Cozzens' magniloquence is not motivated by the pious

reverence of the antiquarian; he uses Victorian mannerisms with a full, ironic awareness of their incongruity in an age which, as Julius Penrose notes, is cheap and maudlin. The ironically artificial speech of some of the characters provides them with a kind of defense against falsity, against too open a revelation of deep feeling. Lieutenant Amanda Turck's "wry phrasing" and intricately formed sentences—"I will stop drinking your valuable whisky, clean up these things, and with heartfelt thanks for your kindness and your cash outlay, make myself, as we said when I was young, scarce"—are not in the normal spoken style of even educated Americans. They are, as Nathaniel Hicks recognizes, defensive; and he is touched by "this controlled and composed, yet ceaseless struggle . . . against that obsessive self-consciousness." He remembers her "in the terrible heat of yesterday's high afternoon pronouncing a little stiltedly: 'The Lybian air adust—' it was defensive, he could see now. It intended the irony, for what that was worth, both ways. Though she reeked, she thought, of sweat, she quoted Milton; and though she quoted Milton, she reeked, she thought, of sweat." Her wry raillery is "aimed at herself; her defense against everything."

The affected speech of Julius Penrose—"the finished phrases, in their level precision almost rehearsed-sounding, the familiar deliberately mincing tones that mocked themselves with their own affectation"—is likewise a defense against hurts to one's vanity. Though not in the ordinary sense realistic, they are realistically appropriate to the hypersensitivity of a proud, crippled man. Julius' habit of speech, ironic at his own expense, serves to hold strangers at arm's length while partially sharing, with old friends, "the privacy, or even secrecy, which alone, at some points, dignifies a man."

Cozzens' own sensibility may well be similar to that of Julius Penrose or Amanda Turck. In a letter written in 1955 he admits that the account of the young writer in *Ask Me Tomorrow* is to some extent autobiographical; and the theme of the novel is pride. Francis Ellery, oversensitive and proud, interposes a series of masks between himself and the world, and Cozzens' use of a central consciousness in the later novels serves as a similar protective device. The point of view shifts in the early novels, but after 1933 it is only in *Castaway* that the author consistently speaks out in his own person. The entire action of *Men and Brethren* is seen through the sensibility of the Reverend Ernest Cudlipp; Abner Coates is unvaryingly the central consciousness of *The Just and the Unjust*; the melodramatic events of *By Love Possessed* are given us only as seen through the normally dispassionate eyes of Arthur Winner. In *Guard of Honor* a few incidents—General Beal on the target range, Sergeant Pellerino at the Knock and Wait Club, the WAC officers at breakfast—are narrated directly, but most of the action of the book is seen through the eyes of the youthful Nathaniel Hicks or the aging Colonel Ross. The device enables Cozzens not only to develop the theme of Hicks' moral education, but to attribute to the colonel a ripened wisdom which a sensitive author might hesitate to offer in his own right.

Another device that serves to establish an exact degree of separation between the author and his characters is the use of full names to designate the principal characters in *By Love Possessed.* A good many readers, including the parodists, have noted, sometimes with annoyance, the frequent repetition of the full name "Arthur Winner." The device may sound mannered, but it serves to establish the slightly formal tone that Cozzens seems to intend. Outside the Society of Friends no one in real life calls another person by his full name; normal idiom would require "Arthur," or "Art," or "Mr. Winner," depending on the degree of intimacy. These names are all used by characters in the novel, but none is really appropriate for the author's use. Garret Hughes, Julius Penrose, Noah Tuttle, and Helen Detweiler are dramatis personae, not personal friends, and in *By Love Possessed* (as in *Guard of Honor,* where military titles are used) the slightly formal note struck by the repetition of the full names helps to detach the characters from the author and to stress the fact that, like actors in a play, their opinions are not necessarily those of their creator.

Cozzens' particular temperament may also be indicated in the frequency with which certain words are used. "Compunction" occurs over and over again throughout the novels, and its connotation—a faint suggestion of arrogance and guilt mingled with pity or sympathy—seems to define the author's contradictory combination of habitual feelings: protectively detached, oversensitive almost to the point of being finicky, yet worried and involved. The impression is reinforced, especially in *Ask*

Me Tomorrow, by an excessive use of other words suggesting a kind of partial disengagement, or shrinking involvement: *mortifying, harassed, crest-fallen; qualms, chagrin, wounded feelings; quailed, shrank, recoiled.* Like his sentence structure, Cozzens' diction reflects his basically Pyrrhonistic temperament, his apoetic intelligence, and his troubled aloofness.

The intricately qualified observations and judgments of the Cozzens heroes are matched by the complexity and magniloquence of the style in which they think and speak, and a very conspicuous trait of this style is its frequent incorporation of quotations, half-quotations, and allusions. It is probably true, as suggested in *Ask Me Tomorrow*, that Cozzens no longer finds satisfaction in writing poetry, but the quotations indicate that he still finds poetry rewarding to read. The English poets of every age since the Renaissance are represented, and references to Shakespeare and the Bible are particularly frequent. Sometimes the quotations are unmistakably indicated by italics or quotation marks, as when Arthur Winner quotes from one of Hotspur's speeches or Julius Penrose recites a stanza from *In Memoriam.* More frequently they are worked unobtrusively into the structure of Cozzens' own sentences. On two of the pages describing the death of Warren Winner there are unacknowledged fragments of *Julius Caesar*, Keats, and Tennyson. An account of the orgies at the Osborne farm, known to the natives as Alcoholic Hill, concludes: "At any rate, the revels, silly or scandalous, now were ended." Mrs. Pratt makes a "fresh deviation into sense"; Arthur Winner thinks of the dimming "image of his late-espoused saint." The appropriateness of such fragments varies. Lieutenant Winner and Tennyson's eagle have obviously a good deal in common, and other fragments are more or less ironic. But some of the allusions are so recondite as to be easily missed by the average reader, who could hardly be expected to think of Sir Christopher Wren when Arthur Winner speaks of his father's monument. Many quotations have no apparent function beyond embellishment. Presumably they just occurred to Cozzens, as fragments from "Abide with Me," echoing the hymn tune played on the carillon, occur to Arthur Winner while he contemplates Colonel Minton's ruin.

The constant casual use of quotations in the novels has something of the effect of a genre of poetry popular in the eighteenth century—the "imitation." Like Pope's imitations of Horace, Dr. Johnson's "London" is neither a translation nor a new poem. The trick of writing an Imitation was to follow the content and plan of the original poem but to supply new, contemporary names and events and if possible to demonstrate a contemporary relevance in the thought of the "Ancients." The relevance might be ironic, as when Pope directed his Imitation of the first epistle of the second book of Horace not to that famous patron of poetry, the emperor Augustus Caesar, but to George II of England, notorious for his philistine scorn of literature and the arts. The effectiveness of a successful Imitation consisted partly in its demonstration of the idea, popular among neoclassic writers, that human nature did not change, that what oft was said could still be relevantly expressed. Partly, too, an Imitation was effective because it flattered the reader. Written for a small group of educated gentlemen, who could be counted on to be conversant with the Latin classics, an Imitation afforded the pleasure of a familiar Latin phrase turned to a new use. Whether the use was exactly apposite was not crucial; the pleasure of recognition was considerable, and it was increased by a flattering sense of belonging to a small, exclusive, superior group. The reader of Cozzens is likewise complimented by an implied offer of admission to the circle of educated professional people in whose mouths and minds the quotations appear.

Similar in use and effect to the quotations in the text are the epigraphs to the novels or to parts of novels. Some are ironic—for example, the text that introduces *The Just and the Unjust*: "Certainty is the Mother of Repose; therefore the Law aims at Certainty." Some are structural in the sense that they announce a theme. The quotation from Acts 2:37, "Men and brethren, what shall we do?" relates the title of the book to the central question answered in the novel. The epigraph to *Castaway* directs the reader to the parallel with *Robinson Crusoe*; the quotation from *Troilus and Cressida* at the beginning of *Ask Me Tomorrow* introduces the theme of frustrated youthful pride. But frequently the epigraphs have no clear, unmistakable relevance. Their significance must be seen, if at all, by peripheral vision, out of the corner of the eye rather than by direct examination. Ariel's speech to the earthbound Caliban beginning "I and my fellows/Are ministers of fate" and stressing his invulnerability to earthly weapons may strike the strictly logical mind as a baffling epigraph for *Guard of Honor.* But it has a kind of glancing relevance in its stress on the intractability of those inexorable forces which, despite our wishes and best efforts, determine a considerable part of what happens to us.

Similarly, the epigraph to *By Love Possessed* may have an indirect significance in addition to its explicit stress on the passage of time. It is taken from a speech by the weak and unhappy King Henry VI, who in the midst of battle wishes that he were a simple swain tracing the uneventful hours of a life that will in due time "bring white hairs unto a quiet grave"; instead of a king who, despite his rich surroundings, is waited on by "care, mistrust, and treason." Arthur Winner, too, had hoped for an ordered, blameless life but is forced to endure an increasingly heavy burden of dangerous responsibility. The epigraphs to the three main subdivisions of the novel are all stage directions, the first two only indirectly relevant. "Drums afar off" probably refers to *Coriolanus*, where the drums are a call to battle. "A noise of hunters heard" is from *The Tempest* and seems to be related to the metaphorical sounds—"Were they of hunting, of pursuers?"—which Arthur Winner takes as premonitory intimations of disaster. Both have a faintly ominous note and thus lead up appropriately to the short, climactic section headed "Within the tent of Brutus."

The parallel between the last section of *By Love Pos-*

sessed and Shakespeare's *Julius Caesar* is too striking to be missed, yet not easily generalized or defined. Helen Detweiler, like Portia too easily despairing, "fell distract,/And, her attendants absent, swallow'd fire." Julius Penrose, who like Cassius "smiles in such a sort/As if he mocked himself," gives Arthur (Brutus) wine to restore his spirits. Brutus, "arm'd so strong in honesty," accuses Cassius of condoning bribery.

> Shall we now
> Contaminate our fingers with base bribes,
> And sell the mighty space of our large honours
> For so much trash as may be graspéd thus?

Cassius' justification of himself is essentially Julius Penrose's insistence that in view of the factual situation principle must sometimes be shelved. Finally, paralleling Cassius' statement that "a friend should bear his friend's infirmities," Julius indicates that he knows, and is able to accept, still loving, the weakness that had led Arthur Winner into adultery with Marjorie Penrose. Those readers who, like most of Cozzens' generation, have studied *Julius Caesar* in school will find a reading of the last section of *By Love Possessed* enriched by half-recognized echoes from Shakespeare's play; just as the scene with Mrs. Pratt in the garden produces a faint resonance—inexplicable on logical grounds since the details are changed with the casual inconsistency of a dream—set up by parallels with Milton's account of the fall of man.

If Cozzens' style, with its usual lucid precision, its

occasional deliberate flights of rhetoric, and its fondness for quoting from the "Ancients," might be described as classical, the same term could be used for another characteristic of his novels: a tight structure, based on the classical unities. The typical Cozzens novel is primarily dramatic; its purpose is the immediate presentation of significant character in action; and an important part of the action is what the characters think. In resolving the dilemma of what Joseph Warren Beach calls "subjective drama in the novel"—if it is to be drama, it must be presented rather than recounted or explained; if it is subjective, it must be told about since it cannot be presented through overt action—Cozzens follows the practice of Henry James. The description of internal, psychological experience is given as it occurs in the consciousness of characters in the novel, rather than by the author in his own person. In *Ask Me Tomorrow* Cozzens deliberately eliminated first-person observations from his original manuscript and lets his main character think about and comment on what happens. It is not necessary for him to "go behind" the consciousness of his characters, since those whose points of view he uses are apt to be, like Colonel Ross or Arthur Winner, almost preternatural in the sharpness of their perceptions, the breadth and depth of their understanding, and the articulate clarity of their thought and speech.

Cozzens does not trace the slow development of character molded by environment and experience over a long period of years. Instead, he confronts us at once with fully formed characters involved in some complication of critical action. The time covered by the novel is characteristically brief—several weeks in *The Last Adam* (the time required for the spread and crisis of a typhoid epidemic); three days in *The Just and the Unjust*; two days in *S.S. San Pedro*, *Guard of Honor*, and *By Love Possessed*; a day and a night in *Men and Brethren*. (*Ask Me Tomorrow* is an exception, both in the looseness of its structure and in the length of time covered.) Into these short periods Cozzens crowds relatively large casts of characters, a variety of crucial incidents, expository flashbacks sufficient to identify and explain both the persons and their actions, and a good deal of comment and speculation.

To present coherently and perspicuously this packed complexity of diverse material is a difficult technical problem even in a short novel like *Men and Brethren*. For the longer novels—*Guard of Honor* or *By Love Possessed*—the problem is fairly staggering. The author's awareness of the difficulty is made clear in a letter to his English publisher:

> What I wanted to write about here [*Guard of Honor*], the essence of the thing to be said, the point of it all, what I felt to be the important meaning of this particular human experience, was its immensity and its immense complexity. . . . I could see I faced a tough technical problem. I wanted to show . . . the peculiar effects of the inter-action of innumerable individuals functioning in ways at once determined by and determining the functioning of innumerable others—all in the common and in every case nearly helpless involvement in what had ceased to be just an "organization" . . . and become if not an organism with life and purposes of

its own, at least an entity, like a crowd. . . . I would just have to write off as readers everyone who could not or would not meet heavy demands on his attention and intelligence, the imagination to grasp a large pattern and the wit to see the relation which I could not stop to spell out between this & that.

The first step in dealing with such a mass of material is a thorough job of organization, and this requires an intellectual effort which many novelists seem unwilling to make. Captain Hicks, in civilian life editor of a popular magazine, comments irritably, in a tone that suggests Cozzens is expressing his own feeling, on the irresponsibility of some modern writers of serious fiction. "One of you prose artists can screw up a simple, factual story until hell won't have it. You never know anything about organization of the material, and most of you won't learn; you think you know it all."

In another connection Hicks speaks of the "austere beauty of order," and the phrase is an apt description of the effect of the Cozzens novels. Order is produced by "the important arts of selection and elimination" and a careful organization of the remaining details. The novels are as scrupulously organized as they are fully researched and documented, but despite the complicated ordering of events and the heavy load of accurate, detailed information carried, they never seem schematized or mechanical. Even so unsympathetic a critic as Irving Howe admits Cozzens' success in creating "the illusion of verisimilitude." The structure of the novels, though tight, appears organic.

Guard of Honor is perhaps the best work to illustrate the point, since it incorporates an especially wide variety of material and the plan is simple enough to permit the bare bones of structure to be easily discerned. The novel opens with a superb account of an army airplane flying back in the late afternoon to Ocanara Air Base in Florida. The military personnel aboard are disposed in a stylized order based on rank. At the controls is General Beal, the commanding officer of AFORAD. Next to him, necessarily but significantly out of rank order, is his copilot, Lieutenant Colonel Carricker. At the foremost of the three navigators' desks is Colonel Ross, the Air Inspector. The other two desks are occupied by Captain Hicks and Lieutenant Amanda Turck, WAC. Behind them, on the pull-down seat by the door, is Sergeant Pellerino, the general's crew chief; and in the tail of the airplane, perched on the seat of a chemical toilet, is T/5 Mortimer McIntyre, Junior, a Negro from the Base Services Unit.

The arrangement reflects the chain of command, which in the Army determines the possession and flow of power, a main theme of the novel. The personnel aboard are key figures in the tense, two-day drama about to be enacted, and they represent the various lines of action that are brought to a practical, if not indubitably moral, solution by Saturday night. General Beal is the dramatic center of the network of events to come; his freezing on the controls when a collision seems imminent typifies the temporary loss of command around which so much later action centers. Carricker, the hot pilot, precipitates by his anarchic defiance of proper military procedure the racial conflict which is another main thread of action. Colonel Ross, the imperturbable man of responsibility, shows even in this introductory scene the qualities of rational, controlled efficiency which make him, in Mark Schorer's words, the "thematic center" of the novel: he is the man who takes over and straightens out the messes produced by the impulsive or emotional behavior of others. Captain Hicks and Lieutenant Amanda Turck are the fated but as yet barely acquainted lovers; and the flight into Ocanara, with Hicks a hapless passenger, parallels his flight out of Ocanara at the end of the book, morally shaken and confused by the disruptive events of the past two days. Sergeant Pellerino represents the group of essential career technicians who really keep the air base operative and whose disciplined competence and assurance are contrasted with the bewilderment of the reserve officers, forced to fit themselves somehow into the immense, ordered confusion of the wartime Air Force. T/5 McIntyre, almost AWOL through ignorance and negligence, has gained the grudging assistance of Captain Hicks in getting back to the base, and his place in the airplane suggests the racial injustice with which much of the subsequent action is concerned.

The flight to Ocanara serves as a kind of overture, sounding all the principal themes to be developed later in the novel. It begins as a routine operation, and in the early hours of the flight Cozzens sketches in, by means of very skillful flashbacks, the immediate background and present situation of each character. General Beal is being watched by the Air Force high command, who hope to give him, if he measures up to his present responsibilities, a major role in the later stages of the war. The account of Carricker's earlier heroism in combat reveals, along with the fact of his skill and physical courage, signs of his lawless, destructive individualism. The frustrating efforts of Judge Ross to get an assignment in the early days of the war, Captain Hicks' daily round of futile hack work, Amanda Turck's gallant efforts to overcome an ingrained maladjustment to life, all are interpolated into the account of the flight.

Thirty minutes from Ocanara, the persistent headwinds turn into a storm, and as the General attempts a landing in a thunder shower he narrowly misses a B-26 that slides into the runway ahead of him bearing one crew of the Negro medium bomb group who are to be tested and trained at AFORAD. The jolting disorder of the landing, with Lieutenant Turck sick and Sergeant Pellerino cut and bruised on the floor of the airplane, anticipates the only other violence directly presented in the book: the injury and drowning of the paratroopers at the review in honor of General Beal's forty-first birthday—the day on which he recovers the authority of command and qualifies as a full adult. Just as the flight to Ocanara serves as an overture to the grand opera that follows, so the whole novel serves as a kind of overture to the impending Götterdämmerung of the final assault on Japan. The first section ends with a superb curtain scene: in the glare of lightning flashes the whole party, from general to T/5, run just ahead of the thunder-shower for the Operations Building, Colonel Ross (the Prospero of this tempest) pausing characteristically to shepherd the new arrivals to shelter.

The multifarious activities of the Air Base—from high policy discussions among the generals to the routine problems of the WAC detachment and the Negro service units—are presented in a series of close-up shots, all organized around a carefully marked time scheme. The novel is divided into three main parts, entitled *Thursday*, *Friday*, and *Saturday*. Each of these parts is subdivided into numbered sections which cover shorter periods of time, usually about an hour. These sections often consist of several scenes in different places, the camera eye moving from one area of the base to another.

Section VII of *Saturday* covers the period just before lunch. The scene is the Base Hospital, and it involves Captain Hicks, Colonel Ross, General Nichols, Lieutenant Stanley Willis (the battered Negro pilot), and his father. That they are all present at the same time is due to a complex of earlier, apparently unrelated—but, as it turns out, providential—incidents. Section VIII includes a number of scenes, and all occur during and just after lunch. The first is at the Chechoter target range, where General Beal relieves his feelings by blasting targets with his 50-caliber machine guns and, as it turns out, solves his personal problems in his own unorthodox way. The second scene shows Sergeant Pellerino and the other master sergeants enjoying an after-lunch game of dominoes at the Knock and Wait Club. In the third scene Colonel and Mrs. Ross, discussing the Negro problem during a belated lunch at home, are interrupted by Mrs. Beal, who has tried to drown her worry about the general by drinking most of a bottle of Scotch and has come to the Rosses' house, drunk and sick.

Though they seem on the surface made up of random incidents, Sections VII and VIII are actually the turning point of the novel since they embody solutions to the two chief problems confronting General Beal. Both have been introduced in the *Thursday* overture. The first is the social and military problem of racial antagonism, which has become acute when Carricker smashes the nose of Lieutenant Willis, the Negro pilot of the errant B-26. The problem has been latent for some time: Army regulations permit no discrimination on account of race, but the Air Base is located in central Florida. In an attempt at compromise the local military authorities have established separate Officers Clubs, but the punching of the Negro pilot, magnified by rumor, leads the other Negro officers to organize a demonstration. They force their way into the main Officers Club and are arrested; the news leaks out to the papers, and General Beal gets a direct order from Washington: straighten out this mess without apparently backing down, without antagonizing the Negroes, and without obviously violating Army regulations against segregation.

The second major problem is personal and psychological. General Beal, accustomed to an active life as commander of fighter pilots, whom he likes and understands, has been going to pieces under the unfamiliar strain of sedentary, large-scale administrative command.

He becomes acutely aware of his loss of assurance and authority when he freezes on the controls Thursday night and almost wrecks the plane. His abdication of authority is confirmed by his flighty behavior on Friday, and his lowest point comes on Saturday morning at the Base Hospital, where his arrogant demand for a sedative conflicts with the professional ethics of a disgruntled young doctor in uniform. One of Colonel Ross's many jobs is to keep the visiting general, who represents the Chief of Air Staff, from knowing that Beal has lost his grip.

Section VII shows Colonel Ross, by a masterly exploitation of accident and coincidence, settling, at least temporarily, the Negro problem. The father of the injured Negro pilot is flattered into accepting an artfully slanted but accurate version of the affair: Stanley Willis was not "beaten up"; he merely got into a squabble—"it had to do with flying"—with "another officer," and got punched in the nose. At the same time a reward is tacitly offered. If Stanley shows the ability to command (*i.e.*, if he is able to calm down the rebellious members of the Negro experimental bomb group), he will be made its commanding officer. After Colonel Ross has read the citation, General Nichols presents Lieutenant Willis with the Distinguished Flying Cross—which, like the Negro father, has providentially arrived from Washington; and it is soon reported that Lieutenant Willis, having made a speech to the rebels, "does not think they will do it again."

General Beal's personal problem is solved over the

target range, though the details are not reported until later. In a fantastic game of "chicken" played with fighter planes high in the air, he makes Carricker flinch.

"Benny's had it close before; but I bet he never had it closer. . . . I moved in on him a little; and he hauled off fast, yelling: 'Stay away, damn it, keep away!' "

Having demonstrated, on Carricker's own primitive terms, that he is still as good a man as Benny, General Beal is restored; and he returns with vigor and assurance to the responsibilities that Colonel Ross has been bearing for him in the interim. The final episode—the accidental drowning of the paratroopers—serves to demonstrate, to the satisfaction of even the "hatchet man" from Washington, General Beal's complete recovery. In a burst of self-assurance, he contradicts his infallible, indispensable mentor, the Air Inspector.

"This way isn't going to work," Colonel Ross said. "But you're the general."

"You're damn right I am," General Beal said. "They have to prove to me they can't do it, not just say so."

At the very end of the novel, General Beal puts General Jo-Jo Nichols and by implication Colonel Ross in their proper places.

He put his hand suddenly on Colonel Ross's shoulder. "Even Jo-Jo knows they could do without him before they could do without me. . . . Jo-Jo can talk to Mr. Churchill; but the war, that's for us. Without me—without us, he wouldn't have a whole hell of a lot to talk about, would he?"

Colonel Ross, "feeling the thin strong fingers, nervous but steadily controlled, pressing the cloth of his shirt," recognizes the gesture—the kindly hand of youth humoring yet firmly directing an aging subordinate. He accepts his position in the spirit of the lines from *Samson Agonistes* which have been running through his mind on the reviewing stand: with new acquist of true experience from this great event, and calm of mind, all passion spent. The final sentences of the book, while they imply another beginning in the interminable cycles of the war, round off this ordered cycle of minor tempest by introducing a different scale of proportion.

The position lights of the northbound plane could still be made out by their steady movement if you knew where to look. The sound of engines faded on the higher air, merging peacefully in silence. Now in the calm night and the vast sky, the lights lost themselves, no more than stars among the innumerable stars.

4

TECHNIQUES

Cozzens seems to be one of those writers who work best within self-imposed limits, and in his novels he follows fairly closely the "unities" so highly regarded by neoclassic criticism. In adapting the unities of time and place he differs from the ancients in that he writes of "existence at a particular locus in space and time," instead of setting the action in the more general, unlocalized short periods and small areas of classical tragedy. But in unity of action Cozzens follows closely the Aristotelian prescription for a good plot, "the soul of a tragedy." "Many events simultaneously transacted" are worked together into an action that is "complete and whole, and of a certain magnitude." Furthermore, the *mythos* of the typical Cozzens novel is apt to be of the kind which Aristotle regarded as especially desirable and distinguished by the term "complex"—that is, one in which "the change is accompanied by . . . Reversal, or by Recognition, or by both. These last should arise from the internal structure of the plot, so that what follows should be the necessary or probable result of the preceding action."

The dramatic irony implicit in a reversal (a change by which a train of action produces the opposite of the effect intended) can be found in most of Cozzens' novels. It colors the funeral scene in *The Last Adam* when Virginia Banning, in a fever to be off on a trip to Santa Fe and in the agony of a child's sense of time standing still, prays, "God, make it a week from Monday"; a week from Monday she will be mortally ill of typhoid fever. An incidental grace note here, dramatic irony in *By Love Possessed* is structural, increasing the tension under which Arthur Winner must make his final desperate choice. It is embodied in scores of comments on the honesty and integrity of Arthur Winner and Noah Tuttle, beginning with Mrs. Winner's protest, "Oh, Arthur. . . . It's absurd to suggest that you, or Julius Penrose either, would ever touch anything dishonorable," and continuing through comments by Judge Lowe, Judge Dealey, and Arthur Winner himself. The comments are backed up by deeds: Noah Tuttle refuses to accept the Sutphen case—perfectly good in law—because certain aspects are the least bit dubious, faintly suggestive of sharp practice. When Arthur Winner discovers that $28,000 of trust funds have gone into Noah's personal account he is astounded at Noah's carelessness: "To say, to know, that such monies were in no way interverted, that the old man by his own methods and in his own good time, would account to the last penny, was all very well; but these procedures were indefensible. . . . Those forms were provided by law!" It is the cumulative effect of these touches that gives the final scene its ironic conclusiveness.

Reversals and recognitions in Cozzens' novels are governed by an iron chain of cause and effect. Recognizing it, Judge Dealey is led to outline a theory of determinism which is summed up in an echo from a college philosophy course, "Freedom is the knowledge of necessity." In *By Love Possessed* the sequences of cause and effect stretch back unbroken into the past to a period far antecedent to the action of the novel proper. Arthur Winner's discovery of his partner's embezzlement is directly due to Helen Detweiler's suicide. The suicide is the result of a variety of pressures, but two incidents are immediate causes: Winner's decision not to tell Helen that the charges against Ralph have been dropped and her discovery that Ralph has stolen money from Colonel Minton, jumped bail, and run away. Winner's decision is based on a desire to spare Helen's feelings and his own stubborn scruple against "half truths": he could not tell her the charges had been dropped without also telling her that Ralph had run away. Ralph steals and runs in a panic at his predicament: "Joanie" is pregnant and Veronica Kovacs has filed a charge of rape against him. He is able to run away because Arthur Winner has insisted, over the objections of the assistant district attorney, that he be released on bail. Ralph gets into trouble with Joanie and Veronica because he has been spoiled by his doting, indulgent sister. Helen's determination to sacrifice herself in order to give Ralph "every advantage" is traceable to the accidental drowning of her parents; and her determination not to marry is the result of a horror of physical contact which, it is hinted, goes back to a childhood experience involving her parents.

A similar "chain" structure underlies *The Just and the Unjust* and *S.S. San Pedro*—a linear pattern of cause producing event which in turn is a cause. The structure of *Men and Brethren* is different; though the book is tightly unified, the pattern is radial rather than linear. Ernest Cudlipp is the center, and his relation to the other characters suggests the spokes of a wheel. Though some of the characters, such as John Wade and Mrs. Binney, are independently connected, most of them are related only to Ernest, and the real unity is inherent in a situation which puts increasing pressure on him. *Guard of Honor*, though with more than one center, has in general a similar radial pattern, and in both novels positive action by the protagonists resolves the tangled situation in so far as it is resolved.

Unity of place is approximated in the narrow sense by limiting the scene of the action to a small area: a ship, a department store, a New England village, a few blocks in New York City, an air base, a small town in the Delaware Valley. Towns are vividly particularized, from the medium-sized county seats of Childerstown and Brocton to the tiny village of New Winton in *The Last Adam*. In this novel the community is one of the conflicting forces, and it is fully recreated, in both its physical aspect and its intricate system of social status based on family and background. It is, in this respect, a small-scale model for the air base in *Guard of Honor*, which, though much larger and more complicated, shows the same hierarchal, interlocking pattern. Cozzens keeps a sharp focus on a relatively small field, avoiding the vast misty prospects of the romantics and the large, often sterile panoramas of the proletarian realists; his exploitation of the "constituted scene" and "discriminated occasion" favored by Henry James increases the reader's sense of a Dramatic Present.

In addition to his technical observance of the unity of place, Cozzens makes effective use of the dramatic potentialities of a particularized setting. The best example is *Castaway*, in which the dim deserted store, crowded with the material wealth of our society, is integral to the action. But the writer's concern for solidly grounded, fully realized background already appears in his earliest novels. *Cock Pit* contains a detailed map of the small area in Cuba which is the scene of the action; in lieu of a preface, *The Son of Perdition* is introduced by a page of inventory, locating Dosfuegos on the map of Cuba and analyzing the organizational structure and plant facilities of the United Sugar Company. Topography is critical in *The Last Adam*, since the typhoid epidemic spreads from the construction camp through the drainage system of the local watershed. Early in the book Doctor Bull, standing on top of Cold Hill, looks out over the snow-covered valley and traces the course of the brooks back up the irregular hillside. The village, actual scene of the impending dramatic action, is out of sight below the crest of the Cobble, but the gray steel towers of the new high-tension transmission line lead the eye to the roofs of the fatal construction camp "behind and above the round spot of the reservoir."

This scene is one of the many landscapes and tableaux which suggest, by their frequency in the novels, that Cozzens has a strong feeling for the picturesque in the original sense of the term—for elements that lend themselves to being composed into a picture. His pictures, moreover, resemble a whole school of landscape painting in their feeling for light and their use of lighting for dramatic effect. The description of sunrise in *S.S. San Pedro*—a bright Sunday morning, with the golden June air "resplendent across the Eastern States"—is similar to the picture of Sunday morning in *By Love Possessed*: "across the enormous panorama of the whole eastern seaboard, the same shining morning, the same serene radiance." But it is only a momentary brightness between human storms, as the radiant morning in *S.S. San Pedro* is a prelude to the foundering of the ship and the final tableau in which the injured Mr. Bradell, experiencing hallucinations of the heat of the engine room and the warmed sweetness of patchouli, mingled with the actual smell of salt and blood, lies in an open boat and sees "only, overhead, the vast sky, pale and white, all around the infinite empty ocean." The picture of the barge party in *The Just and the Unjust*—colored lanterns shining on white dresses and white flannels, the bow ripple running silver in the moonlight—brings in, for Abner Coates at least, the eternal note of sadness. Similarly Arthur Winner, "past the middle of his journey," standing immobile in the "broad and lucid . . . light of evening" at the side of the lake, "with everyone gone from it, spread silent, flat as glass," contemplates "the coming night and the possibly coming storm," and is reminded of the death of his wife, Hope.

Scene, weather, and event are carefully harmonized. Ernest Cudlipp's *agonia* is set among the dismal buildings, sticky asphalt, and hot breathless rooms of New York in summer. In *The Last Adam* the clean, snow-covered hills of New Winton are contrasted with the raw, muddy damp of the thaw that brings on the typhoid epidemic. Arthur Winner's remembrance of his "bad" son, Warren, calls up a vivid image of "the edge of an illimitable parade ground . . . off which blew a hot stale hard wind." A hint of shadow comes into the sparkling warm air of Brocton—"the day's bright look of June (false; since summer was over)"—when Arthur Winner observes Colonel Minton heading for the bar and hears Alfred Revere's report of the doctor's fatal diagnosis. It is really September for many of the characters in the book.

Some of the best examples of the adaptation of place to action are to be found in *Ask Me Tomorrow*. In the sad, interminable rain of an Italian winter Francis Ellery makes his pointless, passionless attempt to seduce Faith Robertson at Milan. Montreux, a health resort at "the damp lake's edge" where an occasional rose blooms in December, is filled with semi-invalids and valetudinarians, absorbed in their symptoms, who take short walks in the "dank thin sunniness." The appropriate incident here is the death of old Rose, Mrs. Cunningham's dog. Grindelwald, a skiing station in the Alps, where a great wind is blowing white flags of snow off the peaks, has its human equivalent in the brisk, tough English guests laughing in the halls of the hotel and the elderly British admiral ogling the social director, Miss Poulter, with "forthright, damn-your-eyes adultery going on in his heart . . . cheerful to see."

A particularly brilliant scene in *By Love Possessed* is the choir procession entering Christ Church on the serene Sunday morning when Helen Detweiler's body is discovered. Arthur Winner and Judge Lowe are wearing the unaccustomed morning coats of ushers; Alfred Revere, the verger, stands near the bell rope, watch in hand; Elmer Abbott, the organist, blows jets of music from his pipes. Leading the procession as crucifer is Chet Polhemus ("arisen from dreams of Ann?"), and behind him come "a dozen scrubbed, starched-collared small boys" and the square-capped sopranos—the "clean thin soar of children's voices . . . warmed, unmistakably colored with sex"; then the tenors and baritones "pulling down the high chant toward male levels of solidity or strength"; and finally the basses "heartily roaring together in their barrel chests." The scene serves as a final, almost nostalgic summary of the stable social order of Brocton just before the picture is shattered, for Arthur Winner at least, by the dramatic events that conclude the novel.

The scene is similar, in its culminating crystallization of significance, to the *tableau vivant* near the end of

Guard of Honor, when the military personnel, from weeping General to naked Negro GI's, seem to pose, immobile, at the edge of the lake in the long flat light of late afternoon.

> The hot sun, nearer the horizon, poured a dazzling gold light across the great reach of the air field. . . . The swimmers, who must have been ordered from the lake, were in the act of coming out. They emerged with shining limbs, their muscular black bodies brightly dripping. Mounting the low bank, they stole guarded glances at the two generals, then glanced respectfully away, going to the little piles of clothes they had left. . . . Around the two generals a circle of officers had gathered, posed in concern. In this sad, gold light their grouping made a composition like that found in old-fashioned narrative paintings . . . —the Provost Marshal indicated the lake with a demonstrative gesture; a young Air Force captain faced him, standing tense and stiff. Bulky in his fighting trim, a captain of paratroopers, and Major McIlmoyle, helmeted and dirty, waited in somber attitudes like legates who had brought news of a battle. To one side, a lieutenant colonel, probably the Post Engineer, in stylized haste gave grave tidings to a thin chicken colonel, that instant arrived—Colonel Hildebrand, the Base Commander.
>
> A deferential distance behind these chief figures, touched with the same sunset light, the mustered myrmidons, token groups of the supporting armies, whispered together—the black engineers, the arms-loaded paratroopers; and in the middle background, borne on a stretcher as though symbolically, the wrapped form of the man who had fallen on the runway was passing.

The tableau suggests the guard of honor at a formal military funeral, and the suggestion is strengthened by one's recollection of a scene occurring a little earlier—the passing in review of five thousand soldiers. Here the color guard, the officers standing at attention, the dropping guidons and formal eyes right of the troops, the airplanes roaring low overhead, and the volleys of rifle fire from the edge of the field, all correspond to authentic details from a military funeral. The two scenes constitute a guard of honor on the grand scale—for the drunken suicide, Colonel Woodman; for the drowned paratroopers; for all the soldiers killed and to be killed in the war; for mortal man.

General Beal, the practical soldier, doesn't see "what good a guard of honor does him when he's dead. . . . Some more goddamn ceremony!" Colonel Ross, "not without grandiloquence," replies,

> "It does us good. Ceremony is for us. The guard, or as I think we now prefer to call it, escort of honor is a suitable mark of our regret for mortality and our respect for service—we hope, good; but if bad or indifferent, at least, long. When you are as old as I am you will realize that it ought to get a man something. For our sake, not his. Not much; but something. Something people can see."

Serving a similar purpose—a symbol of respect for faithful service, something people can see—is the large genre painting of Civil War officers at a critical moment, which hangs in the Union League Club. Both heroic and ironic, it speaks for an age when heroism was venerated and emulated; but it is also, in its lack of historical veracity, a monument to "man's incurable willful wish to believe what he preferred to believe."

Stanley Edgar Hyman first pointed out that "Cozzens is a master of the scenic: he sets a stage that precedes the action and remains after it." His point is illustrated by the writer's vividly detailed descriptions of buildings, static embodiments of the permanence of man's aspirations amid the change of time and circumstance. Cozzens' persistent interest in architecture, suggested by Ernest Cudlipp's remark that "architecture and music are the only arts, anyway" and by Francis Ellery's reputation for knowing "all about architecture," is confirmed by details like the following, which reveal the insider's point of view: "a carved garland of flowers with which the architect had averted the threat of a plain stone casing." Buildings are minutely and lovingly described throughout the novels—the dismal "City Hall" and the ravaged eighteenth century Cardmaker house in *The Last Adam*; the villa at Cap d'Ail and the tawdry splendor of the casino at Monte Carlo in *Ask Me Tomorrow*; in *The Just and the Unjust* the Childerstown courthouse—probably copied from the similar structure at Doylestown, Pennsylvania—and Abner Coates' office, "a small white-painted wooden temple . . . built under the influence of the Greek revival of the 1830s"; the Officers Club and the grotesque Oleander Towers Hotel in *Guard of Honor*; Christ Church and the Brocton courthouse in *By Love Possessed.*

The principal function of this wealth of architectural detail seems to be the grounding of action in a particularized setting. But occasionally architecture is the vehicle for social comment, as when the overornamented Gothic front elevations of Christ Church rectory are contrasted with the blank bareness of the "building's backside, the part to which no polite eye looked" and with the kitchen wing, "where menials toiled" in an almost complete absence of direct sunlight, that being reserved for "the grander rooms, where masters and mistresses were waited on." In *Men and Brethren* the history of Holy Innocents' parish, as well as a century of American history, is implicit in the various buildings that have housed this wealthy congregation throughout its existence. The original church downtown, built in the 1830's, was a little masterpiece, "small and unpretentious . . . [a modification] of the Colonial tradition in the neo-classic Federalist taste." The second church was built in 1873, two miles farther uptown, "a senseless jumble of fake Gothic." Ernest Cudlipp, pondering how those who knew the first church, "a decent and dignified building," could ever have endured the second, concludes that it is "one of those mysteries in which the true course and meaning of civilization doubtless hid." On the one-hundredth anniversary of the founding of the parish, "the fine Byzantine masses of the new Holy Innocents' " had been completed—"the solemn strong nave, the strong low dome of plain pendentives and sweeping smooth cupola on the crossing." The assured power of the building is matched by the "clean functional glass and concrete of the new . . . Dispensary and the parish's day nursery" added on to the "somber, red brick, Romanesque pile of the Chapel House." (The Chapel House, incidentally, seems to have been modeled on the Canal

Street Settlement House, with its day nursery, dispensary, craft shops, and gymnasium, described in *Confusion.*) The only building not fully pictured is St. Ambrose's Chapel itself, and the omission points up the fact that the novel is concerned with the weekday work of a clergyman and stops just short of Sunday in the sanctuary.

The architectural contrasts in *Men and Brethren* also underline the social and economic differences between the rich, comfortable old families of Holy Innocents' and the underprivileged, whose sharing of the spiritual and material benefits provided through St. Ambrose's Chapel soothes the consciences of the wealthy. The sinister, aseptic quality of the expensive private hospital in which Mrs. Binney convalesces is an admirable background for the violation of life implicit in an abortion. The dark, bare bachelor quarters in the vicarage, the fetid heat of the Hawleys' ugly flat on a side street crowded with vegetable stands and fish dealers, the reek of sweat and urine from the locker rooms and gymnasium of the Chapel House are reminders of the inequalities, injustices, and miseries which are the contingencies of human life. Place and action in the Cozzens novels are interdependent, like mathematical functions.

Unity of time in the neoclassic sense is achieved in the novels by limiting the action to a short, crucial period, in which all the narrative lines cross. In addition to being brief—usually a weekend or its equivalent—the period, like the scene, is sharply particularized. *The Just and the Unjust* begins at 10:40 A.M. on Tuesday, June 13, 1939, and fills the subsequent sixty-two hours. *Guard of Honor* opens in the late afternoon of Thursday, September 2, 1943, and ends late in the evening of the following Saturday. *By Love Possessed* covers the forty-nine hours from three o'clock in the afternoon of Friday, September 15, 1950, to four o'clock on Sunday. *Men and Brethren* covers twenty-six hours of a Friday and Saturday in mid-August, 1930. Only in *Castaway* and *Ask Me Tomorrow* are the time and date left unspecified.

Into these short periods a great many critical, often sensational events are crowded—so many as to make a bare synopsis of one of the later novels sound melodramatic. In part, this piling up of incident is attributable to Cozzens' deliberate wielding of the story-teller's chief weapon: "the simple compulsion that makes the reader, whether he likes it or not, have to find out what happens next," as he put it in a letter to another writer. But the concentration of dramatic event is part of Cozzens' conception of the novel as an immediate presentation rather than an extended chronicle. The slow passage of time which shapes character and determines action is implied, or sketched in by flashbacks; what is presented in the novels is only that short period in which causes and effects culminate in a dramatic knotting of event.

Felt, perceptible time is that which is measured in units short enough to be held vividly in a reader's mind—minutes, hours, days, not months and years. The ubiquitous sundials, watches, and striking clocks continually referred to in the novels are important here. To be experienced as time, the dimension of duration must be interrupted by some kind of happening to mark it into units. Doctor Bull, watching the electric clock in Janet Cardmaker's kitchen—"its third hand a slim gilt needle crawling the steady circle without relief or rhythm"—gets "a glimpse of time as it must be, not as man measured it. It was all one, no beginning, no middle part, no end." This is the time of primitive man, barely perceived since only roughly measured. Civilization in its modern technological sense, as Lewis Mumford has pointed out, begins with the invention of accurate clocks, which make possible the precise discriminations of time essential to planned cooperative activities. Janet Cardmaker, living alone in primitive simplicity, eats when she is hungry, sleeps when she is tired, and makes love when she or Doctor Bull feels like it. Doctor Bull's profession makes him a little more subject than Janet to the compulsions of civilization's measured time; but he is capable of dawdling all day on Cold Hill, while Mamie Talbot dies of pneumonia and while the telephone operator—one eye on the clock—tries desperately to reach him and recall him to his duties.

At the opposite extreme from Janet Cardmaker, whose primitive qualities are symbolized in her homemade coat of fox skins, is the correct, disciplined Puritan, Mrs. Banning, whose genteel life is rigorously regulated by the clock.

"Dinner is served, ma'am."

"Oh, Mary, Virginia isn't down yet. Could we have five minutes?"

Although Mrs. Banning is treated satirically in *The Last Adam*, her attitude toward time is that of the class Cozzens usually admires. Despite the occasional appearance in the novels of noble savages to whom time means nothing, most of Cozzens' characters live orderly lives built around a perpetual awareness of measured time. (Arthur Winner, in an early version of *By Love Possessed*, is aware of it even in his sleep and can waken at a predetermined moment.)

Against a background of the steady, measured beat of events, richly ironic variations are played by the horns of fate and chance. The young writer in *Ask Me Tomorrow* sits at dinner in a luxury hotel in the Alps. "While good and expensive food was put before them, while a waiter held in a napkin the bottle of Moselle Francis had ordered and twisted a corkscrew, while they . . . looked down from this high mountain on all the kingdoms of the world in a moment of time," Francis lets his imagination run over the events simultaneously occurring throughout Europe: the Fascists beginning to acquire power in Italy, the last efforts of postwar democratic government in Germany, "the havocs and ecstasies of the Soviet apocalypse." He "would have liked to write about it, if only he could grasp the dramatic inner meaning that lies in the simultaneous occurrence of diverse things."

The statement is an important one; over and over in the novels, Cozzens implies if he does not actually point out the significance in the simultaneous occurrence of diverse things. The device is most effective in *Guard of Honor* and *By Love Possessed*, but there are instances of it in most of the novels. Doctor Bull, having given only casual attention to the little Devon cow dying of pneumonia at the Cardmaker farm—"Devons aren't much use to you anyway"—drinks hard cider with his mistress and takes her to bed at the moment when Mamie Talbot, the Bannings' slavey, dies of pneumonia. While the sedate members of the Calumet Club enjoy the moonlight on their annual barge party, the accused kidnapers—"it was no night to be in jail"—watch the same moonlight through the bars, and in a peculiarly gruesome accident on the highway a Negro is decapitated. At 10:20 Friday morning the foolish, futile Colonel Mowbray of *Guard of Honor* is matching coins with his office staff during the coffee break locally known as the Children's Hour. The wives of the high-ranking officers are folding bandages at the Officers Club and gossiping about Lieutenant Carricker's affair with a promiscuous Navy wife. Carricker is in bed with the wench. A Negro reporter is wandering about the post trying to interview the experimental Negro bomb group. At the same time, "if the weather had been at all possible, Eighth Air Force bombers were turning, a certain number of them damaged with engines out and dead and wounded on board, to try to make their English bases. Perhaps also at this very moment (though for them it was still yesterday) Fifth Air Force fighters were dropping belly tanks as the Zeros came climbing at them over some formerly unimportant Indonesian harbor." Sitting at dinner at the Brookside restaurant, Arthur Winner reflects that men usually have good cause to worry, but unfortunately they seldom worry about the right things. He should be worrying, not about Ralph, but about Helen Detweiler. At just the time when her friends at the birthday party, with a "general slight air of devilishness," are sipping their one Manhattan, Helen in her lonely room is drinking poison.

In the Cozzens novels, time is significant in another sense. Its inexorable progress, bringing man through the stages of green youth, sober maturity, and helpless old age, is a constant reminder, like the motto on the sundial, of mortality. When the light at the sugar factory winks off and on to indicate five minutes till the power is turned off for the night, Oliver Findley is reminded of death, of the illusion of permanence. "He watched thoughtfully; time passing, minute by minute. . . . Gone entirely, without warning. That was the end of it." The tinkling music box in *By Love Possessed* intimates, "with the dying of the half-heard melody," the *lacrimae rerum*, "those only tears the Man of Reason stayed to drop." But though the sculptured figures on the gilt clock represent the joke of things—"Love conquers all"—the clock itself ticks on remorselessly ("the minutes how they run!"), and its inevitable successive strikings conquer all men, too.

It has been charged, as though somehow this were a failure in piety if not an outright sin of omission, that Cozzens ignores the techniques of the modern novel. Without entering into a debate—largely semantic—as to which techniques are, in what sense, modern, one may admit at the outset that Cozzens writes "traditional" novels. His success has led Mark Schorer to say that *Guard of Honor* shows what the twentieth-century departure from tradition has lost. Cozzens has consciously avoided fads and fashions in technique; except for *Castaway*, he uses few devices that have not been used before him by George Eliot or Conrad. But instead of deploring the lack of devices Cozzens does not need, criticism might well concern itself with the techniques he does make good use of.

Cozzens dislikes and avoids sterile bravura effects, but his insistence that he has never consciously set out to construct symbols does not mean that his work lacks depth and richness. He puts down what seems to him "indicated," what feels right in a particular place. These details, in a reader's mind, often connect themselves with others; and, whether symbolic or not, they lend to Cozzens' sober, low-keyed style what may be called a *resonance*—a vibrating of partials and overtones when any note is sounded. Each detail is clear, appropriate, and functional in its immediate context, but taken together they often achieve another dimension of meaning, enriching the story without distracting attention from it. This resonance, usually effective rather than essential, can nevertheless contribute to structure by underlining certain elements of a story.

S.S. San Pedro is a lean, stripped-down, objective account of the foundering of a passenger steamer, and the progressive disintegration of the *San Pedro* is equated with the slow dissolution of its captain. When the ship, still at its pier in Hoboken, shows a slight list to port, Captain Clendening is already ill, and Doctor Percival reminds us that "people grow old. . . . They break down, they wear out." The captain is pale beneath his wind-burned skin; and his hair, "usually a harsh white fur, looked weak and damp." What is most striking about his appearance, however, is that his face, like the ship, droops on the left side. A prosaic explanation is given at once: "An early injury to his jaw—Anthony had heard that it was from a thrown marlin-spike—made itself felt more and more as the captain grew older, and most to-day. His right brow arched up round and steep; the left lay flat. The left corner of the mouth sank in a lump outstanding toward the stubborn chin." Despite the explanation, a reader inevitably relates this detail to the fact, pointed out a few pages later, that the ship does not float quite level; it lists slightly to port. As the captain's illness becomes more acute, the list to port increases until it brings about the progressive breaking up and sinking of the ship.

In a similar slow, seemingly inevitable progression the morale of the officers and crew disintegrates. At the pier the *San Pedro* is a model of efficient discipline, and the high morale is epitomized in the crisp competence of Mr. Bradell, the senior second officer, his white and gold uniform sharply outlined against the blue sky. A boom is loading trunks and luggage, the winch run by a Jamaican Negro so drunk he can hardly stand. Nevertheless "he remained mechanically precise. He and the winch met at an abysmal level of brainless strength. Like the boom on its gooseneck, Packy pivoted blindly on the small hard point of habit. Like the boom, he described invariably the same controlled semicircles." Near the end of the story we get another picture of the boom. It has been swung out, while the ship rolls helplessly, in a desperate attempt to jettison cargo and relieve the now terrible list to port. No longer controlled and precise, the boom "tilted, staggered, mounted uncertain toward the perpendicular. . . ." Then it "hovered in a broken semicircle, balanced dizzily, went into a drunken side movement" and "like a well-directed club out of the anonymous skies . . . knocked Mr. Bradell's poised figure ten feet into the scuppers." Mr. Bradell is the one officer capable of taking command and restoring morale, and when he is incapacitated the captain admits that the *San Pedro* is doomed and finally gives the order to abandon ship.

A similar enrichment of meaning is achieved in the scene in *Men and Brethren* when Carl Willever is recalled to a kind of limited sainthood. The details, simple and realistic in themselves, inevitably remind one of the flash of light from heaven that brought about the conversion of Saul on the road to Damascus. Willever (a homosexual renegade from the monastery of the Order of the Holy Trinity), like Saul "breathing out threatenings and slaughter against the disciples of the Lord," has been sneering at Ernest Cudlipp's belief and denying the Christian faith.

On the clean new back of Holy Innocents' Dispensary one window, high up, without an awning, was catching the afternoon sun in a molten flash, like a mirror. The long shaft of the reflection struck down across the dreary back-yards, through the open window, and began to fall on the piano behind Carl. This unexpected light touched him as he rocked back, and, startled, he turned his head.

He stared a moment at the blinding wink of the window, at the pale beams on the piano keys and the dusty wood. Some intolerable sadness in this false sunshine seemed to unnerve him. The blatant, labored cynicism dissolved visibly away in a baffling transformation which was hardly more convincing. Yet the tears coming into his eyes were real. The torment of mind, which made him shake, must be real too. "Good God, Ernest," he said, "what can I do?"

The answer is: repent and return to the monastery, the vocation to which, despite his lapses, he has been called. The parallel between Willever and Saint Paul is suggestive rather than precise in detail, but it affords a comment on the kind of saintliness possible to the egocentric and melodramatic, and the episode is immediately followed by a revelation of another kind of saintliness—the humble, selfless devotion of Mr. Johnston, a broken-down missionary from Alaska, whose pathetically awkward sermon on the miraculous draught of fishes Ernest Cudlipp despairs of revising. A conjunction of the two types of saint is made explicit in *By Love Possessed* when Arthur Winner wonders what considerations had led Mr. Woolf to give up the faith of his fathers and join the Episcopal Church. "Had light blasted him, like Saint Paul, a little this side of Damascus? Had he, like Saint Peter, seen a multitude of fishes and fallen on his knees?"

The resonance of Cozzens' writing is not a result of

the ambiguity which may lend depth to poetic statement. Auden's "We must love one another or die" can be taken on a number of levels, from the personal or psychological to the political or theological; its profundity—its scope, as distinguished from its truth—is due to its indeterminateness. The overtones of Cozzens' specific juxtapositions deepen the meaning of the events presented, but the range of meaning in each case is limited by the concrete situations that define it. The variety and complexity of human behavior, the difficulty of evaluating it without oversimplification, the contradictions of human character—these make up a large part of Cozzens' material. But such general ideas are expressed in the juxtaposition of concrete details; the reader feels the generalization as an overtone of specific incidents contrasted in a story.

Frequently a tag of poetry worked into a sentence provides a clue, as when Colonel Ross, reviewing the confused, contradictory events of the past two days, thinks of a line from the *Essay on Man*: "All discord [is but] harmony not understood." The reference to Pope's optimistic generalization is ironic, since it would take a literally superhuman intelligence to find harmony in the details he is considering. But part of the resonance comes from the contrast between a period when such optimistic explanations of the condition of man were possible and the present with its uncertainty and doubt. The same tag of poetry might have been used for an epigraph to the scene in which George Bull is called out at midnight to attend the shiftless Peters family. Doctor

Bull is sixty-seven years old, his right hand is painfully swollen from a rattlesnake bite, and for days he has been working singlehanded, almost round the clock, to check an epidemic. Sal Peters, enormously overweight and eight months pregnant, has developed eclampsia and gone blind. In spite of six hours of desperate effort on Doctor Bull's part, she dies. The men of the family are stupid and sullen; a sister, whose long history of sexual miseries had begun at fifteen, has hysterics. Doctor Bull gives the survivors sleeping tablets and just at sunrise leaves them, "three variously drugged, one dead; the house shut up, bleak and gray under the cold blue morning sky. Crossing the bridge into New Winton, he could hear the bells of St. Matthias's ringing briefly for Holy Communion," and he sees the prim form of the village librarian, "pinched and breakfastless" like the spinster in Hogarth's "Morning," entering the church, "her solitary shadow preceding her."

Two successive pictures of women provide another instance of ironic contrast. An eloquent description of the confidence, charm, and grace of Ann Winner concludes with an exalted tribute to woman as the biologically indispensable sex, custodian of life's origin. It is followed immediately by a scene depicting the "obstreperous gay hubbub of screams, shrieks, and jocund squeals" with which the middle-aged women who work at the courthouse celebrate a birthday. "They were . . . mostly, of a certain age, at which, alas, not one woman in ten can fail to grieve the eye and hurt the ear. Providentially unconscious of this depressing fact, they made merry, giggling, babbling . . . ," utterly unaware of their lack of the "dignity and authority of high office" that Cozzens attributes to Ann Winner.

The personalities of the people in the novels are often paradoxical, and the surface contradictions not only make for realism, but serve to check in the reader the stock response, the easy, conventional judgment. Richard M. Ludwig has pointed out that Cozzens' characters "are alive because they are contradictory. Back in 1936 Cozzens had written one of his readers: 'I think a person can be at the same time officious and devoted, self-important and self-sacrificing, insensitive and sympathetic. Indeed, I think that is exactly what most people are most of the time.' " This ambivalent approach to character is also recorded in *Ask Me Tomorrow* when Francis Ellery remembers himself as a boy at boarding school: "The implied contradiction—pity for the child consigned to such a piddling yet effective hell, and contempt for the little whiner—would not resolve itself. Francis felt both."

Such unresolved paradoxes of personality are frequent in the novels. Marjorie Penrose is an unstable compound of the little girl who takes childish delight in domestic orderliness and a latent maenad whose driving power forces her to intermittent excesses of passion and guilt. Harry Wurts, the defense attorney in *The Just and the Unjust*, combines a scornful, aggressive manner with easily hurt feelings. Judge Fred Dealey, the choleric, sensual man of good will, who would "really like to be nicer to more people—the stupid bastards," manifests "the syndrome . . . of angered pity" whose symptoms were "impatience to find that fools must still be suffered" and "indignation at the unfairness of the fact (could they help it?) that fools must still suffer."

Lieutenant Edsell's face displays mixed and contradictory sentiments, "suspicion mingled with contempt; derision never wholly free of resentment; impulsiveness hampered by calculation; vanity unsettled by doubt." His attempts to defend Negro rights are stupidly arrogant, to the surprised annoyance of many liberal readers of *Guard of Honor*; and yet, as Colonel Ross points out, Edsell is also, among all the officers in the story, one of the few champions of human dignity. Captain Wiley, a fighter pilot with the RAF, has learned on Malta that "this death or glory stuff is all bushwah" and his defiantly callous behavior is meant to demonstrate that he believes it. Nevertheless he can quote with innocent appreciation, "Gashed with honorable scars, low in glory's lap they lie," and the contradiction reminds Captain Hicks that the man who protests most loudly against sentiment usually conceals within him a deep love of it. Judge Lowe ponders the discrepancy between appearance and reality: "Behind what man's honorable-appearing face, his airs of sound principle, his manner of rectitude, lay no self-knowledge of at least a few mean secrets?" Not, certainly, the two men immediately called to our attention: Arthur Winner and Noah Tuttle.

The contrasts are not limited to paradoxes of the human personality. Over and over again Cozzens stresses the ironies of circumstance by juxtaposing scenes and incidents. Captain Duchemin, a genial, extroverted hedonist, shares a room with Captain Andrews, an awkward, naïve mathematical genius; and Duchemin's seduction of his empty-headed Emerald is contrasted with the graceless, devoted love episode between Andrews and his ailing wife. The trivial squabbles of the Air Base personnel in *Guard of Honor* are put in their proper proportion when the petty recriminations of a conference are intermittently interrupted by sounds of the real war outside the open window: the rumbling passage of a "motorized heavy weapons company," a little later the racket of "a motorized anti-tank company, the carriers trailing the towed guns," and finally, as a kind of *reductio ad absurdum*, "the shrill female yelp"—"brisk, and carefully brusque; but soprano, just the same"—of a company of WACs, counting cadence as they march. The "excessive muliebrity" of Mrs. Pratt is contrasted with the weathered marble copy of the Medici Venus in the garden where she talks—"bumps of stone breasts wasted too far to be worth notice; below, the retiring pubes worn blankly neuter, all sexual definition lost."

At the beginning of *The Last Adam*, the towers of the new high tension transmission line with their clean, swooping arcs of wire march across the snowy hills, an embodiment of abstract, inhuman beauty. Later, Doctor Bull encounters the line again as he drives to the Peters farm just after midnight. His headlights pick out the base of a tower on which an enamelled sign reflects a skull and crossbones with the warning DANGER OF DEATH 220,000 VOLTS. But the lethal power is almost a hundred feet up in the air, harmlessly out of reach. What has made the transmission line deadly to New Winton is not the high, clean thunderbolt of electric power but the human dirt and carelessness of the construction workers who have caused the typhoid epidemic; and the *Danger* sign is much more appropriate to the nearby Peters farmhouse, where human folly and lust have actually brought death very near.

A striking instance of the resonance of meaning possible to concrete presentation without generalized comment is the dream, recreated with great psychological realism, which begins Part III of *By Love Possessed*. That Cozzens worked hard on this episode is indicated by the nine manuscript versions of it now in the Princeton Library.* Arthur Winner has gone to sleep worrying about his decision not to tell Helen Detweiler that the charges against her brother have been dropped. In the course of the dream all the women who have been brought to his mind in the last two days appear, merging into one another and producing in him a feeling of deep anxiety. The proctor of Perkins Hall at law school, who had been obsessed with the suspicion that graduate students smuggled women into their rooms at night, appears as a censor, a slightly ridiculous voice of conscience. Someone does have a woman in his room, and the room itself changes to the garage attic in which Winner had carried on his adulterous affair with Mar-

* Photostats of a page from each of four of these versions are printed as illustrations to Richard M. Ludwig's article, "A Reading of the James Gould Cozzens Manuscripts," in *The Princeton University Library Chronicle*, XIX (Autumn 1957), 8.

jorie Penrose. The woman on the bed becomes Veronica Kovacs, and Winner suddenly realizes that he is the man on the bed, about to engage in intercourse with Sue-Ann, the youthful mistress of his prodigal son, Warren. The scene shifts to an airfield in Texas, at the time when Sue-Ann was introduced to Clarissa. But in reality it was not Clarissa but Arthur Winner's first wife, Hope, who had gone with him to see Warren get his wings. "With a jump of the thankful heart . . . Arthur Winner detected the error . . . the interpolated falsity" which proved to him, still only half awake, that he was only dreaming. But the "running engine of phantasmogenesis" carries him on to his later visit to the airfield after Warren's death. There, examining Warren's effects, he is interrupted by the arrival of Helen Detweiler, deathly pale, her eyes sealed, exhausted and spent. A military band plays strains from "The Son of God Goes Forth to War" and some of the words run through his mind: "Like him with pardon on his tongue / In midst of mortal pain"—the martyr who, like Christ, prayed for them that did the wrong. Helen asks, "Do you want me for anything, Mr. Winner?" and he replies, "No; there's nothing more you can do. I'll take care of things. Go and rest . . ." and he sinks back into deep, peaceful sleep.

The time of his starting, half-awake, from sleep is not precisely specified, but it must be near midnight—about the time, according to Doctor Reggie Shaw, when Helen, comatose for hours, had finally died. Thinking back the next day, Winner's reason angrily rejects as nonsense the idea, so vivid the night before, that Helen, released from her hated body, had come to pay "some blind last calls." But his irritable denial only serves to remind a reader of the obsessive force of the dream itself; and the immediate transition to the hard-boiled, scientific unfeelingness of Doctor Shaw confirms one's sense of dissatisfaction with the positivist's rational explanation of all things in heaven and earth. Moreover, it is made clear immediately that Reggie Shaw's hard-boiled manner is a protective affectation, a way of concealing from the world that he, too, like Arthur Winner—like (for the moment at least) the reader—is possessed by feeling, unable to nourish himself on the bare bones of dispassionate reason.

The meaning of the dream is not clear to the rational, discursive mind; but the aroused feelings are sure that it has significance. It is at once a recapitulation and a prophecy—one of the presages Arthur Winner has referred to earlier, an intimation of mortality and an implicit demonstration of the tight interweaving of hidden causes and effects that men have called Fate or Fortune. Its resonance echoes through the remaining pages of the book.

Cozzens may have had no conscious intention of writing in symbols, but some images recur frequently enough throughout his books to suggest that they have, perhaps subconsciously, some referential significance for him. In any case, the consistency with which certain images recur in similar contexts suggests a special significance to the reader. The most obvious instance is the storm; in nine of the twelve novels a storm occurs at a crucial point, and when it is a thunderstorm the context is usually love.

In the earliest novel, *Confusion*, the pattern is set. The heroine takes refuge in a barn from a sudden thunderstorm, and for the first time falls in love. In *Michael Scarlett*, during a period of tense, threatening weather Michael takes shelter in a deserted chapel. There he meets Lady Ann, disguised as a boy, and when she refuses to draw her sword he flogs her with his saddle whip. Thunder, a wink of lightning, a silver sheet of rain—and Michael recognizes Lady Ann and falls in love with her. A hurricane with thunder and lightning accompanies Oliver Findley, the son of perdition, into Dosfuegos; he spends the night with a native girl, and as a consequence Osmundo Monaga is killed next morning by his own father. The *San Pedro*, already listing to port, runs into a heavy storm off the New Jersey coast, and the violent rolling of the ship causes enough internal damage to make its foundering next day inevitable. In *The Last Adam* a winter rainstorm, bringing about an unseasonable thaw, causes the typhoid epidemic which is the climax of the book.

The problems of the vicar in *Men and Brethren* come to a head in a thunderstorm: the rector forces him to violate his principles, the arrival of a renegade monk confirms the rector's decision, and his former mistress turns up dripping, deranged, and moribund. *The Just and the Unjust* opens with a description of the police, in a heavy rain, grappling for a body in a muddy stream, and at the climax of the murder trial the clouds thicken and steady rain falls all day. In *Guard of Honor* General Beal's plane lands at Ocanara in a tropical thunderstorm and the lightning flashes illuminate the white and Negro soldiers and the fated lovers who are key figures of the novel. Thunder and rain are a background to Arthur Winner's first compulsive, adulterous encounter with Marjorie Penrose in the summerhouse. (A summerhouse, incidentally, is also the scene of an adulterous affair in *Michael Scarlett.*) Lightning rends the Ponemah oak at the moment when Arthur Winner consummates the most satisfactory of the love episodes depicted in *By Love Possessed*, and the thunder is an ominous prelude to the suicide, twenty-four hours later, which makes inevitable his final tragic recognition. Whether deliberate symbol or not, a storm in the Cozzens novels seems to be equated with a violent, wanton act of the gods—the bolt of Zeus hurtling from the blue to change irretrievably the lives of mortals.

The shafts of late afternoon light—which shine on the tableau of white and black soldiers at the edge of the lake where the paratroopers have drowned; which turn Carl Willever back to the monastery; and which, in *The Just and the Unjust*, illuminate the marriage license that Abner has finally persuaded Bonnie to sign—are another recurrent image. And there are more: the pocket watch, proud symbol of efficiency to the Brazilian quartermaster in *S.S. San Pedro*, which is smashed as he gets the wounded Mr. Bradell off the foundering liner, and the watch in *Castaway* which has stopped mysteriously at quarter past five and only begins to run again when the body in the basement struggles painfully up the stairs. The opossum, frozen in the glare of headlights and crushed under Arthur Winner's car, is recalled explicitly when the dazed, doomed Alfred Revere reports the doctor's hopeless diagnosis. And the Ponemah oak,* over three hundred years old, is a constant symbol of vitality and permanence, a living link with the past. Blasted by lightning it still has, according to the tree surgeon, a chance to survive; as Arthur Winner may, with luck and the skillful aid of Julius Penrose, recover from the blow of Noah's embezzlement.

One final example of a recurrent image which seems more than a simple descriptive detail is provided by the snakes in the novels. Some of them, beyond question, are mere props. The rattlesnakes mentioned in *The Just and the Unjust* are introduced as part of a metaphor referring to the kidnapers. The grass python kept as a pet by a woman artist in *Confusion* is just a detail of Bohemian life, and the milk snake in "Something about a Dollar" is used as part of a schoolboy's practical joke. But the rattlesnake hunt in *The Last Adam* manages to suggest a significance beyond the immediate context, and the overtones recall both classical myth and Biblical story. The serpent was the living emblem of Aesculapius, god of medicine, who was commonly represented carry-

* The word *Ponemah* appears first in *Confusion* as the name of a lodge on the edge of a lake. It occurs again in "Something about a Dollar" as the name of a boy's summer camp in the pines by a lake, and finally as the name of the private lakeside resort in *By Love Possessed*. An actual camp named Ponemah flourished in the early twenties near Kent, Connecticut.

ing a clublike staff with a serpent coiled around it. The serpent-entwined caduceus of Mercury, now the symbol of the medical profession, was in its oldest form a rod ending in two prongs. Doctor Bull, going hunting with a forked stick and a roughly finished oak bludgeon, is bitten in the hand that holds the cudgel. However, his favorite method of killing a rattlesnake—jumping on the "son of Satan" and crushing its head with his hobnailed heels—recalls Genesis 3:15 and relates the Doctor to the seed of Eve—the last Adam.

In *Guard of Honor* and *By Love Possessed* the snakes have marked sexual overtones. The childlike, sexy blonde wife of General Bus Beal has for two weeks been sleeping alone, avoided by her overtense husband. When the general disappears she is forced to turn for information to Lieutenant Colonel Carricker, the potent fighting male, whom she dislikes intensely. Then, humiliated and lonely, she sees a bottle nearly full of Scotch and says to herself, "How's about a little drink? That'll put some lead in your pencil." She wanders, drunk, over to the Rosses' cottage.

"I came around by those bushes. Almost stepped on a snake. Coral snake."

"Did you really?" Colonel Ross said.

"No, silly!" said Mrs. Beal. "I just said that. You don't know where Bus is, I bet."

The dream of Lieutenant Amanda Turck, following her flight to Ocanara with Captain Hicks, is traceable, on a common sense level, to an incident that had occurred a month earlier. A water moccasin had appeared between two of the enlisted women's barracks; a guard had killed it, and Lieutenant Turck had given the hysterical WACs a standard, schoolteacherish lecture on dealing with venomous snakes.

In the dream version, however, it was she, and not the calm, lumbering guard who had the snake to deal with. Though she hit at it repeatedly with a file drawer full of index cards which she was for some reason carrying, she struck with no force, and the snake's gross folds kept edging closer—not with any apparent hostile intent, yet with a loathsome dumb determination. A Girl Scout leader she had known twenty years ago told her, tapping her shoulder, that rattlesnakes seeking warmth sometimes crawled into the blankets of campers sleeping on the ground.

Lieutenant Turck's sexually unsatisfying marriage, her obsession with physical cleanliness, her repressed attraction toward Captain Hicks, and her dream of the moccasin fall into a familiar Freudian pattern.

The copperhead in *By Love Possessed* calls up the richest tangle of associations. "Original sin, man's baser nature, the subconscious (named as you chose)" is described as a crowded snake pit, from which strays occasionally escaped, "creeping above ground, insinuating themselves where nature had fallen." (Arthur Winner says, "We don't know where they breed; but every now and then one turns up in the hollow, here.") A stray from the nest of "unholy gross urges," of "unavowable dark desires," manifests itself in Mrs. Pratt's pleasure at turning the conversation inexorably from the general to the particular, from love to the details of

Arthur Winner's own sexual experience. Just as she is saying, "You know now who was really responsible," she sees the copperhead in the garden. (It is worth noting that the garden is complete with roses, two crab apple trees, and a man who, like Adam, names the plants for the benefit of a quintessential female.) To Mrs. Pratt the copperhead is a harsh, intolerable bit of reality, bringing down to the level of actuality all her ecstatic imaginings, her "glad gushings of pure tenderness" over matters that were none of her business. Her horror "in the face of one solid sense perception—the true, tangible (if not very big) hideous serpent in the garden" forces her to retreat unsteadily from Paradise to the house, where she encounters another bit of rude reality—the angry Mr. Moore, whose "bitter-looking round small mouth," spitting poison and threats, recalls the tiny, gaping, venomous mouth of the copperhead. Meanwhile Arthur Winner, with assurance but some distaste, decapitates the snake with a long-handled hoe. The "ensuing convulsive thrash of muscular reflex, the violent castings-about" of the body recall the real subject of Mrs. Pratt's talk: the adulterous encounter with Marjorie Penrose, her "paroxysms of pleasure" and her "flings-about in her extremity."

All of the Cozzens novels, including *Castaway*, have the traditional virtue of being rich and meaningful on the simplest level of narrative: they tell a story that is realistic, compelling, and representative of universal human experience. They accurately reproduce the speech and behavior of particular individuals; they evoke a vivid sense of place; and through a careful unity of time, they achieve a heightening of a dramatic present. Characters are not merely presented, as on the stage; they are analyzed with shrewd psychological insight by the central consciousness of each novel. Accordingly, instead of the gossamer insights of poetry a reader feels the firm iron of a controlling intelligence. But this traditional framework of the realistic novel is enriched by the devices of a highly literary style, full of allusions and quotations that provide both embellishment and ironic contrasts. Less apparent, but highly important in creating the pervading resonance of this author's writing, are the devices of juxtaposed or echoed incident, which may explain Cozzens' demand for readers with "the wit to see the relation which I could not stop to spell out between this and that."

5

THE RANGE OF HUMAN DIFFERENCES

The picture of society in Cozzens' novels is in a double sense static. For one thing, the writer is more interested in situation than in process; he does not, characteristically, trace in chronological order the slow changes in an individual or family or social group. Instead he presents people as they are at a given dramatic time and place, only incidentally offering, through flashbacks, some explanation of how they got there. In a more important sense, the picture of society is static in its implicit denial that change is equivalent to progress and the implied doubt that progress is possible at all. Although Cozzens does not go to the extreme of the Augustan poet, complacently insisting that whatever is, is right, his attitude toward social inequalities and injustices is not at all reformist. On the whole, Cozzens seems content to limit himself to an examination of things as they are, rather than as they might or should be.

As things are, or at least as Cozzens sees it, a significant aspect of American society is the variety and spread of differences among people. Most human characteristics do not appear in sharply defined, mutually exclusive categories, like male and female. Rather, human differences are apt to be a matter of degree, and any range of differences in degree constitutes a kind of continuum, like the range of pitch in which, at some point, every musical tone has its place. The quality of a particular tone is important to the musician, and the quality of individual characters is the basic material with which the novelist works. Beyond this, however, Cozzens seems to have an unusually keen interest in the range of difference itself; his characters are "placed"—of a certain age and level of ability, product of a carefully defined family background, involved in a particular kind of work, and living at a particular social level. In his attempts to fit individual deviations into some kind of intellectual framework, he is related more closely to George Eliot or Aldous Huxley than to, say, Emily Brontë or D. H. Lawrence. Cozzens shows little interest in exploring the subtler nuances of the individual sensibility; his major theme, as R. P. Blackmur is said to have remarked in conversation, is "the organization of modern society."

In Cozzens' view, the organization of modern society is hierarchal. It is possible to regard the ranges of human difference as spread out horizontally, with no implication of better or worse attaching to various points in the continuum. High *C* is different from low *C*, but it would be uncommonly foolish to argue that one is better or worse than the other. But it is also possible to consider a continuum of variations vertically, as though it were standing on end and represented a gradation of differences, better and worse. Of the various ranges into which Cozzens fits his characters, a few are nonevaluative, like his treatment of the differences between men and women, but most ranges of difference are treated as though they constitute a hierarchy. The novels clearly imply, for example, that differences in degree of maturity are evaluative: a good middle-aged man is usually shown as better than a good young man. More important for the structure of society are differences in intelligence or aptitude, and along this range (fully explored from moron to near-genius) Cozzens' picture of society is as hierarchal as the system of rank in the Army which provides a framework for *Guard of Honor*. He is particularly interested in exploring the extremes of the range of aptitude, in contrasting the intelligently competent with the stupidly shiftless.

Stating the point so flatly oversimplifies the fertile complexity of Cozzens' view of men in society and the subtlety of his value judgments on them. Nevertheless, he does see society as ordered by the existence of certain ranges of difference in man, and three of these seem worth detailed discussion: his treatment of youth and age, the differences between men and women, and the differences in aptitude and ability that account for his view of society as static and hierarchal.

Unlike many of his contemporaries, Cozzens does not write about growing up; he writes about grown-ups. Only the short stories published in popular magazines during the thirties are concerned with the agonies of adolescence; the novels put away childish things. Ripening is an inevitable part of the cycle of human life—the achieving of a temporary balance between the negative incapacity of youth and the positive infirmity of old age. We may see, as in *The Just and the Unjust* or *Guard of Honor*, the hero, under pressure, make the next step toward maturity; but the events leading up to the change are sketched in retrospectively. What is stressed is not the long process of maturing but the contrast between different stages in the process.

The main differences between youth and age have been neatly summarized by a writer with a similar judicial habit of mind, Sir Francis Bacon.

> Young men, in the conduct and manage of actions, embrace more than they can hold; stir more than they can quiet; fly to the end without consideration of the means and degrees; pursue some few principles which they have chanced upon absurdly; use extreme remedies at first; and that which doubleth all errors, will not acknowledge or retract them. . . . Men of age object too much, consult too long, adventure too little, repent too soon, and seldom drive business home to the full period, but content themselves with a mediocrity of success.

Cozzens could well agree with Bacon that "it is good to compound employments of both"; but his novels flatly contradict another of Bacon's conclusions: "For the moral part, youth will have the pre-eminence. . . . Age doth profit rather in the powers of understanding than in the virtues of the will and affections." On the contrary, Cozzens' novels suggest a belief that the virtues of the will and affections can be perfected only through the powers of understanding, and that consequently, despite the existence of old fools and old devils, age will have the pre-eminence; a good older man is better, because more understanding and controlled, than a good young man.

In the major novels the typical Cozzens hero is middle-aged, fully formed, aware of his powers, and not inhibited by the knowledge of his limitations. Abner Coates, the hero *manqué* of *The Just and the Unjust*, is in his middle thirties. Ernest Cudlipp is forty-four. Arthur Winner is fifty-four, and Julius Penrose seems to be his contemporary. General Beal, the central figure of *Guard of Honor*, is forty; and the real hero, the always admirable character, is Colonel Ross, aged sixty-odd. "Youth's a kind of infirmity," says Arthur Winner, momentarily glad of his fifty-four years; he echoes Lancy Micks of *Cock Pit*, who calls youth "a disabling disease" and gives it "no more quarter than life itself did." But extreme old age is also a disabling infirmity, as we see in the faltering grip of Noah Tuttle; the pathetic formal courtesy of the very old man in *Ask Me Tomorrow*; the windy pomposity of Mr. McKellar, that "super-annuated buffoon" from the same novel; the busy inefficiency of Colonel Mowbray in *Guard of Honor*; or the physical disability of Judge Coates in *The Just and the Unjust*. Old age, however, appears only incidentally. Cozzens' real interest is in contrasting the competent assurance of his middle-aged heroes with the uncertainty, ignorance, and pretensions of youth.

Two of the best examples are Wilber Quinn, assistant to the vicar in *Men and Brethren*, and Francis Ellery, to some extent a self-portrait of the author as a young man, in *Ask Me Tomorrow*. Wilber Quinn is thoroughly likable. With an air of amiable common sense rather than intelligence, he enjoys "the buoyant, optimistic insensibility of the so-called sound mind in a strong and healthy body." Rushing in where angels fear to tread, he dabbles in Marxism and Buchmanism, sustained by "the enthusiasm of his inexperience." He seems to be, in the words of Ernest Cudlipp, "really a case of arrested development—one of the little children suffered with no other requirement to come to Jesus."

> You could rely on him, not merely in great matters of principle, but in every small matter. When he failed, it was only poor judgment, or human forgetfulness. As far as his intention enabled him to be, he was perfect in the first-named fruit of the spirit. What more could you ask of any man? You could ask better sense!

The fault is described in *By Love Possessed* as typical of youth: "the ordinary far-reaching flaws in judgment, the usual failures in discrimination" of young men. Wilber's flaws and failures—the belief "that argument served some purpose . . . beyond giving pleasure to those who already agreed with its contentions," his antagonizing of the rector, his patronizing of Ernest Cudlipp—are shown as amiable and amusing. But the inadequacies of Francis Ellery are painful, since his is neither optimistic nor insensible. Rather, he is oversensitive, proud, and poor. His failures in judgment come from an unresolved struggle between contradictory urges. As a writer, he wants to be published, but he is agonized at the thought of readers, "perhaps privately derisive . . . tchick-tchicking with the satisfaction of superiority over faults that Francis was already aware of." He recoils from "the intolerable advertisement" to other people in the room that he wants to see Lorna in private, though he wants to desperately. He recognizes that Miss Imbrie and Lady Bardo, though old, are better company than Lorna, who appears to the reader as colorless and empty-headed. But to Francis, hardly less astute than most readers but young, she is infinitely desirable.

He tries to practice "the painfully acquired elements of the art of not making a fool of yourself" but is so self-conscious that his continual attempts to impress people make him appear ridiculous. Recognizing, like the British public school boys, the hollowness of Miss Poulter's attempt to pass for a person of distinguished family and background, he is at once aware of his own similar attempts and of the ironic circumstance that, despite his pride in his superior intelligence, he too is a hired servant, used and tolerated, however graciously, by the wealthy. Cozzens' treatment of Francis Ellery is typical of his generally critical, unsympathetic attitude toward the young. Far from sharing the naïve popular admiration of youthfulness per se, which Ortega y Gasset characterizes as a "half ridiculous, half disgraceful phenomenon of our time," Cozzens leans toward the other extreme. The selfishness, pride, poor taste, and bad judgment of such characters as Guy Banning, John Wade, Lieutenant

Colonel Carricker, Ralph Detweiler, or Warren Winner suggest that he has stacked the cards against youth.

In contrast to the young—and to those "superannuated children" like Colonel Mowbray who carry over into middle age "the boy's long, long, illogical thoughts; the boy's unwarranted entertainment and unfounded terror in a state of things systematically misunderstood"—are the men who have been ripened by the years, who have learned something from their experience. It is significant that Arthur Winner should so often ask himself "What do I learn from this?"; and the other Cozzens heroes are equally eager to profit by their experience. One of the things they learn is the necessity of giving up youthful illusions in favor of "an undeceived apprehension, a stern, wakeful grasp of the nature of things." General Nichols, like Ernest Cudlipp, Martin Bunting, Colonel Ross, and Julius Penrose, looks at things calmly "in well-earned assurance of rightly estimating the possibilities and limitations of the Here and Now, and so of being ready for what might come." If what comes is, as Colonel Ross suggests, usually less satisfactory than one would like, the Cozzens heroes have learned to resign themselves.

Young men have no need for resignation. Even if they cannot change the things that are not as they would wish, they can, like Lieutenant Edsell, derive a bitter, compensating satisfaction from the contemplation of their own unbowed, though bloody, heads. As old Judge Coates puts it,

"Young men are great ones for facing facts! Even when they don't like the facts, there's a kind of tonic in them. Dwelling on how all-wrong the world is may help them enjoy more the feeling . . . that they're strong, they're well, they'll live forever, they're all right."

Lieutenant Werthauer, a young neurologist who has been honored by an invitation to read a paper on causative factors in somatic chorea before the Neurological Society and who has spent his time in the Army treating blisters and prescribing laxatives, is far from resigned. He thought

that intelligent planning would not have put the hospital area directly up the prevailing winds from the air field. Yet the fact that there they had it afforded him a regular bitter pleasure. A hundred times a day [when planes went low overhead] his poor opinion of the military mind was recalled and increased.

This dubious solace is denied the men in charge, the responsible generals, judges, clergymen, and district attorneys. In their own areas, at least, they make the decisions, and they have only themselves to blame if things turn out badly. When Abner Coates complains about the power of the local Republican boss, district attorney Martin Bunting defines Cozzens' notion of adult responsibility.

"Standing off and saying you don't like the way things are run is kid stuff—any kid can work out a program of more ice cream and less school and free movies and him telling people what to do instead of people always telling him. . . . Until you have some responsibility, do something besides kick, or try to heave in a few monkey wrenches, you aren't going to know what you're talking about. . . . Wait until it's been up to you for a few years, until you've had to decide, until you've seen how a few of those brilliant ideas turn out."

Bunting displays the failings, as well as the virtues, of the typical Cozzens hero. He has no sense of humor; neither has Abner Coates. "When he saw a sense of humor in action, it always seemed to Abner a lucky thing, since somebody had to do the work of an unappreciative world, that a certain number of people could be relied on to lack it." Bunting also lacks a certain kind of imagination. In his summing up of the case against the gang of kidnapers he is clear, logical, and simple, but "along with the virtue, he had the vice of unselfconsciousness. Absorbed in what he wished to say, he never thought of standing off and looking at himself to see how he was doing, or of asking himself if this were the way he would like to be talked to. His custom was to instruct juries." When the jury, swayed by the melodramatic appeal of the defense attorney, ignores Bunting's instructions, Abner Coates realizes that "though he could not now, and perhaps never could, match Marty's skill and experience . . . he had a temperament better suited to meet difficulties like this. . . . He would not have summed up in such a take-it-or-leave-it way; and he could easily have brought himself to stoop to Harry's level."

In spite of these shortcomings, Bunting is an admirable man. Cozzens takes some pains to describe his appearance, and the description takes on significance in view of the opinion, many times repeated in the novels, that people are in fact exactly what they look like to an experienced observer.

> Starting, when young, with no claim at all to handsomeness, Bunting's face could be seen to have gained, as the years passed, a fineness of finish. His pointed, convex profile and long neat-lipped mouth took on character. The use of good sense, the habits of control and judgment, informed every feature with strength.

Moreover, when Bunting made a mistake "you recognized that it wasn't 'like' Marty. The things that were like him were wisdom and foresight, patience and temperateness."

One of the rewards of being competent and responsible is the pleasure of patronage. Abner Coates recognizes it as "a fairly pure pleasure."

> If it made him feel good to be able to give what was plainly so much wanted, the good feeling was at least in part the good feeling of being able to adjust the fallings-out of a too impersonal and regardless chance so that the deserving got some of their deserts. It would be . . . the one real pleasure, when all was said and done, of power.

The patron, both protector and benefactor, corresponds in some respects to the figure of the father. Ernest Cudlipp is referred to as Father Cudlipp only in jest, but his behavior toward the young poet John Wade is essentially fatherly: Ernest provides him with food, lodging, and credit, motivated by "the general paternal hope, the fond urgent wish for every good thing to be John's." In time he might "see John develop into a person of character, intelligent and responsible, master of the simple secret of a good, happy, and fruitful life." Like Arthur Winner, who had hoped the same things for his son Warren, Ernest Cudlipp is disappointed.

"The size of it is, I don't know what to do with him. I couldn't know less if I were his father. It's time I gave it up, and I ought to be glad that I can give it up."

He ought to be; but he felt instead a frustrated soreness of heart.

It is a feeling known to many of the fathers in the novels: Mr. Jennings, distracted with anger and disappointment, "taking a strap to the incorrigible Jimmy" and beating him "in what was truly and largely a frenzy of love"; Julius Penrose noting that everything today is for the children and speculating that they might be better prepared for life if they were "soundly cuffed into ministering a little to their elders"; Mr. Banning, looking ahead with some dismay to the time when "the patronage of today would be reversed" and Guy, seeing his father as "an aimless old putterer," would take care that his vagaries "didn't do him any real harm."

Not all fathers are disappointed; Judge Coates has found Abner a great source of satisfaction just as Noah Tuttle has found his son-in-law, Arthur Winner, "a good boy." Colonel Ross's real sons are mentioned only in passing in *Guard of Honor*, but he finds a substitute son in General Beal. Why should he take responsibility for the problems the general has run out on? The answer, in part, is the Army tradition of loyalty; Colonel Ross has been connected with the Army since World War I, in which he earned the nickname of Grandpa from the young pilots he looked out for as supply officer. But the nickname suggests that Colonel Ross is by nature fatherly—indulgent toward the failings of his quasi-son, determined to make something out of him and willing to "pick up after him." In analyzing his motives for trying to save the general from himself, Colonel Ross concludes that "in some . . . important ways, his relationship to the general might resemble the general's relationship to Benny Carricker. . . . that difficult, erratic brat, put only one real claim on General Beal; Benny needed somebody to look out for him; and who else was there?" To his wife Colonel Ross gives another explanation: "I think Benny is what Bus wishes he were; what Bus thinks he might have been, if they'd only had the war fifteen years ago, not now when he's forty and too old."

Both explanations are applicable to Colonel Ross. He admires, even envies, the general, and the general needs him. General Beal is, in fact, Colonel Ross's "grand project," and he is willing either to take over for him or pick up after him. Throughout *Guard of Honor* he does both, in small matters as well as in great. When a WAC spills Coca-Cola on the general's trousers Colonel Ross not only sees that the mess is cleaned up but restrains and consoles the embarrassed, weeping girl; it will not do to have a rumor circulating in Washington "that WACs are constantly running out of the general's office in tears." When the general's party, landing in a rainstorm, run for the Operations Building, Colonel Ross stops to direct and shepherd the newly arrived Negro group to shelter. When the Negro officers bring the latent problem of segregation to a head, Colonel Ross settles it. When General Beal runs out on his job and goes flying, Colonel Ross does his best to cover up for the general. His sense of responsibility is made effective by astuteness in judging men, a realistic view of circumstances, a judicial habit of mind, and the capacity for quick, confident decisions. Colonel Ross is the exemplar of the middle-aged heroes in Cozzens' later novels.

The differences between youth and age are a matter of degree; the temperamental differences between men and women, also analyzed in considerable detail in Cozzens' novels, are more absolute and are presented more objectively. There are, to be sure, occasional hints that the Cozzens hero, if not Cozzens himself, shares the widespread masculine conviction that woman is the inferior vessel, possessed by feeling instead of guided by reason. What mainly appears in the novels, however, is a sensitive analysis not of woman's inferiority to, but of her generic difference from, man. The mere insistence that such differences exist may strike some readers as evidence of prejudice, and women in general seem to dislike Cozzens' novels, perhaps because of a fancied tone of condescension in his attitude toward them. It may be impossible to write with complete impartiality on a subject so charged with normal sex antagonism, but it seems likely that the question which of the sexes is "better" would only be raised by a person already emotionally committed to one side or the other. It is, in fact, usually raised by those who, whether consciously or not, share the militant, aggressively defensive attitude of the professional feminist.

The reasons for the emotional charge generated by feminism are clear enough. Like the Negroes in America, women were for centuries deprived of their full human rights and dignity. Militant action, sustained by a sense of grievance and a theory of basic equality, was needed to bring about a change. But the paradox inherent in the theory of feminism is indicated in the fact that the movement has encouraged women to emulate men in masculine activities rather than to perfect their own feminine qualities. The heroines of the novels demonstrate that Cozzens understands the rights, dignities, and special emotional problems of women. His dislike of the European concept of the dominant, superior male is made clear in the story "Whose Broad Stripes and Bright Stars," in which only gross Prussians like Mr. Bechtel, who eats larks spitted on little silver skewers, insist that girls don't count. The basic antagonism between men and women is sensitively analyzed in a short story, "The Way To Go Home," and even more fully and compassionately in a scene between Colonel and Mrs. Ross in *Guard of Honor.* But the later novels also make clear that sex antagonism is not abated if women try to turn themselves into lesser men.

The picture of women in the early novels shows the effects of youthful, romantic idealization; the beautiful and accomplished Cerise d'Atrée of *Confusion* is all too clearly a young man's wistful projection of desirable qualities. She is followed by the more dynamic Ruth

Micks of *Cock Pit*, who plays a man's role in the novel, even though, somewhat incongruously, she is also represented as a paragon of feminine attractiveness. This image of woman as young men would like to have her—peer and perfect companion, with the added charm of sex thrown in as a bonus—appears for the last time in Janet Cardmaker, of *The Last Adam*. An outspoken, ruthless individualist, living alone camp-style on her hill farm outside New Winton and utterly contemptuous of the talk in the village, Janet still has the essential female attribute: a "vital, almost electric sensuality" that has irresistibly drawn George Bull to her for twenty-eight years. Her role as companion to man is indicated by her dress: boots, corduroy breeches, a flannel shirt, and a home-made garment—"eight or ten red fox skins sewed over an old cloth coat." It is appropriate clothing for the mate of a cave man like Doctor Bull, but her type disappears from the novels along with Cozzens' nostalgic portrayal of the vital, unkillable last Adam.

Subsequent heroines may retain some supposedly masculine traits—the candor of Bonnie Drummond, the magnanimity of Mrs. Cunningham (whose "regard for truth was not . . . regard for the benefit or credit of a reputation for being truthful, but for the thing itself"), the cool precision of Clarissa Winner, the sturdy good sense of Mrs. Ross in *Guard of Honor*. But the latter book, with its sardonic picture of women gone to war, stresses the fact that women trying to be like men are pathetic or absurd. Though Colonel Coulthard may be titillated by the sight of "these bright respectful women, all soldiers if often full-breasted ones, to the girdle; piquantly, all girls in skirts down from the waist," the implied split in personality is damaging. It is also ludicrous, and some of the best comic scenes in the book are those that demonstrate the truth of Lieutenant Mary Lippa's despairing conclusion: "I don't think a woman ought to be in this business." There is, for example, the scene in which the upright, serious commander of the WAC detachment ponders the best ways of discouraging the wandering hands of male officers; three walnuts placed under the stocking top seem to give them pause. And there is the scene in which Colonel Ross inspects the WAC barracks and, "sternly putting down the ribald, highly unsuitable impulse to laugh," solemnly considers the problem of peeping GI's at the base hospital dressing rooms. Women trying to act like men, even when they are fairly successful, appear in the Cozzens novels as also slightly ridiculous.

When women, accepting their difference from men, act like women, they display a quality summed up in a phrase which some readers may find offensive—"a sort of vital, sustaining bitchiness." The girl to whom Francis Ellery makes this remark is insulted, and even more insulted when Francis tries to explain his meaning. But the staid Arthur Winner comes to a similar conclusion as he watches his well-loved daughter comforting the spaniel bitch at Roylan, and Clarissa Winner uses the term to describe something in her own nature. Francis Ellery insists that his remark is "at least two-thirds a compliment," but the girl is not convinced. Perhaps part of the essential feminine quality (in contrast to the reaction of men, who are not insulted when compared with bulls, or bucks, or fighting cocks) is a refusal to admit the femaleness which is, after all, what "a woman [is] supposed to make you think of." Bitchiness, in its two-thirds complimentary sense, seems to include and sum up such feminine qualities as toughness of mind and feeling, which leads to a realistic view of life; a vital charm which often manifests itself as outright sexual aggressiveness; and a sense of incompleteness which appears as a need to be dominated and cherished. All of these traits are abundantly illustrated in the novels.

That women generally are tough in spirit and body—resilient and enduring to a degree which men can seldom equal—is suggested in a remark Julius Penrose makes about his wife; and Ernest Cudlipp, another confirmed antisentimentalist, refuses "to feel the least pity for women as such" or "to regard the disabilities of women with reverent awe." Doctor Bull's Aunt Myra, well on in her eighties but still sound and spry, illustrates in her attitude toward her nephew the saving realism and common sense, the ability to accept disagreeable things and put them in their proper place, which Cozzens attributes to women of all ages. Ann Winner, on the threshold of womanhood, is already endowed with "a woman's disinclination to cry for the moon; a woman's sagacity about true interest . . . a woman's reliable sense of where substance is and where shadow is." Although rudely shocked by her discovery of the passage of love between Arthur and Clarissa, by next morning "the child's corrosive thoughts" have all been packed off "to their proper place out of mind, the place of safe deposit where in normal balance the normal woman kept the less good, the too true, the unbeautiful. . . ." Ann's mother was also supported by "the female's saving, tough-spirited, matter-of-factness . . . enabling her, like any woman, to face unblenching and unsqueamish every anguish and every nastiness that life could inflict on her." A similar acceptance of the "rank offenses to dignity or reticence that a woman thinks nothing of" appears in May Tupping, caring for her paralyzed husband in *The Last Adam.* Woman's psychic resilience may be traceable to a lack of the peculiar male vanity which finds a public humiliation an almost insupportable blow, instead of a minor incident to be put in its proper place out of mind.

Another element in what Cozzens seems to regard as the essential feminine quality is woman's awareness of her charm and a willingness to employ it. Clarissa Winner demonstrates the "scheming," as her husband calls it, by which intelligent women exploit their attractiveness—the calculated effect of dressing and staging and behavior. A wise assurance of her charm is implicit in Ann Winner's "pert vivacity," the "turn of her dark head and knowledgeable lift of chin . . . femininity without age," as she and her friend comfort the cocker bitch that "might have the most awful puppies" if she were allowed outside the dog-run. The sexual overtone of feminine attractiveness appears continually. "What else is [woman] for, anyway?" asks Francis Ellery. The charm may be full-blown, as in Mrs. Pratt, or meager and desperate as in Joanie Moore; but Cozzens' women instinctively know how to manipulate it to get and retain the upper hand over their elected mates. This "inherent female know-how" leads Peg, Wilber Quinn's radical girl friend in *Men and Brethren*, to brave the scandal of her friends in the Young Communist League and accompany Wilber to church. It produces in Alice Breen a "naïve feminine transformation" when even so unlikely a male as the chapel organist shows by his embarrassed confusion his helpless admiration. "Her charm acknowledged . . . Alice became at once more charming —a definite, deliberate sweetness."

Consciousness of charm blends into deliberate exploiting of charm, and this into overt sexual aggressiveness. Cozzens makes clear again and again that woman is the hunter, not the hunted. On the crudest level there is the frantic physical offering of Veronica Kovacs in *By Love Possessed*. A good many degrees higher is the pursuit of Mr. Bradell, senior second officer of the *San Pedro*, by the flapper Marilee or the deliberate campaign which, according to Mrs. Pratt, was carried on against Arthur Winner by Marjorie Penrose. The signaling of "little invitations . . . bolder each time and more alluring" by which the sixteen-year-old Mary Beach leads a high school teacher into trouble induces Abner Coates to speculate on "the fact, so well known to the district attorney's office, that, unless the man were insane, or very drunk, the woman was always to blame for what happened to her. She could end it any time by an honestly meant flat refusal." Even so proper a girl as Mrs. Geraldine Binney does not make the flat refusal which, as Ernest Cudlipp points out, would have put an end to her affair before it actually got started. "You'd have to let him see that it was a pushover before he'd make any serious advances." Amanda Turck is a sensitive and decent woman whose principles would prevent her from throwing herself at a married man, but when the widely separated details of her meetings with Captain Hicks—her first wry half-confidences, her dream of the water moccasin, her self-consciousness when they meet at his office, her casual invitation to stop in for a drink on Saturday—are brought together, it is clear that Cozzens meant to show her, perhaps unconsciously, taking the lead in an affair which on the surface is completely accidental and unpremeditated.

The sense of female incompleteness is defined by Lieutenant Turck in a memorable passage.

> A girl who's pretty isn't as likely to think of it so often; but even she must occasionally pull up and reflect that a woman really has to have a man, or men. I don't mean just for purposes of romance or reproduction. You need one for all kinds of things. Your whole economy is based on it, like some primitive tribe and its domestic animal. You know, the yak, maybe. They eat it, and drink the milk, and make clothes out of its fur or hair or whatever it has, and shoes out of its hide, and use it to pull a sledge, and on and on. If you haven't got one, you are really on a spot. You can't lead a full life. You're definitely underprivileged, or on submarginal subsistence.

Mrs. Ross, though happily married, is described as being caught in the same dilemma: a dislike of maleness per se coupled with a need for man. In the privacy of her mind she is certain that a woman's world would be better than the actual world mismanaged by men, but she is resigned to her husband's dominance.

> It was, after all, necessary to her happiness as a woman that he should retain that male ascendancy of strength, courage, and intelligence, in the notion of which she could take refuge when she was tired of exercising her superior wits. . . . It was one of those moments, fairly numerous in life, when a normal woman must wholly and heartily hate men for their folly and hypocrisy, their callousness and their conceit. There he sat, talking away—all that nonsense! —and who would want him, who would mind losing him? The heavy answer was: she would.

The outrages to woman's sensibility brought about by the selfish bluntness of masculine behavior lead a girl in *Ask Me Tomorrow* to say of men, "I could kill them all —sometimes." But the qualification is significant; she also needs them—sometimes.

> The conflict of her feeling came out of the subconscious —its archetype perhaps in childhood memories of being happy playing some intricate, orderly game with other little girls; and, at the best moment, having it broken up noisily and stupidly, for no reason, by horrid boys—all the horrider, since she might have been wishing that boys would come, admire, and play nicely, too.

What women need, according to the Reverend Ernest Cudlipp, is to be dominated and cherished, and most of the unhappiness between the sexes in Cozzens' novels comes from a failure of the male in one or both of these respects. Abner Coates, like the man in the short story "My Love to Marcia," is an unsatisfactory lover partly because he is so indecisive and uncertain. Francis Ellery, overcivilized and self-conscious, fails to dominate Lorna, "to his past faults . . . adding now the inexpiable one of doing nothing, of letting her have her own way." He knows how her furious spitefulness should be handled. "Confronted with it, a man's right instinct was to beat the little hell-cat until pain and fear brought back her senses (and, at the same time, brought back his; because her fright or injuries would rearouse tender feelings)." But, he adds, "Nowadays this was seldom done."

Domination by force, though it may give a woman a sense of male strength and consequent security, is not enough. It must be complemented by cherishing, by a warmth of affection which, as Bonnie Drummond sadly notes, is not constant (all normal men must be part-time lovers), but which should be vehement and absorbing at the appropriate times. Looking at Alice Breen, Ernest Cudlipp "could recognize, with a painful, reluctant pity (painful, since he did not believe it could ever be appeased; reluctant, since pity was a form of disparagement), the uneasiness of loss, the insecurity, the restless resentment of a woman not cherished." The point is made most poignantly in Lieutenant Turck's account of her platonic marriage of convenience, which failed so utterly because she "also wanted to be loved." Judy O'Grady and the colonel's lady are juxtaposed in two successive episodes in *Guard of Honor*: Mrs. General Beal getting drunk because her husband has been neglecting her and Private Sybil Buck on the carpet for her drunken conduct in a car with some AA men. However much they seem to differ, women are alike in that they all need men more than the men, with a different biological foundation and wider opportunities for self-expression, need women.

This dependency does not imply that women are inferior to men; Cozzens is quick to point out that they have compensating gifts which most men lack. Particularly notable is a quick perceptiveness that flies to the heart of a truth which the more lumbering, logical masculine mind may miss completely. Clarissa Winner knows at once, intuitively, what Mrs. Pratt is like and what she wants. All the admirable women of the novels share the ability to see more, more quickly, in a social situation or in a personality than men are able to. The gift, to be sure, may shade into an accompanying fault—a reliance on the logic of the heart which is all too ready to ignore what the swift mind beholds at every turn. Even the high-minded Helen Detweiler displays a quirk that is "integral to most female minds—seeing a so-much-wanted end, no means could ever be unjustified." Lieutenant Turck contributes a bit of the sad wisdom distilled from her experience: "Of course it would be Eve who ate the apple. She had no ethical sense. Anything women deeply and seriously want, or want to do, they *know* is right. . . . They know it isn't really wrong because it couldn't be when they want to do it so much." She is exaggerating, but the kernel of truth in her remark is not entirely to the discredit of women. The wisdom of the heart may come closer to moral truth than the cold abstraction of science, and in any case it is a distinctively human, as well as humane, quality. It appears at its best in Hope Winner's dismissal of the "figments of the reason" and her cleaving to "the realities of feeling." Her "woman's capacity for the persisting wish, for patient expecting of the impossible, for knowing a thing to be true while simultaneously not believing it," leads her to a moral truth which, in moments of illumination, is shared by men as well as women. What a man does should never be confused with what a man is. The kind of love that transcends blame or guilt and accepts people as they are is the second greatest commandment.

If Cozzens has sometimes been criticized for his supposedly superior attitude toward women, he has been much more widely and seriously attacked for his hierarchal view of society. By stressing men's differences in ability he has seemed to some critics to reject the egalitarian sentiments which, European observers tell us, are a conspicuous trait of the American mind. At a time when aptitude tests are ubiquitous in schools, government, and industry it can hardly be denied that, in respect of whatever qualities aptitude tests measure, men are born unequal; and the social results of inequality are likewise distressingly apparent. Cozzens can hardly be reproached for pointing these out in his novels, but his unsympathetic treatment of the underprivileged has been unfashionable enough to elicit strong protest.

Actually, what seems to be objected to most is Cozzens' correlation of native ability with wealth, privilege, and status. The debate between John Adams and Thomas Jefferson has not been concluded, and Cozzens' novels serve to sharpen the issues. It would seem difficult to disagree with the contention of John Adams—and Cozzens—that wealth and status frequently adhere to persons endowed with unusual abilities, and that status and privilege tend to persist in families, since (quite apart from the statistical probability of good genes reproducing good genes) members of the favored group have unusual opportunities to develop what gifts they may be born with. Conversely, able children born into the underprivileged classes are less likely to be able to make full use of the abilities they inherit. In this sense the Cozzens-Adams picture of a class favored by heredity (either social or biological) seems justified. But all Americans recognize the tremendous social potential inherent in the concept of "natural aristocracy," and most of us would agree (with Jefferson and Cozzens) that no amount of family background can guarantee the special abilities which are the only moral justification of status and privilege; and that, on the other hand, the lower levels of society often produce individuals who, if their capacities are given an opportunity to develop, deserve the highest degree of honor and reward.

Cozzens presents both points of view: the hereditary privileges of families for generations responsible and competent, like the Coateses and the Winners, do not rule out the possibility of a Judge Ross, a Garret Hughes, or a J. Jerome Brophy rising through native ability and hard work into the privileged class. Judge

Ross had run away from the farm as a boy of fifteen. Garret Hughes is also the son of a small farmer, and Brophy's father had been the town saloonkeeper. Abner Coates' efficient secretary is the daughter of "old Dan Starbuck," who used to drive the ice wagon; and the highly successful district attorney, Martin Bunting, "had prepared for his bar examinations at night school, and in Judge Irwin's office."

If the number of these natural aristocrats in the novels is small, so is the number of men with really superior gifts. "The observable inequality of men in every known society" is typified in the curve of normal distribution which represents graphically, and with at least statistical accuracy if the numbers are large enough, the range of variations in any measurable human trait. When the thinning upper end of the curve reaches the degree of aptitude epitomized in Paul Bonbright of *The Just and the Unjust*, or Captain Andrews of *Guard of Honor*, the number of persons represented rapidly approaches zero. The fact is brought home to Abner Coates "with dismay and some chagrin" when his acquaintance with Bonbright shows him that his own are "not first rate abilities handicapped by laziness, but second rate, by no degree of effort or assiduity to be made the equal of abilities like Bonbright's." Captain Andrews, handed five samples of a Navy code by a cryptographic expert, innocently sits down in a corner and, in his head, in about an hour, works out the principle to the astonished horror of naval security officers and for all practical purposes breaks the code. Andrews possesses "a brain of the very first order, a brain whose specially developed capacities exceeded those of the ordinary, so-called intelligent human being's as much as the ordinary, so-called intelligent human being's brain exceeded in its capacities those of, say, a fish's cerebellar nerve mass." It does not necessarily follow that Lieutenant Andrews will have the wealth and status that go with Bonbright's partnership in a big New York law office; but the two men exemplify Cozzens' persistent, fascinated interest in the extreme of the range of human ability, and this interest seems a more likely motive than vulgar snobbery for Cozzens' preoccupation with the highly competent few.

Cozzens shows no trace of John O'Hara's obsessive concern with the finer shades of snobbery. O'Hara can spend an entire page distinguishing those friends who call Mr. and Mrs. Sidney Tate "the Tates" as superior in social prestige to those who call them "Sidney and Grace." Cozzens makes only the broadest distinctions. In his novels wealth and status appear as the normal concomitants, if not the actual causes, of success in American society; but his *aristoi*, exemplified in the members of the Calumet Club, include a wide range of natural abilities. The common element seems to be the cultivation of aptitude and sensibility, with a resulting similarity of tastes and interests. Cozzens identifies himself, like Abner Coates, with "the ordinary, so-called intelligent human beings" who people his books, and his natural inclination is toward the class that has improved its natural endowment by hard work and discipline. The family of Geraldine Binney in *Men and Brethren* is typical—"a breed or stock which, succeeding by its strength, was toughened and encouraged by its success. . . . If, relatively, it had been fortunate; relatively, too, it had been superior in intelligence, in responsibility, in perseverance."

The extent of Cozzens' leaning toward the Adams view that ability and privilege tend to run in small groups of families is indicated in his analysis of such institutions as the Calumet Club in *The Just and the Unjust* or the Ponemah Association and Union League Club in *By Love Possessed*. The Calumet Club, founded in 1825 as a reading circle and self-improvement association by the professional folk of Childerstown, had come in the course of a century to have chiefly a social function. It held two cotillions (in practice, if not in name, coming-out parties) in the winter and barge parties in the summer. The account of one of these barge suppers stresses the simple, unpretentious congeniality of comfortably well-off people with similar tastes and backgrounds. Moderate drinking, some childish horseplay, and a hint of sexual irregularities serve as a reminder that these solid professional people have normal human failings, but the comfortable informality, the easy talk, and the spontaneous singing after supper contribute to the total effect of orderly, unaffected pleasure in each other's company.

Qualifications for membership in the club, though loosely defined, are rigid. "Of the four thousand odd inhabitants of Childerstown, about a hundred belonged to the Calumet Club. About thirty-eight hundred had not the least desire to belong. . . . That left a few people who did have a desire to belong, but had not been asked . . ." and these, of course, included the critics of the club, who spoke bitterly of its snobbishness. Cozzens' discussion of the problem is tinged with irony, but he seems on the whole to be on the side of the club.

> Calumet Club members thought the accusation of snobbishness absurd. Qualifications for membership were ordinary respectability and education, and some interest in the avowed objects of the club. You did not have to have money, and your grandfather did not have to have been a member. It was not their fault that most of the members were in fact children or grandchildren of former members. It was not their fault that respectability and education so often went with an adequate income. If people with means but no grandparents were congenial they were invited to join; if people with grandparents unfortunately lost their means they would certainly not be invited to resign. Since giving parties was now the club's principal activity it would be silly to have members who did not fit in. That was all there was to it.

That is not, of course, all there is to it, and it is disingenuous to pretend that a club, which by its nature is exclusive, does not exclude. How one feels toward clubs is apt to depend on whether he is looking from the inside or the outside, and Cozzens' view is chiefly from the inside. But he has also an insider's knowledge of the limitations of the club set that tempers his sympathy for their virtues.

The Calumet Club, like the Ponemah Association and the Union League, exemplifies the configuration of family-money-education-taste; but Cozzens makes it clear that such organizations, and possibly the social stratification on which they are based, are moribund—an anachronism in the changing social patterns of the twentieth century. Judge Fred Dealey, with his brusque common sense, readily admits the fact, and Arthur Winner's nostalgic regret is mixed with his appreciation of an irony inherent in the situation: J. Jerome Brophy, condescendingly invited to join when the club needs money, has deflated the "best people" of Brocton by a firm and dignified refusal. *Men and Brethren* has similar passages attacking the complacency of the respectable and well-off. There is, for example, the bitter contrast between the flower-filled, air-conditioned room where Mrs. Binney is recovering from her abortion, and the hot, dismal bedroom in which Mrs. Hawley is wretchedly dying —"close, dim, definitely fetid," with the elevated screaming along at window level only fifteen yards from the bed. Ernest Cudlipp, in what seems an excess of Christian charity, can consider the contrast "without irony, simply thoughtful"; but a reader cannot.

Sardonic reference is made to the difficulties experienced by a proper young clergyman, used to the private school girls who make up the Saturday Morning Club at Holy Innocents' church, when he finds himself in charge of a group of tough neighborhood girls at the summer camp sponsored by St. Ambrose's Chapel. Ernest Cudlipp thinks—and again the reader feels an irony at the expense of the "compassionate" rich members of Holy Innocents' (the name of the wealthy church that supports the Chapel is in itself ironic)—that "the general genius of the Church" has more to do with the polite girls of the Saturday Morning Club than with the girls who go to the St. Ambrose camp.

> St. Ambrose's Chapel was all very well, and might be said to have done great good in its time, yet really no good so great as the good it did Holy Innocents' soul. Essentially, the Chapel was Holy Innocents' answer to the lesson of the Good Samaritan. . . . They were acutely distressed to hear of the poor and miserable. Although, in fact, the poverty and misery around the Chapel was not extreme, it was terrible enough to them. . . . They, too, poured in oil and wine, anxiously illustrating the new parable of the Good Levite.

The shepherd of this flock of holy innocents, Doctor Lamb, has "an arresting air of elegance" in dress and carriage. "Given the finest materials and perfect fitting, clerical garb became positively novel—a dress of unsuspected grace and distinction." With his close-cropped silver hair, his finely formed face and aquiline nose, Doctor Lamb "showed the perfect noble definition of an eighteenth-century medallion." But Cozzens at once points out that "this whole effect of glacial, genuinely aristocratic dignity . . . had no special foundation. Doctor Lamb came of plain, far-from-distinguished people—his father, he once told Ernest, had been a locomotive engineer." Nor had Doctor Lamb himself any special distinction of mind or character; he had, rather, a gift for "smoothing things over . . . preserving decent harmony—even, his relatively few enemies declared, at any expense of principle."

Men of outstanding achievement or cultivation are

generally treated in the novels with respect, but for a decaying hereditary plutocracy Cozzens feels pity qualified by contempt. An intellectual snob like Harry Wurts, fatuously "pluming himself . . . not on what he knew, which would be absurd enough, but with an ultimate, almost indescribable absurdity, on where he had learned it," may be ludicrous at times, but in his way Harry is able and Cozzens does him justice. Flabby characters like Elmer Abbott, the ineffective, effeminate organist in *By Love Possessed*, are treated as unsparingly as is the Banning family of *The Last Adam* whose sterile gentility serves as a foil to the rude vigor of Doctor Bull.

Herbert Banning represents the third generation of wealth, and he is intelligent enough to "see his life as really one long, half-expressed apology for being born superior, for being kept there by money not earned, for eating when other men went hungry, riding when other men walked, living at idle ease when other men struggled to death." He tends his roses, is dutiful in public and private benefactions, and finds refuge and consolation in an habitual exercise of gentle irony. Descendant of hardy, hard-living ancestors, he has achieved refinement at the expense of strength; his sensitivity has been corrupted by his weakness. Mrs. Banning represents the old New England strain. She is a New Haven Brooks, accepting the privileges but also the "exact obligations" of her class.

Vulgar reliefs were closed to her. Without perfect success, but with all her heart, she held to a tradition, not in the easy right of an established aristocracy, but, if possible, prouder for being less public—the deliberate ascetic superiority of the dying Puritan strains. Make the willful body do right! Make the doubtful heart fear nothing!

Like her husband, Mrs. Banning is shown as admirable in her aspirations but a little ridiculous in the sterile gentility of her life. Their son, Guy Banning, represents a reduction to absurdity of John Adams' hereditary aristocrat. Without special gifts of intelligence or sensitivity, he is innocently selfish; his family position and his social education at Yale have given him an unshakable assurance which will enable him to assume, untroubled by doubts or qualms of conscience, a dominating position in the plutocracy of big business.

Guy could already please people worth pleasing; probably he was learning to command people not worth pleasing. . . . Of greater importance than not fearing or envying people more fortunate than himself, Guy would never feel embarrassed and apologetic to people less fortunate or weaker.

In his short story "Whose Broad Stripes and Bright Stars," published in 1936, Cozzens gives a highly unsympathetic picture of the *Junker* class in prewar Germany. The American equivalent of the correct, arrogant Prussian noble is Guy Banning. His expert cruelty in cutting down Larry Ward, the hired boy he has known since childhood, when Larry's friendly gestures suggest that he is stepping out of place, is in the worst *Junker* tradition, and the whole scene makes a pointed contrast with his father's rueful hospitality to Bert Ward, the brother who later arrives to make funeral arrangements for Larry. Bert and a friend have driven up from Bridgeport in an open car on a bitter night in March so as not to lose time from their jobs at Remington Arms. Mr. Banning, uneasily aware of his comfortable house, with the "bright, unnecessary fire" in the library, offers them supper. They have eaten four hot dogs on the road, but they accept some whiskey and Mr. Banning's offer to pay the funeral expenses with almost tearful thanks for his generosity, "a kind of holy joy at man's humanity to man."

The irony is characteristic. The hereditary plutocracy, the men like Judge Irwin's drunken son in *The Just and the Unjust* or the spoiled rich boy, Lieutenant Phillips, in *Guard of Honor*, who enjoy wealth and status without the ability, the effort, and the accepted responsibility that justify such privileges, are consistently painted in unflattering colors and provide a foil to Cozzens' idealization of the natural aristocrat, the man who makes full use of his endowments and is rewarded accordingly.

Cozzens is critical of the upper classes; though he idealizes their virtues, he ridicules their vices. Toward the underprivileged his attitude is consistently detached and objective. Though he sympathizes with their miseries, he reveals none of the spontaneous indignation in the presence of injustice that motivates the reformer. Cozzens' attitude is more like the detached sympathy of a physician for the suffering of an incurable patient. The weaknesses and failings of the incompetent are depicted with unsparing realism, but there is seldom any trace of the sarcasm with which the Bannings are described. The "insolent manner" of Doctor Casali in *Men and Brethren* is analyzed by Ernest Cudlipp, who concludes that "it's his misfortune, not his fault." Doctor Casali's objectionable behavior means that "he hasn't forgiven his parents for begetting him and bringing him up in a slum."

He means that he hasn't forgiven the people at his medical school who cold-shouldered him because he was poor and vulgar and didn't dress properly. He means he hasn't forgiven the people who, with half his ability, had the pull to get good appointments. He means he isn't forgiving Holy Innocents' for being able to hire him to do work of this sort instead of whatever work he may want to do.

In a competitive society relative misfortune must be the lot of a large number of people. Abner Coates is reminded of the fact when he sees a stone shield bearing the seal of Childerstown High School. Beneath the figures of Greek runners with a torch is a line of Scripture, "So run that ye may obtain the prize." But in a race only one person, or one team, can obtain the prize; "the others were, when you got right down to it, bound to be running for nothing." So long as men differ in ability, the less able in a competitive society are going to feel, and be, unfortunate. Cozzens' explanation of Joanie Moore's desperate efforts to secure a husband is compassionate, but it includes a remorseless analysis of Joanie's inadequacies—"no looks, no social standing, no money, no anything."

Other novels introduce the suggestion that the misfortunes of the underprivileged are the inevitable consequence of folly, incompetence, or lack of energy. "People who are poor, while they may be estimable and virtuous, confess in the fact of poverty an incapacity for mastering their environment," according to Francis Ellery. His opinion echoes an observation made by the author in *The Last Adam*. "Doubtless luck is the chief factor, but, dispassionately considered, almost every financially unlucky person is a plain fool to start with." Incompetence goes hand in hand with failure of all sorts, and the novels multiply instances of people whose lack of ability, or of courage, or of energy, dooms them to an inferior position in society. The Talbots and the Peterses of *The Last Adam*, the Kovacses and Dummers of *By Love Possessed*, are like Mr. Moore—the angry father of "Joanie"—in being numbered among the many score thousands whom, Arthur Winner remembers, the Lord God himself described to Jonah, as being unable to discern between their right hand and their left.

Mr. Moore's situation is typical: a newcomer to Brocton, he is an outsider as well as a perennial failure. His face shows his history of frustration, "the long hard-luck story of the incompetent." His angry threats are quickly overcome by "the level, hateful voice [in this case, Arthur Winner's] of that part of the superior practical world which would always have been his master and his enemy, which was forever brushing him impatiently aside, or beating him casually down." It is easy to understand and sympathize with Mr. Moore, but we are at once reminded that his whipped-up rage is a real hazard; he has a revolver in his pocket. There is good reason for his anger, but he is partly to blame for his trouble in that he has never paid attention to the actions or whereabouts of his now pregnant daughter. Still, Arthur Winner reflects, what father can really know his children or control their behavior? But still, again, Moore's actions are dangerous as well as foolish; like the copperhead in the garden he must be disposed of. When he has been reduced to bitter impotence, Arthur Winner's relief is tinged with sympathy. The reader, his feelings pushed first one way and then the other, is left with dislike for the "loud-mouthed little vulgarian," despite a certain sympathy for the "weak blusterer, surely incompetent in life and probably incapable in business."

Outsiders—whether social, racial, or moral—are seldom assimilable to the Cozzens circle of the competent, prosperous, and respected. Jewish lawyers from the metropolis—Mr. Servadei in *The Just and the Unjust* and Mr. Woolf in *By Love Possessed*—are not shown actually engaging in sharp practice, but the possibility is hinted. When Mr. Woolf is invited to join a party at Ponemah Lodge, he gives himself away as not belonging partly by the bold vulgarity of his speech, which is immediately contrasted with Judge Lowe's bookish style. "A lot of men they put up statues to might not look so good if we knew what they really did," says Mr. Woolf; and Judge Lowe replies, "Yes; men, perhaps unfortunately, are men. . . . If no secrets were hid—each of us, I think, might do well to consider just where that would leave him personally, whether he'd still be quite so well regarded as he may be now." The judge's measured sentences are almost a parody of Cozzens' own style; the realistic vulgate of Mr. Woolf underlines his differences. Mr. Woolf also gives himself away by his increased respect for Arthur Winner following a quick estimate of the value of the house at Roylan and by his delight at recognizing that he is being entertained by the "best" people of Brocton—"not, as he might have feared his getting an invitation meant, the second best." He is unduly admiring of Noah Tuttle's readiness to apologize, unduly jovial in slapping shoulders, unduly complimentary and apologetic. Nevertheless, he behaves with admirable dignity in the face of Noah Tuttle's unforgivable outburst at the auditor's meeting. And as for sharp practice, has Noah Tuttle a right to cast the first stone? The "cultivated, intelligent, and affable converted Jew whose name had been changed from Steinthal to Stonington" is mentioned in *Men and Brethren* only to increase the irony at the expense of the "shrewd, kind, rich old men" who have added him to the vestry of Holy Innocents' "to show their broadmindedness." Captain Manny Solomon in *Guard of Honor* comes off the better man in his painful scene with Lieutenant Colonel Carricker; and Mr. Rosenthal, an interior decorator from New York, is represented as superior in taste to the villagers in *The Last Adam* and superior in dignity to that sharp-dealing Yankee, Henry Harris. Arthur Winner Senior, "a fair and just man, a man absolutely unbigoted and unprejudiced," still did not want Jews for neighbors, but his is the voice of an older generation. Judge Fred Dealey says that such a feeling today "wouldn't make much sense. My personal observation is that Jews behave as well as other people; and you can trust them just as far

—which isn't saying much!" Cozzens' treatment of Jews in the novels is not unsympathetic, but he shows them to be, in the minds of many Gentiles, outsiders.

The foreigners—Poles, Italians, Czechs, Slovaks—who work in the factories of Hartford or Mechanicsville are typified in the picture of the Kovacs family in *By Love Possessed*: the father an economic slave and domestic tyrant, the mother a noisy virago, and the daughter a slut. More surprising, at least to a reader brought up on the Pacific Coast, is the treatment of the Irish. Judge Lowe explains the prejudice, which he says "existed," but which obviously still exists.

> "Seventy years ago . . . the term 'Irish Catholic,' at least to this community, meant the base and obscure vulgar. Few had anything that could be called education. Their mostly low standards of living—all they could afford—resulted in objectionable habits and manners. Politically, they were a troublesome mass vote at the disposal of their own highly purchasable politicians. Religiously, they seemed to be the willing dupes of their priests, of a superstition to the Protestant mind corrupt and alien."

Their descendants in the novels, even when they have more cultivation than the doorman with "the broad, loutish, Irish face" outside Mrs. Binney's apartment, give evidence of "a permanent, if hardly noticeable, defect in breeding"; and they are apt to be climbers like the parents of Monsignor Vincent McNamara, "born bog-trotters who made a fortune and then turned Episcopalian for social reasons." The Monsignor in *By Love Possessed*, though more cultivated than the parish priest who says "modren" for "modern," is still "the least little bit cheap." Julius Penrose thinks it's really serious when his wife's "new emotional needs are so imperative that they transcend all fastidiousness as well as all reason."

Another kind of outsider, the criminal, is analyzed in *The Just and the Unjust* with a complete lack of sentimental sympathy. Half-sick, stupefied with alcohol or drugs, the gangsters share the repeated failures of more virtuous incompetents. Their depleted bodies cannot enjoy the crude pleasures made available by occasional success, and their successes are few. On the witness stand a kidnaper who has turned state's evidence describes life in the "routine world of professional crime." It is not much different from the world in which the law-abiding struggle.

> In one, as in the other, the principal problem was how to make a living; and criminals who made good ones were as rare as millionaires. The rank and file could count on little but drudgery and economic insecurity; and for the same reason that most men in lawful pursuits could count on little else. They had no natural abilities, and lacked the will and intelligence to develop any.

The treatment in the novels of another class of outsiders—the Negroes—has evoked bitter reproaches from a number of critics. Their feeling is understandable. The injustices suffered by colored people in this country are so glaringly obvious that they must arouse the indignation of all decent persons. But no matter how generous in origin, feelings of indignation are apt to petrify into oversimplified antitheses of good versus bad; and where racial discrimination is concerned, the average well-intentioned person usually proceeds to a compensatory but not necessarily well-founded prejudice in favor of the oppressed race. Ideally, the proper attitude toward the Negro or the Jew would be no attitude at all; a completely unprejudiced person would treat individual Negroes or Jews not with special (and therefore condescending) consideration but exactly as he treats any other fellow citizen.

Perhaps no American can be completely free from prejudice, favorable or unfavorable, in his view of the Negro. It was on this assumption that the Carnegie Corporation in 1937, seeking a man to direct its monumental study of the Negro in America, chose the Swedish sociologist Gunnar Myrdal. Myrdal's conclusions parallel to a surprising degree the unsentimental conclusions implicit in Cozzens' picture of the Negro. Potentially, all anthropologists agree, the Negro is equal in aptitude to his white fellow citizens, but a long history of mistreatment and injustice has prevented Negroes as a group from developing their capacities, and they remain thus far unassimilable, outsiders deprived of the most elemental decencies of life and blamed for the results, in ignorance or shiftlessness, of this deprivation. The injustice of the situation produces an acute dilemma in the American mind, a conflict between a passionately held "American creed" of equality and justice and a complex of "personal and local interests; economic, social, and sexual jealousies; considerations of community prestige and conformity; group prejudice against particular persons or types of people; and all sorts of miscellaneous wants, impulses, and habits."

The essence of the moral situation, according to Myrdal, is that the conflicting attitudes are often found in the same person. "The moral struggle goes on within people and not only between them." Even the poor whites who are most hostile to the Negro share the American creed in some compartment of their minds; even New England liberals have some race prejudice, however sternly repressed from consciousness. Accordingly, a sense of guilt is apt to accompany the admission by an American of the fact, "obvious to the ordinary unsophisticated white man, from his everyday experience, that the Negro is inferior." Myrdal goes on to say that this inferiority is no illusion: under scientific study, the Negro does show up to be, on the average, poorer, less healthy, lower in "intelligence performance, manners, and morals." A similar conclusion is recorded in *Guard of Honor*. Captain Andrews, formerly "a statistical expert for a firm of consulting engineers," has been working on a special job—"a control analysis on Negro flyers." He has studied

> a lot of stuff processed right off Statistical Unit reports on Negro fighter pilots in Africa last spring—every damn thing; percentage airborne effective; aircraft aborting by type of cause; operating rates figured on required maintenance and return from maintenance. . . . The truth is, they didn't stand too well compared to some white squadrons.

This inferiority is, of course, environmental rather than biological—the inevitable result of injustice, discrimination, and oppression. A widespread recognition, even in the South, that the old dogma of biological inferiority is scientifically unsound has deprived southerners of a comfortable device for rationalizing the mistreatment of colored people and has accordingly aggravated their emotional resentment. In the North, acceptance of the idea of biological equality has led many goodhearted people to ignore the real cultural poverty of the Negro in this country and to idealize the oppressed race to a degree unjustified by science or practical experience.

Cozzens has stubbornly resisted the pressure to idealize the Negro. His views have changed somewhat in the course of thirty years, but he still writes of colored people with chilly objectivity, avoiding the generally applauded attitude of sympathetic special consideration, an attitude which, if not offensive snobbery, is apt to be mere sentimentalism. In the early novels, drawing on his firsthand experiences in Cuba, he depicts the Caribbean Negro, in the stokehold or in the sugar mills, as a kind of savage. Packy, the giant Jamaican Negro in *S.S. San Pedro*, is typical: brutally strong, stupid, ignorant, and childlike. In the later novels the range of Negro types and classes is considerable, from the lazy, shiftless handyman with his "mild, faintly cretinous gape" in *The Just and the Unjust*, or that preposterous Uncle Tom, the aged headwaiter in *Guard of Honor* "whose tufts of white wool and striped waistcoat had long delighted those . . . Northern visitors who knew a real, old-time darky when they saw one," to the Revere family of *By Love Possessed*, intelligent and self-respecting, the younger generation on the way up to careers in business or the professions.

The top of the scale is represented by Rodney Revere, great-grandson of a fugitive slave, now in his second year at dental college, or Lieutenant Willis, probable commander of a picked group of Negro airmen "all with GCT scores of one-thirty or better." At the other extreme, uneducated, shiftless Negroes like Ernest Cudlipp's aged cook share the struggles and frustrations of the white mill hands and dirt farmers of the novels. Near the middle of the scale is the appealing figure of T/5 Mortimer McIntyre Junior, black, shy, clean, and bewildered, and the coffee-colored quartermaster who gets the injured Mr. Bradell into a boat when the *San Pedro* founders. The third-class passengers on the ship, black or negroid, are reduced by well-justified terror to a "mess of paralyzed muscle and brain and will . . . lumps weighing some hundred and fifty pounds, too yielding to grasp, too misshapen to handle." But the second officer, at first infuriated by their flaccid despair, is finally moved to pity "their wretched humanity, their common helplessness against the inhuman ocean."

Since the fictional account of the sinking of the *San Pedro* parallels so closely the details of the actual foundering of the *Vestris*, it provides an opportunity to see whether Cozzens has slanted the story to the discredit of the Negroes. In the novel the Negro stokers desert their post, come up to the well deck, and are prevented from swarming the boats on the promenade deck by an armed officer. Among the boats that finally get away, the one containing Mr. Bradell has more than thirty Negro crew members on board, and the mulatto quartermaster recognizes this as shameful. Cozzens seems to have taken these details from the published reports of the sinking of the *Vestris*. Survivors charged that "some of the crew became panic-stricken and rushed the boats, crowding out passengers"; and they blamed the captain for the lack of discipline among the motley crew—white, yellow, and black. The British Board of Trade seriously debated the necessity of a law prohibiting the hiring of Caribbean Negroes in the stokehold. It was reported that four Negroes in a lifeboat refused to pick up a white man struggling in the sea. The chief engineer testified at the investigation before the Board of Trade in London that the Negro firemen mutinied, only three remaining on duty. The charge had been supported by other engineer and deck officers, though the NAACP had vigorously denied it. Finally the chief engineer admitted that conditions below were so bad that the stokers could not be blamed for leaving; but it seems certain that they did leave. On the other hand a Negro quartermaster, Lionel Licorish, was played up as a hero in the same issue and was credited with saving twenty lives. He seems to have been the model for Cozzens' mulatto quartermaster who saved Mr. Bradell.

Cozzens has used details from the conflicting reports to fill out the basic theme of his novel: the destructive effect of rigidly following a traditional pattern. Mr. Bradell, unable after desperate efforts to jettison a crated automobile, holds his hands behind his back to keep from beating hysterically at the Indian's head stenciled on the crate. The Negro Packy, equally frustrated but less inhibited, drives his crowbar into the stenciled head. Though childish and useless, his act is a normal human response to defeat. It is Mr. Bradell's inhuman self-control, his refusal to break discipline and take command, that really causes the disaster. Cozzens' account may imply that Negroes are less inhibited than whites, but his use of details of the disaster can hardly be cited as evidence of race prejudice.

The Negroes in the novels display a variety of attitudes toward white people. The grotesque, obsequious servility of the aged headwaiter in *Guard of Honor* contrasts with the cheerful assurance of northern Negroes like the Reveres of *By Love Possessed*, who follow their ancestor in the "freeman's dignity of choosing to serve." The airmen's justifiable resentment of the segregated Officers Clubs contrasts with the melancholy submission of Mr. Willis, father of the battered pilot.

> Never resigned to life in the land of Egypt, yet wasting no breath on useless protest, he mourned the recurrence of a phenomenon of insult and injury for which he found no understandable explanation, a woe of his people about which he could not do anything.

The attitudes of the white characters in the novels are more complex; after all, as Myrdal points out, the Negro problem exists primarily in the mind of the white man. The extremes are represented by Captain Wiley and Lieutenant Edsell. Wiley, a southerner, is built up as a fairly sympathetic character, so that it is the more shocking to find his ingrained, blind conviction of Negro inferiority leading to the prompt, brutal action that checks the Negro officers in their attempt to force a way into the forbidden club. Edsell, a northern writer of leftist leanings, is portrayed throughout as an obnoxious person; but he argues with informed intelligence, if not benevolent good judgment, the case for integration. Colonel Ross admits that Edsell is one of the few outspoken defenders of the dignity of man to be found on the post. Nevertheless, his violent dogmatism can only lead to conflict, and his delight in stirring up trouble is matched by his willingness to sacrifice individual Negroes to his inflexible principles and cynical policy of using any means to serve his end.

Other characters and incidents represent a variety of intermediate attitudes. Colonel Mowbray is an incompetent old fool, violently certain that colored boys are always second-string. Yet he makes one telling point, which underlines the widespread tendency to compensate for a sense of guilt by doing the Negro, on occasion, more than justice. In bringing in his plane without being sure he was clear to land, Lieutenant Willis has been guilty of inexcusably reckless flying; in strict justice he ought to be reprimanded, "grounded for a while, and docked some pay," as a white officer who had nearly wrecked the general's plane would have been. This deviation into sense, however, is exceptional, and its effect is cancelled by an emotional tirade in the course of which Colonel Mowbray repeats all the standard clichés in defense of segregation. "By and large, man by man, they just haven't got it! The Bible says hewers of wood and drawers of water, and that was no fooling!" The local newspaper editor, born in the North, thinks that differences of opinion "arise between those who have to deal with facts, and those who are free to deal with theories," and he concludes that "violence and disturbance will not help . . . those, black or white, who must live together, and who want to live together amicably."

Cozzens' picture of race relations has its paradoxes. When Judge Lowe is polite to young Rodney Revere, amazement is plain on the face of Mr. Woolf, the Jewish lawyer from New York. "Though holding with religion the concept of all men as equal, Mr. Woolf, humanly enough, meant to say that *he* should be any man's equal, not that every man should be *his* equal." Paralleling this bit of prejudice on the part of a victim of anti-Semitism is the scene in *Guard of Honor* in which the black Sergeant Rogers demonstrates that the way to get good work out of a happy-go-lucky company of Negro service troops is to treat them with a tyrannical severity worthy of Simon Legree himself. What is apt to happen when they are undisciplined and unsupervised appears in the juxtaposed incident of the ruining of the Lake Lalage rescue boat by a Negro who runs the motor "without a drop of oil in it and freezes both engines solid." The complexity of Cozzens' picture of race relations is increased by the spectacle of Alfred Revere serving Colonel Minton at the bar of the Union League with "the dogged respect of some private estimate—something perhaps atavistic, a feeling passed over to him from his slave forebears; an old South concept of a largely mythical 'quality' which you were, or you weren't." The scene is made ironic by the presence in the club's entrance hall of a more than life-size statue of Lincoln, near whose feet, "looking up with hope, crouched a basalt Negro whose shackles had been broken."

The Cozzens heroes, such as Colonel Ross, Captain Hicks, or Arthur Winner, confront the Negro problem with troubled minds and ambivalent feelings. Arthur Winner admires the "natural rule of self-respect" that keeps Alfred Revere from trying "to intrude where, he saw at a glance, he did not belong"; and he appreciates the aristocratic sense of courtesy which leads Alfred to take Communion last so that "members of the congregation need never hesitate to receive the blood of Our Lord Jesus Christ because a cup from which a Negro had drunk contained it." The irony is savage, and it is entirely directed against the white churchgoers who persist in so unchristian a prejudice. Yet Arthur Winner understands the attitude of old Dr. Ives, the former rector, who, observing "the observable inequality of men in every known human society," concludes that the differences in men, being ordained by their Creator, were not to be disputed or made light of. "God's great enjoinment was only charity, love of one another; the kingdom not of this world's motto was never stated to be: liberty, equality, fraternity."

Captain Hicks, an enlightened northern editor of a popular magazine, has "no conscious prejudice against Negroes," and he is "irritated by the note of self-esteem necessarily present in all assertions on the subject." He is made uncomfortable by the epithets of Major Post, who damns the Negro corporal as a "brainless black bastard"; but, contemplating the corporal's predicament (he has sold his return ticket in the hope of catching an Army plane to Ocanara and he will be AWOL unless a ride turns up), Captain Hicks shares the major's annoyance. "It was up to the man himself to see that he got back." But since the man himself is obviously incapable of managing his affairs prudently, Hicks is duty-bound to help him, even at the cost of considerable personal inconvenience. He is both sorry for the Negro, who is almost at the point of tears, and angry at him for being, so needlessly it seems, in trouble through sheer incompetence.

Colonel Ross's feelings are equally ambivalent, but for different reasons. He is confronted with the difficult problem of handling Negro officers assigned to an air base in Florida, and his native feeling for justice and decency is in conflict with a hard fact: the Base Commander has ordered that the Negro officers be segregated. It is Colonel Ross's assigned duty—distasteful but necessary—to face the rebels down, and he feels sure, with his "gloomy working knowledge" of what to expect from Negroes, that he can do it. Addressing the group of resentful colored officers, whose "sullen, half-heartedly scheming, black faces, so suited to their old role of the abused, the betrayed, mooned up at him in righteous protest," Colonel Ross forces himself to think rationally. These officers "had faced the standing injustices of their world; they had overcome great handicaps, with little or no assistance, in order to sit here as commissioned officers. . . . They were an unusually sensitive, intelligent, and courageous lot." And yet he is startled to realize how close to the surface of his mind is a dangerously explosive antipathy. The most trivial detail might set it off. These officers are still boys, and all boys are apt to glance aside in the presence of authority. "It was not these boys' fault that the movement of white eyeballs in dark faces was more noticeable than the movement of white eyeballs in white faces. It was not fair to form the conclusion that they were an unusually furtive, sullen, and shifty lot."

Despite his shamefaced feelings of the injustice of the whole situation, Colonel Ross "handles" the Negro officers with cold-blooded skill and checks their incipient revolt. He justifies his conduct in the course of a long conversation with his wife, whose unconscious prejudice—revealed in her remark about getting "awfully fed up with these colored girls"—is disguised by her emphatic statements that discrimination is outrageous. Colonel Ross says that she is reacting to a theory rather than the actual conditions.

"For reasons of justice and decency; and also for reasons of political policy, the War Department decided that colored men must be given a chance to qualify as officers. . . . In the Air Force, we have now somewhere around three hundred thousand white officers. A certain number of these . . . an unmanageably large number, hold that a nigger is a nigger. They will not have anything to do with him socially. . . . I don't say this couldn't be changed, or that it won't ever be; but it won't change today, tomorrow, this week."

When Mrs. Ross protests that "there must be many more, a big majority, who feel that a Negro is a human being, and who want to see him treated fairly," Colonel Ross replies,

"That big majority may feel that a Negro is a human being all right; but when you add that they want to see him treated fairly, you're wrong. . . . The condition is that the big majority doesn't *mind* if he's treated fairly, a very different thing. The big majority does not want him to marry their sister. The big majority does not want to insult or oppress him; but the big majority has, in general, a poor opinion of him. It gets awfully fed up with these colored girls."

The "good" characters of the Cozzens novels show signs of the inner conflict that Myrdal has pointed out as the heart of the problem, and which, more recently, Robert Penn Warren has so eloquently illustrated in his book *Segregation.* In so far as Cozzens implies a solution, he agrees with Warren's rejection of the possibility of immediate change. Segregation is morally wrong and outrages every decent instinct, but the latent power of the forces that have produced it suggests that, like sin, it may be with us for a long time. For the present, the inner conflict—"the rub," as Warren calls it—must be endured. The Edsell type of trouble-making only puts off the day when the slow forces already at work—industrialization, centralization, education—may make equal justice for colored people an achieved reality, at least so far as an ideal can ever be translated into practice.

Cozzens' attitude toward Negoes and the problem of racial discrimination is another facet of his most constant theme: the difficulty, quite possibly insuperable, of reconciling abstract right with the refractory nature of man and the contingencies of human existence.

6

"MEN AND BRETHREN, WHAT SHALL WE DO?"

The Cozzens novels provide no clear evidence of the author's commitment to any religious faith. *Men and Brethren* is an eloquent and sympathetic account of the works and faith of an Episcopal clergyman, but the Reverend Ernest Cudlipp is a dramatis persona, not a mouthpiece for the author's own belief. The *aristoi* of the other Cozzens novels are members, at least in name, of the Episcopal Church, usually in its middle-class, low-church form; but the Church is depicted with the mild irony reserved by Cozzens for institutions he does not disapprove of but to which he does not want to commit himself. Cozzens' own attitude toward religion seems to be very similar to the deism of the Enlightenment. A letter written in 1950 states explicitly his inability to share beliefs which transcend reason and common sense.

It has long been my opinion that in the affairs of life the Law's rational design to have the facts and to prevent more being made of them than unassisted reason makes is in flat opposition to the usually triumphant emotional wish (sometimes merely sentimental; sometimes gravely religious) to down mere 'facts' and to rise over them by a different logic where feeling counts as Higher Knowing.

I have to acknowledge that I work under a limitation here in that such Knowing is utterly beyond me; yet I think it is true when I say I have no hostile feelings and no wish to deride what I do not understand; on the contrary, seeing it as I see it, I find it affecting—an example of the general wistful human persistence in make-believe. Naturally I will deal [in *By Love Possessed*] only with what I am able to know, which is the cold dismay or unhappy amazement which those whose minds can get no higher than the Law's level of common sense must find themselves experiencing when they come up against the goings-on whose origin is spiritual—specifically, my lawyer's difficulty in imagining what can possess his wife in slowly going Catholic.

This somewhat bald statement of deistic rationalism is refined and qualified in the thinking of the Man of Reason. Arthur Winner's father is skeptical at heart; he regards the articles of Christian faith as "allegorical fantasy, a laborious attempt in symbols to relate the finite known to the infinite unknown." Christian myth is to be taken "not as shedding light on, but as admitting, the mystery, awesome and permanent, of life." Nevertheless the Man of Reason, with his "detached, dispassionate, well-tempered mind" has a due regard for decorum.

The stuff of this myth had long been the sacred fiction of the Man of Reason's people, his race. A fable so venerated, around which their civilization, for century on century, had formed itself, had a vested right. Were such established uses of piety to be lightly scouted? . . . Shows of doubt had the offensive smack of *hubris*. Professed skepticism was a vulgar sin against taste. Whether or not any given doctrine was true, any particular rite efficacious, any specific rule of conduct divinely ordained, didn't matter, was not of moment. Of moment, could be only the simple question of what was seemly and what was unseemly.

In this as in other respects the Cozzens heroes show their acceptance of the Renaissance virtues manifested by the urbane gentlemen of the Enlightenment. For the magnanimous man the virtue of courtesy requires behavior suited to one's position in society, and both the Man of Reason and Arthur Winner Junior serve, gracefully and effectively, as pillars of Christ Church, smothering, like old Judge Lowe, any expressions of doubt as to "the point of it all."

The attitude toward the Roman Catholic Church expressed in the later novels suggests the deists' distrust of authoritarian religion. The Cuban novels, written in Cozzens' youth, are in general tolerant toward the Catholic Church. Fray Alejandro, the altruistic, disillusioned priest in *The Son of Perdition*, "had never conceived his mission to be reforming men. He did not think men could be reformed, only helped; and at the end, by God's grace, saved." His attitude implies a criticism of optimistic liberal Protestants, and *Cock Pit* pokes fun at Protestant ministers "whose duties were never done, whose manifold activities and good works kept their churches in a turmoil of classes, benefits and uplifting programs all the week through." *Men and Brethren* marks a change; the Reverend Ernest Cudlipp has outgrown the optimism and missionary zeal of his youth, and he no longer accepts the Catholic Church with the tolerance of the religious liberal. He is able to admire the Church's realistic understanding of human nature, its unblinking acceptance of man's imperfections, and its skill in manipulating human beings into prescribed patterns. But like most of the admirable men of the later novels, he regards the Roman Church with distrust even while admiring its efficiency as an organization.

The elements of Roman Catholicism that come under attack in Cozzens' later novels emphasize the author's natural affinity for the modes of thought and the values of the Enlightenment. The theological casuistry that Swift and Pope distrusted in the medieval schoolmen is attacked when Julius Penrose analyzes the dogma of the Assumption. What he objects to is the needlessness, rather than the absurdity, of the doctrine. It has been made a basic article of belief not because of its intrinsic theological significance, but because it helps to round out an elaborate logical structure which would otherwise be open to forensic attack. Though the Church will split hairs to preserve an outward logical consistency, it does not rely on logic to convince its adherents. Basically the Church relies on its authority; its flat statements of dogma, which must be accepted entire, are precisely what attracts such desperate converts as Marjorie Penrose: theatrical people, alcoholics, former Reds—in short, according to Julius, "men and women who must long have been ill-balanced." In addition to the sense of security afforded by dogma, "all the slightly troublesome, perpetually recurring, obligations of worship . . . help the players feel this game is real." For people like Marjorie Penrose, frantically seeking relief from accumulated frustrations and regrets which have been aggravated by the emotional disturbance of the menopause, turning to the Church seems to offer an escape from personal problems—a motive for conversion sternly rejected by the theology of Ernest Cudlipp.

The 1950 letter already quoted indicates that a wife's conversion to Catholicism was originally intended to be a major source of conflict in the plot of *By Love Possessed.* As the novel was changed and revised the conversion became less important, but the husband's hostility to the Church remains. Marjorie's turning to Rome seems to Julius "a futile little ignominy," with "the sheer vulgarity of all frightened acts." Whether it be his wife or Blaise Pascal, he hates to "think of anyone cowed that way"; and his feeling echoes a remark by Judge Coates, "There's something about their organization that seems to me to debase a man." Even the temperate Doctor Trowbridge, rector of Christ Church, thinks that the Roman Catholic laity "tends just to pay its money and take its faith. They have, of course, any number of saintly, spiritually vigorous individuals; and I would not wish to speak uncharitably; but the rank and file do give one an impression of passively buying magic, rather than actively practicing religion."

More serious, because of its political implications, is what Ernest Cudlipp calls "the unique, peculiar air of authority and condescension; the bureaucratic . . . everyday voice of Rome," found even in the lesser parish priests. Francis Ellery may feel tolerantly superior to the ignorant superstition of the Cunninghams' Irish servant, but the long line of cars parked each Sunday outside Our Lady of Mount Carmel Church fills Julius Penrose with somber speculations about the political power that has reduced New Hampshire, Massachusetts, Rhode Island, and Connecticut to the condition of "virtual papal states."

Arthur Winner supplies an illustration of the operation of this power. As a member of the School Board he has heard Father Albright argue—with a bigoted conviction of right which leads Julius to invoke John Locke's query why those "who do not . . . tolerate should themselves be tolerated?"—that a moving picture on sex education should not be shown in the Brocton High School. Since the Church cannot afford a parochial high school, Catholic children are forced to attend the public schools, and though they are not required to see the film, excusing them would amount to discrimination, singling them out "in an open and invidious way." Father Albright is not yet in a position to enforce his preposterous demand that *nobody* be allowed the benefit of sex education; but as the Delaware Valley fills up with the immigrant labor for whom the millowners raked "every area of Europe where, life being wretched, superstition was rife," Julius fears that it may not be long till, through the "whisper of blackmail to nervous newspapers, to nervous advertisers, to nervous politicians," this state within a state will be strong enough to fill the velvet glove with the iron hand of power.

Arthur Winner listens without comment to the monologue containing this ominous forecast. But his sympathy is indicated later on by his comparison of Mrs. Pratt's rapt, emotional absorption in the Church to Caroline Dummer's moronic pleasure in the sterile security of the county jail. Characteristically, Arthur Winner qualifies his basic agreement with Julius by attributing it to prejudice, "an antagonism or enmity of mind, residue of the abhorrence and distrust by ten generations of forefathers passed down to him . . . the Puritan's warlike wariness, become now mostly disdain." Nevertheless, whether motivated by outworn prejudice or an open-eyed recognition of potential danger, the admirable characters in the later Cozzens novels distrust the Roman Catholic Church.

The sentiments voiced by dramatis personae cannot with assurance be attributed to the author; but whatever Cozzens may himself believe, there is a good deal of evidence in the novels that he has had a persistent interest in Christian doctrine and apologetics. In *Confusion* (1924) a minor character, the Reverend Robert Breck, is a preliminary sketch for Ernest Cudlipp in *Men and Brethren*, who as the youthful curate of Saint Matthew's had been "passionately, priggishly broad-minded and liberal." Like Ernest, Robert Breck has informal evenings for people who are seeking self-expression, and at one of these he debates the problem of predestination, arguing that no one, not even Judas, is irrevocably lost. Cozzens here follows a theory elaborated by De Quincey, and the episode is significant of his early interest in "liberal" theology. In *Michael Scarlett* there is a good deal of sophomoric wrestling with the problem of man's destiny, mainly by Christopher Marlowe. *The Son of Perdition*, as its title suggests, is centered on the problem of intrinsic evil embodied in the composite figure of Satan/Judas. The question of determinism and free will, raised by Judge Dealey in the philosophical language he remembers from college, is discussed in theological terms as part of God's providence by Ernest Cudlipp, and the agonized question, "Men and brethren, what shall we do?" is the equivalent of Judge Dealey's "What can we do?"

In the other novels Christian doctrine is not often discussed or argued, but an implicit theology may afford important clues to the evaluations of character that Cozzens is prompting his readers to make. Three ideas recur often enough to indicate the trend of Cozzens' theological interests: the concept of vocation, or calling; the idea of special providence; and a sense of intrinsic and irremediable evil which suggests Calvinism.

Despite the urbane skepticism of his admirable characters, Cozzens seems to have a natural leaning toward the Calvinist view of man. *Men and Brethren* contains frequent references, on the whole approving, to that neglected masterpiece, Calvin's *Institutes*. Ernest Cudlipp, speculating on the triumph of the infralapsarians in the modern Presbyterian Church, contrasts them—"no better than Lutherans"—with the genuine supralapsarian Calvinists, "who didn't blench at a little sound logic" and who "accepted easily teaching so desperate and awful" as the doctrine that man's fall was preordained by

God's eternal decree of reprobation. The Puritan background, common to the heroes of the major novels, takes for granted an hierarchal order in society, which stems from Calvin's insistence that class differences are inevitable and that "those in narrow and slender circumstances should learn to bear their wants patiently," since "it is unlawful to overleap the prescribed bounds." Accordingly the righteous man, whatever "his particular mode of life, will, without repining, suffer its inconveniences, cares, uneasiness, and anxiety."

More important, however, is the Calvinist conception of "calling" with its related stress on the necessity of good stewardship. Aside from the general "calling" of all men to salvation, an invitation to turn to God in the hope of proving to be among the elect, there are occasional special summonses to careers of notable Christian service, like the calling of which Saint Paul was continually aware. But on a humbler level, every man has a calling, a vocation or way of life, in which he may best serve God. "Lest all things should be thrown into confusion by our folly and rashness, [the Lord] has assigned distinct duties to each in the different modes of life [which] He has distinguished . . . by the name of callings." This idea, according to Carl Weber, was soon interpreted as involving a duty to labor in one's vocation, since good works, while useless "as a means of attaining salvation . . . are indispensable as a sign of election."

The Cozzens heroes recognize themselves as belonging, like Captain Hicks of *Guard of Honor*, to "that undistinguished majority of men for whom . . . work was an end in itself, not a necessary detested means to make a living." Conversely, the renegade monk in *Men and Brethren* suffers from the "dull, horrible melancholy of an enforced idleness; a helpless, hopeless inanition. He had nothing to do." *Cock Pit* (1928) is the first novel to reveal Cozzens' interest, later to become absorbing, in the technical minutiae of an occupation and the shoptalk that goes with it. "As a matter of fact, Cozzens' characters perform more actual *labor* in the course of one of his books than those of any other novelist writing today. The work is the man, and it is in his work and by his work that the hero finds himself and is revealed to the reader."

Cozzens has been criticized for his "quite routine American fascination with the routines and demands of professional life," which is said to imply "an unconcealed admiration for the man who uses his mind for precise utilitarian ends." It is doubtful that Cozzens' gospel of work reflects an aimless pragmatism which values accomplishment without regard to what is accomplished. The Cozzens heroes seem, rather, to exemplify the Puritan tradition that considers laboring in one's vocation not only as intrinsically satisfying, but as virtuous. This is borne out by the stress, particularly in *Men and Brethren*, on the idea of stewardship. Whatever a man's status in society, Calvin insists that "earthly blessings have all been given us by the kindness of God, and appointed for our use under the condition of being regarded as trusts, of which we must one day give account." Or, as Doctor Trowbridge puts it, "Talents aren't meant to be buried;

and, by the grace of Our Lord, they aren't allowed to be!"

What one's calling is, one discovers only as his powers, abilities, and limitations are made evident; vocation depends on the kind of person one is. And the kind of person one is appears, not in spectacular achievements or occasional lapses, but in what one does every day. Mrs. Binney's adultery, Ernest Cudlipp points out, is not really like her. By temperament and training she is a good girl, born into an upper middle-class family, nurtured in the low church faith, educated at an eastern woman's college, inclined by schooling as well as preference toward marriage and motherhood. Ernest recognizes in her "the one convincing possibility of steadiness, of virtue and integrity, in the dissolving turmoil of an unlimited transition." Like other people, she has struggled from time to time against what she was meant to be. After the tedium of a blameless wedded life in Cincinnati, she is easily swept off her feet by the young poet, John Wade, and is recalled to her vocation only by Ernest's providential aid.

The characters in the novel who are, even in limited degrees, saved—and it is worth noting that some are not —are those who recognize their calling: what Ernest Cudlipp calls an obligation "to do or be every good thing I have learned I ought to be, or know I can do." The intuition of God's providence which is the climax of *Men and Brethren* leads Ernest to read aloud to Mrs. Binney the "terrible twenty-fifth chapter of Saint Matthew's gospel"—the parable of the talents and their use by the faithful and the unprofitable servants.

Despite the Calvinist insistence on good stewardship, the central theme of *Men and Brethren* stresses, not good works, but faith, humility, and repentence. The question "What shall we do?" with its overtones of guilt and despair, is asked in some form or other by most of the characters in the book. The epigraph, more structurally significant than most of Cozzens' obliquely relevant quotations, is the conclusion to a sermon delivered by the Apostle Peter to the Jews on the day of Pentecost.

> Therefore let all the house of Israel know assuredly, that God hath made that same Jesus, whom ye have crucified, both Lord and Christ.
>
> Now when they heard this, they were pricked in their heart, and said unto Peter and to the rest of the apostles, Men and brethren, what shall we do?

The answer given by the Apostle Peter is "Repent, and be baptized every one of you in the name of Jesus Christ for the remission of sins, and ye shall receive the gift of the Holy Ghost." The Reverend Ernest Cudlipp, in answering the people who appeal to him, gives this injunction a wide variety of interpretations, some of which would no doubt shock the conventionally orthodox, but all his answers are at bottom the same: Repent and be forgiven. Repentance means admitting one's sinful imperfection in the eyes of God, giving up selfish pride, and reconciling oneself to God's providence. Not all who ask the question accept the answer, but those who do, find some degree of salvation.

Mrs. Hawley's question is easy to answer; though she has lived most of her life as an Episcopalian, she was born a Roman Catholic. Should she, on her deathbed, call a Roman Catholic priest? Ernest not only calls a priest for her, but finding him somewhat reluctant to put himself to extra trouble, neatly plays on his jealousy of the Dominican fathers to force him to come to Mrs. Hawley. To Bill Jennings' question about his delinquent younger brother there is no simple answer. Jimmy is stubbornly unrepentant, and Ernest decides to leave him in jail for a few days, in the hope—probably as vain as that of the father who tried to beat Jimmy into virtue—that he may be frightened into good behavior. John Wade, stiff-necked and contemptuously independent, does not even ask the question, but Ernest with fatherly concern answers it anyway, and is roundly snubbed. Lulu Merrick is so far sunk in alcoholic befuddlement that she can no longer phrase a clear question, but her arrival, bedraggled and desperate, at the vicarage door is an implicit appeal for assistance. She is beyond receiving advice, or any real help for that matter, and Ernest can only conceal from her the hopelessness of her situation in life and send her back to the sordid hell of idleness in a New Jersey boarding house.

The actor Lee Breen wants to know whether or not he should join the Roman Catholic Church. Ernest tells him that whatever he does will make little difference, since Lee has confused the search for happiness with the search for God. Until he is repentant enough to seek God wholeheartedly, giving up "this indecent anxiety about his happiness," he will never achieve the realm of significant religious experience. Lee's wife Alice is dissatisfied with her marriage and the kind of life it entails, and is frankly, though hopelessly, in love with Ernest. She has two questions: Shall she divorce Lee, and does Ernest want her to join the Anglican Church? Ernest's answer is lengthy and comes out in the course of several extended conversations, but in essence it is the answer he gave to Lee. So long as her own feelings seem to her the most important things in the world, she will neither seek nor find the kind of salvation that the Church offers. Ernest urges her to go on with her marriage; Lee, though vain and often foolish, is also often kind and sometimes amusing. Given her values, a true marriage in the Christian sense is impossible ("You could get just as much married as you needed to be at City Hall"), but her present situation is not intolerable. She will feel better in the fall. As to her joining the Church, Ernest would not be able to receive her; he would be bound to suspect her motive. When Alice insists that it is his duty as a priest to want her to join the Church, he replies that conversion comes to the individual from God, not through faulty ministers.

> If, perhaps many years from now, anything I ever said or did, anything you remembered about me, persuaded you that I was right, and you had always been wrong, all my religious duty toward you would be done.

The climax to the dramatic structure of the novel comes with the questions raised by Geraldine Binney and Father Carl Willever, O.H.T. Mrs. Binney, a casual acquaintance of Ernest Cudlipp's, has telephoned in despair, and Ernest arrives at her apartment just in time to prevent a suicide. She has left her husband; she has been in love with John Wade and has wanted—in a fit of frantice possession by love—to have a child by him. Now she is pregnant and John, having lost interest, is weekending on Long Island with a girl from his publisher's office. What shall she do?

The practical answer involves a difficult moral choice for which Ernest must take the responsibility, a choice not between good and evil but between two evils. Abortion is a serious sin, and Ernest makes no attempt to conceal its gravity. The alternative, however, if Geraldine goes back to her husband, would be the long-continued violation of another person's rights. Ernest decides for abortion, forces her to accept the idea, and makes the arrangements. Mrs. Binney must go back to her husband and children and live the kind of life that all her past training and experience have prepared her for. If, as she says, she can never forgive herself, that is because she has no power to forgive herself. Forgiveness comes from God, and a necessary condition is a contrite heart. Ernest has seen evidence enough of her contriteness. Repenting, she will be saved: it will be all right, he assures her.

Carl Willever's question, "Good God, Ernest . . . what can I do?" is brought on by a sudden insight, penetrating the defensive layers of bravado, into his real plight as man and sinner. In the six years since Ernest has last seen him, Carl has changed from a strikingly handsome, brilliantly eloquent preacher, the pride and chief ornament of the Order of the Holy Trinity, to a middle-aged confessed homosexual, "lax, bloated, pasty. He looked like a furtive, obscene old man." His release from police custody is the result of an ironic mistake: the Irish police captain thinks that any monk must be a Roman Catholic and accordingly dismisses the charges. Carl has left the monastery after a series of extravagantly emotional scenes, unable, he says, to stand the hypocrisy any longer. Now in a violent outburst of despair and resentment he reviles the brothers, baits Ernest, sneers at the Christian faith, and finally bursts into tears and implores Ernest's advice. His practical situation is indeed desperate. Such things, Ernest thinks, usually don't get better; they get worse. Next time he'll get a jail sentence. The taint of homosexuality will prevent a career in the secular clergy, and Carl is too old to make a fresh start in another field.

In all these circumstances, he advises Carl to go back to the monastery. When Carl protests "I can't go back —I don't believe anything, I tell you!" Ernest answers, "You don't have to believe anything. . . . All they ask of you is that you should be penitent. It would be hard to doubt that you're that." Carl hardens; this is the final proof, the evidence he has been looking for that Ernest, too, is a hypocrite. Ernest begins to explain, "Call it hypocrisy, if you must. There's a greater sin. It's presumption. I've committed it too many times. I know all about it. I think you would be blamed less for considering what is expedient than—" But Carl cuts him off. Restored to his former arrogance he strikes Ernest in the face, spurns his offered aid, and announces that he will set off for the monastery on foot.

"There are roads. Better men than I have walked them. It's not comfortable. Oh, no. It's not expedient! A Pullman seat would suit you better. I want none of your money. I want nothing of yours. . . . When I see the devil," he said, "I know, at least, that I am God's child."

Ernest speculates on Carl's future at the monastery: the melodramatic scene at the gate when the dusty and footsore pilgrim returns, "all the great drama ready and waiting for him. . . . prodigies of fasting, exhausting vigils, perpetual prayer [which] would soon make Father Willever a legend." Perhaps a hair shirt, or permission to keep a cord discipline—eventually, even, beatification: Blessed Carl Willever, O.H.T. Carl has "the temperament to support the awful rigors of emotional religion"; he might "prove to be, once he had found his formula, among the few chosen from the many, on occasion, called."

Nothing so spectacular, so nourishing to a certain kind of ego, awaits Ernest Cudlipp. Bitterly repenting the follies of his youth, he is now content to minister to the pharisees—a job that someone must do and for which he seems specially qualified. If doing that job requires him to subordinate his own likes and dislikes, even his social conscience, to the authority of the Church, he will accept his lot. It will be neither distinguished nor easy. Given his temperament and his age, it is not likely that he will rise much higher than his subordinate role at Saint Ambrose's Chapel. He has no illusions about the people who come to the chapel; they are making good their part of a bargain, in return for such benefits as summer camps, the Dispensary, and the sweat-soaked gymnasium in the Chapel House. Far from being a meek ascetic, Ernest is a full-blooded, sensual man, harried, like his young assistant, by the urges of the flesh. Thinking of Alice Breen's freely offered favors, he falls back on the promise in I Corinthians, 10:13. "God is faithful, who will not suffer you to be tempted above that ye are able; but will with the temptation also make a way to escape, that ye may be able to bear it." Without the comfortable support of a monastic order or even a well-ordered domestic life, half-convinced that his labors among people like the emotionally infantile Mrs. Hawley and the incorrigible Jimmy Jennings are futile, poignantly repentant for his past sins of presumption and pride, Ernest admits the providence of God and accepts the station in life, the duties and the renunciations, for which his whole past experience has prepared him, to which he has been called.

The Christian concept of providence is central to the meaning of *Men and Brethren.* To an Episcopal minister, the necessary working out of events as part of a long and incredibly complicated system of causes and effects is purposeful, the providence of God. Even what, with our limited view, we call accidents and disasters are "capable of being made to subserve the Divine Purpose," as discords may ultimately prove to be part of a new harmony. "There is no event, and no aspect of any event, even those due to human sin and so contrary to the Divine

Will, which falls outside the scope of [God's] purposive activity."

When Geraldine Binney asks Ernest Cudlipp why he went into the ministry, he gives a variety of partial causes: temperament, the influence (not, however, intentional) of a priest he admired, a chance to earn pocket money singing in the choir, a desire to influence people, a recognition that the Church offered him an opportunity to express himself. "In short, the Church gave me an opening. I saw it." Mrs. Binney, evidently expecting something dramatic and spectacular, like Saul's vision on the road to Damascus, is surprised. "You mean . . . that that was all?" Ernest explains that the way he has described it "can be understood by people who are satisfied with chance as a sufficient cause. To those people who have faith in the miraculous and believe that there is a purpose in the world, it is just as purposeful and miraculous as the conversion of Saint Paul." As he speaks Ernest realizes, reproaching himself for his blindness, that all the unhappy, crowded events of the last two days have also been providential. Geraldine could not have returned to her husband to lead the kind of life she was meant from the beginning to lead, without this disciplining. Carl Willever's fall from grace may be the means of turning him into a kind of saint. Even "the last inevitable indignity" of Lulu Merrick's suicide has been a part of the means by which Ernest Cudlipp's youthful pride and presumption have been chastened into the humble and contrite heart essential to service as a minister of God.

In the other novels, this comfortable assurance of God's providence is treated ironically. May Tupping, whose common-sense reading of the philosophers (she is plowing through the Harvard Classics) has thrown her back on a Hardyesque conviction of an immeasurable, indifferent universe, finds her whole outlook changed when her paralyzed husband begins to recover. Although his recovery is as mysterious and accidental as the paralysis, she now finds (she has advanced to Milton in her reading) a radiant significance in the "great harmony" of the closing lines of *Samson Agonistes.*

> All is best, though we oft doubt
> What the unsearchable dispose
> Of Highest Wisdom brings about. . . .

But even as she reads, the telephone brings news of another discord which, in the providential view of things, must be attributed to God's unsearchable dispose: Virginia Banning has died of typhoid as inexplicably as Joe Tupping has recovered.

Colonel Ross finds himself thinking of the same lines from Milton as he stands, tired and aging, on the reviewing stand. The lines have been supplied by his subconscious in the hope that they would satisfy his need, provide an answer to his not yet formulated question.

> The answer . . . came in the only terms possible for this kind of communication. They were terms of symbol or image, perfectly related to the meaning that was intended to reach you in the flawless logic that things equal to the same thing are equal to each other. It was again unfortunate that the conscious mind was not too bright, and so never

could work out the perhaps-worthwhile meaning of most of these messages.

The "message" of some lines from Pope seems equally enigmatic:

> All nature is but art, unknown to thee;
> All chance, direction, which thou canst not see;
> All discord, harmony not understood. . . .

As Colonel Ross considers the random, violent events of the past two days—discords certainly not easy to understand—he seems to be on the point of announcing a revelation: "From this, we learn—" But he is interrupted by the emergency siren signaling a new discord, the disaster at the lake.

The providence so eloquently illustrated in *Men and Brethren* is deterministic as well as teleological, and the problem of determinism, raised in several of the novels, is introduced in *By Love Possessed* by a consideration of guilt. Judge Fred Dealey asks whether, if a man lacks free will, he can be blamed for what he does. Since Arthur Winner did not know his wife was pregnant, is he guilty when a miscarriage brings about her untimely death? Dealey, citing the law on negligence and liability, thinks not. But in his blunt, naïve way, he goes on to outline a theory: Maybe what's going to happen is just as much settled as what has happened.

"When it gets to where you come in—well, it's bound to be pretty late in the day. Things have been fixing for whatever this is for a long time; and . . . what you're going to do or not do has been fixing for a long time, too. Freedom, I read at college, is the knowledge of necessity."

Cozzens, like Arthur Winner, seems to "reserve judgment on whether or not an unalterable, already finished design determined your future." It is a useful idea to men in trouble. Something like it, a debonair fatalism, has sustained Captain Wiley, the fighter pilot with the outnumbered British squadrons on Malta, just as it sustained the young pilots of World War I with whom Colonel Ross had served in his youth. One may reserve judgment as to the future, but can one deny the "iron chain of effect following essential cause by which the past had so plainly determined [the] present?" Cozzens' answer is given by the intricately linked chains of events which comprise the plot of *By Love Possessed.* If—to take one small example—Mr. Woolf's manner had not aroused Noah Tuttle's angry prejudice, Arthur Winner would not have made the propitiatory gesture of inviting Woolf to dinner at the lake; Woolf would not have been flattered into dropping his questioning; and the normal course of the hearing on the McCarthy trusteeship would have brought to light the fact that the accounts were irregular and short. Throughout the novels a reader can't help seeing "that there had been a point in every course of events (and usually countless points) at which the littlest, most incidental change in any one of a hundred interlocking details of time, place, or human whim, would have turned the whole present into something entirely different." Discussing the way in which the past determines the future, "the limit put on what we could do next by what we had already done," General Nichols tells one of his ironically relevant stories. Suppose a paratrooper approaching the ground sees that the terrain and enemy dispositions make it impossible to carry out his mission. What should he do? "Why, unless the man's a bloody fool, he climbs back into the plane and tries somewhere else."

In all the Cozzens novels since *S.S. San Pedro*, the same tightly knit chain of events leads inexorably to the conclusions; the same intricately unified plots are built around interlocking details of time, place, and human whim. The heroes, however, do not act as though, things being determined, they lacked free will. On the contrary, in sharp contrast to such passive weaklings as Mr. Banning of *The Last Adam* or the giant Numidian prince in *Michael Scarlett*, a philosopher who "believes that all is written, already decreed" and who accordingly allows himself to be burned at the stake without resisting, the principal Cozzens heroes take it for granted that they can make significant choices, and they continue to fight even though they have no assurance that effort will be effective.

Doctor Bull's comments on the statistics of typhoid illustrate the problem. Forty-three of the townspeople are stricken with a virulent strain of the disease. Statistics show that "the mortality is about seventeen per cent. . . . Consequently we're going to have seven or eight deaths. That's perfectly certain. Only question is, who'll they be?" This statistical certainty may be "a kind of Fate," as Doctor Bull says, but it does not stop him from requisitioning a house for use as a hospital nor from filling himself and the townspeople with typhoid vaccine. The indeterminism implicit in the question "Who'll they be?" demands positive action. Whether man has free will or not, he ought to act as though he had; and the Cozzens heroes do generally so act, whatever they may think. In this they again parallel Calvinist precept: one cannot be certain that he is among the few preordained to be saved, but one is supposed to act as though he were, glorifying God by both faith *and* good works.

Another Calvinist idea may be reflected in the emphasis throughout the novels on the extremes in human society. Cozzens' contrasting of the competent and responsible with the shiftless and incapable parallels the sharp dichotomy which, according to Calvin's theory of predestination, divides men into the elect and the reprobated. In the Cozzens novels we find a continuing contrast between good people, potentially redeemable despite their faults and lapses, and what Ernest Cudlipp calls "cheap people," who "have no chance because they are no good." Economic and social status may be contributing factors, and in the later novels there is a marked tendency to associate virtue with privilege and achievement. In *Men and Brethren* the division is in terms of basic, inherent aptitude; the bad people are born bad. "Many of them seem to be simply bad stock, bad blood—just what those things really are doesn't matter. Whatever they are, I have seen what they mean. The matter is practical, not theoretical." Good people, like those predestined in Calvinist theology, manifest their election to God's kingdom by good works; those foreordained to damnation by "the sentence of God's Predestination" are thrust "either into desperation, or into wretchlessness of most unclean living, no less perilous than desperation."

Cozzens does not divide his characters into the chosen and the damned with Calvin's rigorous, unsparing logic; most of them fall into a middle group, neither saints nor hopeless sinners. But the outline of a dichotomy similar to Calvin's is apparent in the treatment of the extremes. Only an occasional person achieves the ascetic saintliness of the Reverend Mr. Johnston of *Men and Brethren*, but most of the novels contain at least one instance of the hopelessly reprobated, men who are basically and unalterably evil.

These sons of perdition are not to be confused with the victims of environment, bad because they have never had a chance—the familiar case histories of the social worker's textbook. The novels show many instances of such "conditioned" bad people—the criminals in *The Just and the Unjust*; the spoiled children, male weaklings and female sluts; the unfortunate and incompetent. These people may be difficult or impossible to save, and there is little evidence that Cozzens thinks they will be saved from what modern Episcopal doctrine calls their "social inheritance." This theory, not unlike the social views of John Adams, dodges the question of the transmission of acquired characteristics and assumes the molding effect, for better or worse, not only of immediate environment but of the traditions of one's ancestors, "the efforts, gains, and failures of countless generations." Most of Cozzens' admirable characters show, like Geraldine Binney, the beneficent effects of social inheritance, and it constitutes their vocation to a life of responsibility and accomplishment. Many of the "cheap people" from whom Ernest Cudlipp expects so little are products of bad backgrounds, and Cozzens follows the practice of most novelists in offering some explanation of these characters through a study of family tradition and immediate environment.

Cozzens, however, goes beyond the hopeful assumptions underlying the social worker's explanations. Wilber Quinn, agreeing that Jimmy Jennings is "a bad egg," explains with the easy optimism of immaturity that "he's never had a chance" and is "the natural product of a society in which property is the source of privilege." Wilber's habitual naïveté goes far to discredit his opinions in the reader's mind, but to remove all doubt the author has Ernest Cudlipp enunciate a concept of evil as real, inexplicable, and irremediable. Personifications of this kind of evil appear in most of the major novels.

The archetype of the damned individual is Oliver Findley, whose nature and behavior explain the title of the early novel, *The Son of Perdition.* On the level of everyday reality he is a well-known type, the man of good family gone to seed in the tropics. Despite his education and background, he has degenerated in the course of fifteen years in Central America and Cuba into a drunken, lying ne'er-do-well and trouble-maker. The superstitious Alcalde at Dosfuegos is convinced that Findley is the Devil, and Cozzens carefully builds up the symbolic truth of this identification. Like the Father of Lies, Findley delights in deceit and wanton malice.

"Where he goes," says the Alcalde, "there goes death." As Findley watches, a roller falls and kills a Negro at Central Chicago; when he arrives at Dosfuegos, the lights mysteriously go out and a hurricane sweeps over the village. Old Cuchita, the witch, is poisoned that night; in the morning, as a result of Findley's seduction of a native girl, Vidal Monaga kills his only son.

Stoically enduring pain and punishment, Findley is the eternal rebel and outcast, fighting the Company which has no place in its disciplined ranks for such a self-centered anarch. Fray Alejandro, "priest in the ranked order of hierarchal authority outstanding against the chaos of such individuals, saw no good in the man." And Joel Stellow, Administrator General of the powerful United Sugar Company—its initials appear like a brand on all the people and property of Dosfuegos—concludes, "Wherever you go there'll be trouble, and it's not going to be here. It's too late to make you over, Findley." When Findley stumbles up the gangplank of the dark freighter that is to carry him to permanent exile abroad, the Second Officer, the gilt initials on his cap gleaming with reflected light, says coldly, "There is a place prepared for you." The slightly stilted phrasing of these last words in the book suggests an allusion, and Milton supplies a parallel.

> Such place Eternal Justice had prepared
> For those rebellious; here their prison ordained
> In utter darkness.

Cozzens identifies Findley not only with the rebel Satan but also with the traitor Judas, "the son of perdition," who is the only one of the Apostles to be lost. Like Judas, Findley is a traitor to his class and to those who try to help him; he steals from the young engineer who has recognized his background and treated him as a gentleman, and he betrays Stellow's trust. Concerning Judas, Cozzens draws on a tradition that goes back to Irenaeus. It appears first in *Confusion*, when the Reverend Robert Breck explains that although Judas "went to his own place" he was not necessarily damned. His betrayal is explained in human terms: wanting a sign of God's power, Judas "sold Christ that he might force God's hand, and when he saw the Lord led off to die without sign of Heavenly intervention, he doubted and despaired." As Satan, Oliver Findley is damned; as Judas, the human sinner, his fate is left uncertain. He waits outside the office window hoping to hear that the godlike Administrator General, by saving Vidal Monaga from the death penalty, will also save Stellow himself from complete dehumanization. When Vidal Monaga refuses to permit the whole matter to be hushed up, Oliver Findley is struck by "the great joke of the machine . . . confounded so inevitably by the rooted folly, the poor stubborn pride of man," and he stumbles laughing up the gangplank to the place prepared for him.

The son of perdition, combining the human sinfulness of Judas with the unalterable, unforgivable pride of Satan, has a number of descendants in Cozzens' later works. An instance in miniature appears in a short story, "The Animal's Fair." Emerson Hicks, a new boy at school, is a born rebel and trouble-maker. He has learned to use his candid, innocent expression to win over adults and boasts that he got a teacher fired "at one school I went to once." His shrewdness is used to gratify his malicious delight in making trouble for those in authority, and he betrays his schoolfellows with no compunction whatever. Indifferent to punishment, he is likewise unamenable to kindness or sympathy. Finally, caught in his own trap, he is expelled from the kingdom of the just —the latest in the series of schools he has briefly attended. Robert Basso, one of the criminals in *The Just and the Unjust*, exhibits a similar defiance of authority, a heartless malice, and an indifference to punishment that leads Abner Coates to suspect him of being a mental case. The same unsparing disregard of suffering makes Lieutenant Colonel Carricker a law unto himself. He ignores orders that do not please him, calmly disregards the feelings of others, and recognizes only the most primitive of loyalties—that to a comrade in arms.

None of these characters is explained in terms of environment. The two most fully developed examples of the damned character—Jimmy Jennings of *Men and Brethren* and Warren Winner of *By Love Possessed*— are presented simply as existing, inexplicable facts. Both boys come from "good" stock, and by giving each a "good" brother Cozzens sets up a kind of control to demonstrate that environment is not a sufficient explanation of the sons of perdition.

Of Arthur Winner's two sons, Lawrence was "tractable, brought readily by reasonings and mild admonitions to do what Father said was best." Warren, on the other hand, had always been disobedient, self-willed, unamenable to instruction, and impervious to punishment. Consequently, he was the object of continual worried attention, and his occasional return on his own contemptuous terms to the parental roof was an occasion for rejoicing which aroused mixed feelings in his brother Lawrence. A little jealous of the special attention lavished on the prodigal, as compared with his own "routine tokens of approval," Lawrence could only conclude that his father was weak, permitting his feelings of joy that the lost had been found to overcome both his reason and his sense of justice. Arthur Winner, thinking of Warren's long record of trouble, is reminded of a question raised by Judge Dealey: Could the father have changed Warren if he had done differently by him? The answer he arrives at is a flat no. How can one establish communication with the infant squalling at the baptismal font; the three-year-old throwing his silver mug across the floor instead of drinking his milk; the disobedient, heedless ten-year-old; the teen-ager expelled from private school? Communication being impossible, changing Warren was impossible —"In the acorn was the oak"—and Arthur Winner realizes when he opens the telegram announcing Warren's death that he had always known it was bound to end this way; that Warren's death had been twenty years in the making. "Except in some short-term view, limited and, so, ignorant, *accident here this date* was just what Warren's death hadn't been." The details come out later. The malice that had made Warren in his teens seek an opportunity to beat up the effeminate organist appears again in his cynical corrupting of a young Texas girl and in his arrogant disobedience of military orders, which results in a collision with an experimental bomber carrying nine men, two of them distinguished aeronautical engineers. The closest that Arthur Winner can come to an explanation is suggested by the note of reluctant admiration in the voice of the general describing the crash. Warren was "the true heathen berserker of the skins and tusks, the dreadful champion of Nordic myth. He was indifferent to iron and fire. For others and for himself he was uncaring. He was outside all law."

A similar contrast appears in the Jennings brothers of *Men and Brethren.* Bill Jennings, with his "clear, dumb, honest face," does secretarial work for the vicar and worries about his brother Jimmy's latest troubles. Jimmy has ordered a revolver from a mail-order house and has been picked up in the act of claiming it. Since he is eighteen he is being held for bail, and could be sent to Sing Sing for violation of the Sullivan law. Bill Jennings is baffled by his brother's behavior: "Nothing has any effect on him. Pa's licked him until he couldn't sit down. . . . He don't—he doesn't care. What can you do with a person like that? It isn't any use telling him what he does is wrong. He just laughs at you." Bill, who knows "plenty about him," concludes that, although it's an awful thing to say of one's brother, jail seems to be the proper place for him. Jimmy's father, as desperately ineffectual in establishing contact with his son as Arthur Winner has been with Warren, thrashes him in "what was truly and largely a frenzy of love," a desperate attempt to hurt or frighten him enough so that he would keep out of trouble. Why he should need such beatings, "why he couldn't be like Bill—furious, his father must have asked him that a hundred times. There was no possible answer."

The existence of such characters, in whom the heart of darkness common to all men is so imperative that no amount of social conditioning can repress and contain it, is one of the circumstances which the Cozzens heroes have to admit and adapt themselves to. Though he shares many of the traditional values of liberalism—the appeal to reason, a high valuation of individual liberty, a tolerant open-mindedness—Cozzens does not share the liberal's belief that education and reform can eliminate the basic evils of society. Rather, he seems to agree with orthodox theologians that a better society is possible only if its architects adapt it to such immovable objects in the social landscape as the succeeding generations of the sons of perdition.

7

SELF-DIVISION'S CAUSE

At the opposite pole from such monsters of moral insensibility as Warren Winner are two potential saints: Father Carl Willever, who despite his sins and his neurotic urge toward melodrama may be able to sustain "the awful rigors of emotional religion," and achieve some kind of mystical beatification; and the Reverend Mr. Johnston, Ernest's middle-aged assistant. Mr. Johnston is grotesque in appearance and stunted in personality. Years of service as a missionary in Alaska have ruined his eyes and his constitution and brought about "what really seemed to be a mental impairment, a simplicity very close to silliness." In company, his voice a weak, stammering croak, "the muscles of his throat twitching behind the sagging curve of the too-large clerical collar," he shakes with "disjointed confusion." His intellectual level is indicated by the pathetic sermon about the miraculous draught of fishes—in which, drawing on his knowledge of the Alaskan salmon fishery, he explains at unnecessary and awkward length how "the float line came loose from the net proper"—or in the "senseless bombast" of his favorite hymn, "Fling Out the Banner." Requesting that the accomplished Alice Breen sing "There's a Long, Long Trail Awinding," he demonstrates his cultural poverty. His room in the vicarage is as dismally bleak as the picture that hangs on the wall—a photograph of Eskimos in a terrible landscape of rock and snow. On Saturday night he has only the choice of spending a hot evening alone at the vicarage or going to watch Mrs. Hawley die. Ernest feels a momentary pity for this empty life, but is unable to think of anything that might provide Mr. Johnston with amusement. Earlier in the evening he has been urging the renegade monk, Carl Willever, to look closely at his fellow men in order to see "in what just and unpredictable ways [God] fills the hungry with good things." Now he recognizes in Mr. Johnston an instance of the hungry being filled. "Mr. Johnston needed no amusements, no suggestions. The rewards of his hard, bare, devoted life, the unsearchable riches of Christ, were given him in the perfect freedom and perfect joy of needing nothing."

The majority of mankind, falling somewhere between the ascetic selflessness of Mr. Johnston and the extreme malice of the sons of perdition, do not escape from "the self-centredness normally incidental to finitude" which is the modern Episcopalian definition of original sin. Man's angle of vision makes him tend to see and judge the world from his own point of view. "But the world is not centred upon him; it is centred upon God." Original sin is man's inability to recognize, or failure to remember, that he is a creature, not the Creator.

What might be called the average degree of self-centeredness appears in Lee Breen's concern about his own happiness. A successful actor getting on toward middle age, he has had a serious illness in the course of which he thought he was going to die. Ever since, he has been aware of a certain emptiness and futility in his life. In a rambling search for significance he has gone through Yoga exercises, Christian Science, theosophy, and a nudist nature cult in Germany. Now, skillfully played on by a Dominican father who specializes in the conversion of celebrities, he is thinking of becoming a Roman Catholic. The scene in the Chapel House office when Ernest Cudlipp is asked whether joining the Catholic Church will make Lee happier ("for certainly Lee didn't mean to go to a lot of useless trouble") combines high comedy with moral depth. Lee's wife, Alice, is less vain, more intelligent, and much more sympathetically portrayed; but she too thinks of religion in selfish terms as a possible remedy for the restless dissatisfaction of her life. Alice takes it for granted that happiness, if not actually a human right, is at least the chief end of human life, and she is accordingly blind to what the Church regards as the most vital element of worship, "the submission of our wills to the Divine Will."

The problem can be put in terms of secular morality rather than theology, and in the other novels it is usually so stated. The self-centeredness of the finite can be translated as pride or passion, and in place of the Divine Will one may read "the factual situation," the nature of things. Passion and reason, in the words which Julius Penrose quotes from Fulke-Greville, are self-division's cause. Blinded by pride, by one kind or another of selfish passion, most men disregard what reason shows them about the actual nature of things and pursue, at any cost, the immediate satisfactions which their feelings so urgently demand. By so doing they put themselves on the Fool Killer's list. The function of reason in the Cozzens novels is to clarify the limits of the possible, and to warn men not to work outside those limits. Cozzens is often referred to as a pessimist, and in the basic theological sense he undoubtedly is. But what is often mistaken for pessimism is a reflection of his underlying moral belief: man is, in varying degree but always to some extent, limited in his abilities and circumstances; feeling—the "wild, indeterminate, infinite appetite of man"—is unlimited. If an infinite appetite coexisting with limited powers is not restrained by reason, frustration and unhappiness are bound to result. Man in general, however, is possessed by love, so much at the mercy of his feelings that he rejects reason's sober injunctions in favor of "youth's dear and heady hope that thistles can somehow be made to bear figs."

The normal human impulse to ignore facts and choose the view of things recommended by the passions is exemplified in the heroic oil painting that hangs in the lobby of the Union League Club. The picture shows, in scrupulously realistic detail, the bearded, gauntleted, jackbooted men of the Eighth Pennsylvania Cavalry waiting in a grove outside Chancellorsville.

They were being pictured at the supposed instant when the major commanding imparted to them orders from their division's general. Horrifying intelligence had just begun to reach Hazel Grove. . . . In the appalling, altogether unprepared-for emergency, concentrated artillery fire offered an only chance of saving the army. Time must be gained to get guns enough in battery. There was one fearful way to gain that time. If a cavalry charge (who could hope to come back?) was thrown against Jackson's van, the all-important momentary check might be effected. Those were the Eighth Pennsylvania's orders. A plate attached to the ponderous gold frame carried, as a title, the major's reputed calm response to the aide with the message: *Sir, we will do it!*

Over the hanging of the picture a serious dissension had in 1880 split the club into two angry factions. Was the event depicted historically true? Judge Lowe, with an antiquarian's enthusiasm, dug out the official records and discovered—what any reasonable man would have found out long before—that the scene was pure fantasy, an invention by a certain general to build himself up. Why, then, did a majority of the club, ignoring the records, insist on hanging this depiction of the "mere vaporings of a braggart," this heroic bit of false history? For that matter, why had the Historical Society constructed a memorial at the grave of twenty-three militiamen massacred by loyalists in 1778, in the face of documents which "seemed to prove that what was actually buried in a pit there was about that number of pigs," dead of swine fever? "Willard Lowe knew an answer. These were the ways of man. This was man's incurable willful wish to believe what he preferred to believe. If a fiction pleased him more than a fact, he threw the fact away."

The best example of man's throwing away the fact in favor of a pleasing fiction is to be found in the cycle of love and marriage. Abner Coates has seen, in the course of suits for divorce, plenty of evidence.

> The primary trouble was the same. Differences were only in detail. . . . Someone had married someone that he or she (usually she) did not really know. Ruling out occasional cool moves to get money or deliberate resolves to take a last or only chance, it would seem that those about to marry avoided rather than sought real knowledge; and were content to investigate nothing but their own feelings; and were satisfied if, among their feelings, they discovered some truth, such as: every time my honey leaves me, I get the blues.

A precise illustration of this general statement appears in the history of Lieutenant Amanda Turck, whose desperately unhappy marriage was brought about by her own determined ignoring of her real needs and of the ingrained homosexual bent of her intended husband. Kirkland, the extroverted athlete in *Ask Me Tomorrow*, having failed to see that Mrs. Hartpence is an alcoholic trollop, is naïvely outraged because "she he loved had swindled him. He had taken her with the understanding that she was romantic and desirable," but she "had misrepresented herself."

No such painful surprise is apt to befall Abner Coates, whose tepid wooing of Bonnie Drummond has sometimes been cited as evidence that the author's head is too much in command of his heart. It is true that Cozzens often treats romantic love as a mere incident in a well-ordered life. Though Abner "loves" Bonnie, he can hardly be said to have lost his head over her. His proposal and acceptance take place in the kitchen while Bonnie is preparing a bowl of milk toast for a sick child, and the episode is more comic than romantic. Furthermore, the implication is clear that their married life, like that of Captain Hicks in *Guard of Honor*, will be happy precisely because neither partner regards the world well lost for love.

However, it would be a mistake to assume that this relationship epitomizes Cozzens' view of love. In his analysis of the relations between the sexes, he goes far beyond this simple, sensible marriage of true minds. Greek mythology has two traditions regarding the god Eros. Whether sprung from the primal Egg or, as in Hesiod, a son of Chaos, in the older tradition Eros, a young man, is the god of generation; and his power, terrible and universal, is the creative principle in all things. The later tradition of Eros embodied in the Roman Cupid represents the god as a willful child, often blind, who shoots his golden arrows indiscriminately. A true son of Venus, he is the god of physical passion, and it is his effigy that appears on the gilt clock in Mrs. Winner's parlor. His power is pictured, in full and frank detail, only in *By Love Possessed*, but all the novels—the language varying from the Elizabethan bawdiness of *Michael Scarlett* to the dry, legal matter-of-factness of *The Just and the Unjust*—are full of references to sexual intercourse. *The Last Adam* may serve as an example. It contains, in addition to the long-standing, generally accepted, and hence almost "regular" relations between Doctor Bull and Janet Cardmaker, allusions to irregular affairs between Janet's hired man ("the village satyr") and a number of women including Belle Rogers and Mamie Talbot; between Larry Ward and Charlotte Slade; between Robert Newell (proprietor of a summer camp notorious for its freedom) and both the Clark sisters. There are references to Doctor Bull's appreciative ogling of Doctor Verney's nurse, "her short face sweetly sensual, her pert flanks shifting"; to Guy Banning's thoughts of a night in New York with "the shamefully attractive and obscenely available DeFoe girl . . . a slut of good family"; and to Betty Peters' "long history of sexual miseries—she had begun at fifteen by spending a night with a group of men from Sansbury in a tobacco barn."

In a moment of disillusion Francis Ellery considers "the conventional French proposition that, in life, the really important (but not serious) thing was love." "It's like a picture in *Le Rire*," whose advertisers also "spoke to you of love. What about the pied-à-terre grand luxe always open and the articles d'hygiène en caoutchouc? . . . What about the disorders of the voies urinaires, the pilules and pastilles good for impuissance, acte bref, and frigidité féminine? You couldn't say they hadn't told you!" This sardonic view of sexual relations is echoed later in the book when Francis Ellery thinks how the amorous behavior of grown-ups must appear to the twelve-year-old eyes of Walter Cunningham.

> Suddenly abandoning everything that they said or implied to Walter or the world about their dignity and reasonableness, adults, seized by love, went into a sort of vaudeville act, side-splitting at first, but much too long; holding hands, kissing, bandying pet names; until, for no ascertainable reason beyond their own silliness, they fell to fighting and yelling, and the women at least to crying. . . . All Walter maintained was that love looked funny; and who could deny that from the first infatuated ogles and formal beatings-about-the-bush to the last ridiculous position and brief pleasure, it did, it did?

The Chesterfieldian disillusion of such passages, frequently repeated in *By Love Possessed*, is balanced by descriptions of love, not as it appears to the indifferent small boy or adult nonparticipant, but as it seems to the lover transfixed by the golden shaft of Eros. Seeing Lorna after a long absence, Francis Ellery is smitten by a helpless longing which, going beyond the imperative urge to physical possession, would use sex only as a means to make her give him "the something more, he did not know what, that, over and above her body, have from her he must." Between these extremes is the mean, represented by Lorna's friend Gwen, "progressing gravely and intelligently from a neat happy child, to a neat, amiable young woman, to the neat comfortable marriage whose reasonable affections would operate to make her the mother of more neat happy children." That this mean is not the norm of human behavior is shown by the number and variety of the people throughout the novels who, for better or worse, are possessed by love. Francis Ellery's passion—"she could despise or cheat you and that would be all right. She could be a nun or a motion picture actress . . . she could be a dirty old worn-out tart; she could be dead; while you . . . groveled through the hopeless days or years, still loving, still locked out"—is only a prelude to the full development of the theme in *By Love Possessed.*

Possession by love, as represented in the latest of Cozzens' novels, goes beyond sexual desire or passion to the endlessly varied complications caused in life by the "manifold manifestings of the amative appetite." In its sexual form, it appears at its simplest and crudest in Ralph Detweiler and Veronica Kovacs, victims of a sharp, undiscriminating itch. On a more impressive scale is the tyranny of physical infatuation, exemplified by Marjorie Penrose, whose normal "little girl" personality conceals a maenad—an irresistible urge which is perhaps the female equivalent of Doctor Bull's unkillable "good greedy vitality." Even the rational, controlled Arthur Winner is conquered by the contagion of her "oestrual rage" and is led to desecrate his wife's memory and deceive his best friend. Less spectacular but more typical is the sharply drawn contrast between the self-possession of Lieutenant Mary Lippa, WAC, when she is performing her duties as "a first-rate company officer" and the "eloquent, distinctive shyness . . . the light tremble of the heart, the low quiver of the womb" which reduce her to helpless doting when Lieutenant Edsell appears. At four-thirty she marches at the head of her company past the reviewing stand—alert, trim, rigidly at attention. Two hours later she is in the hotel lobby with Edsell, flushed and clinging to his arm with an "effect of sensual abandonment . . . so marked that she was getting a good deal of attention."

Joanie Moore's "utter unreason of feeling" comes, not from physical passion, but from another kind of possession—an imperative need for recognition and affection. The conventional, self-generating, low-pressure romance that accounts for Arthur Winner's first, unsuccessful marriage to Hope Tuttle brings about also a convenient sober union between the young rector and his earnest, modest Midge. Parental love is analyzed in a number of instances, ranging from the blind carelessness of the Moores and the helpless stupidity of the Dummers to the equally blind overcarefulness of Helen Detweiler and the equally helpless intelligence of the Winners as they try to redeem the prodigal, Warren.

Many of the forms of amative appetite reduce to love of self—or, what amounts to the same thing, love of an imagined self. It is this cherished picture of himself as irreproachable man of honor that Arthur Winner at the end of the book is forced to exchange for the moral ambiguity in which Noah Tuttle has lived for years. Noah's determination not to let down the townspeople who had invested in the Traction Company reduces ultimately to love of a picture of himself as the wise infallible adviser. The driving ambition of J. Jerome Brophy comes from a picture of himself as a good deal more than the son of an Irish saloonkeeper from the wrong side of the tracks; and his determination to make the town accept this self-estimate is "an obsession, one of those things that take a person over."

Colonel Minton—the reasons are not made clear—is possessed by love of oblivion and is rapidly drinking himself to death. A secret, helpless, destructive sympathy for suffering humanity has cracked the protective shell of Doctor Reggie Shaw's scientific objectivity and is leading him inexorably, through the stages of hopelessness and disgust, to the brink of collapse. The portrait of Judge Fred Dealey is a little masterpiece of passionate self-division. Impatient "that fools must still be suffered," indignant that they "must still suffer," he denounces "the intractability of circumstances, the random brute works of mischance" with the "vitriolic passion of outrage" until he is embarrassed by his own unreason. "Now what fool, simultaneously suffering and insufferable, had allowed feeling once again to make a fool of him?" Mrs. Pratt is possessed by an overripe, self-centered emotionalism, which she mistakes for the love of God. Even Julius Penrose admits to "human weaknesses of vanity and self-regard"; his honor, referred to with a grimace, obliges him to sacrifice his own fortune if Arthur Winner sacrifices his. Even the sternly self-denying Helen Detweiler "just couldn't help" trying to dissuade Miss Kovacs from pressing her charge, though Arthur Winner has warned her of the legal dangers involved. "She had to do what her feelings pressed her to do! Possessed by her feelings, she couldn't help it! On the real nature of the human will, on all vaunted self-control, on all admired self-discipline, were those words the last word?"

The question, ignoring the insoluble problem of determinism and free will, asks for an answer in the human terms of passion versus reason, and Cozzens' answer is unequivocal. For most men, the will is subject to the tyranny of feeling, and the result is trouble. But the heroes—though they may be subject to lapses, temporary fits of possession by feeling—have the ability to live by some measure of rational control. Colonel Ross reminds himself that "if mind failed you, seeing no pattern; and heart failed you, seeing no point, the stout, stubborn will must be up and doing"; and all his actions show his ability to live up to this stern prescription. Ernest Cudlipp, putting into practice one of the principles of the spiritual life—that "appetites depend a good deal on what you spend your time thinking about"—maintains the celibacy that his convictions demand. Francis Ellery, torn between what he knows is right (his responsibility for Walter) and what he passionately desires (Lorna), chooses duty and, aided by some ironic quirks of chance, makes himself do what he knows he should do. Judge Coates, Ernest Cudlipp, General Nichols, General Beal, Julius Penrose—indeed all the men Cozzens invites the reader to admire—demonstrate that within limits man can make choices and will to live by them. Nevertheless, the common practice of most men, and the occasional lapses of even the superior man, demonstrate the basic truth of the motto inscribed on the clock; all men, at some time and in some ways, are possessed by love. Love, indeed, conquers all.

In regard to most problems of ethics, Cozzens' distrust of oversimple solutions leads him to answers which are ambiguous if not actually equivocal. It is not merely that he makes us aware of the exceptions to every rule; there are a bewildering number of rules, and though each may seem convincing as presented in a particular context of character and action, taken together they lead to contradiction and tension.

The sexual ethics implied in the novels illustrate this moral ambiguity. Except for a youthfully defiant insistence in his early novels on such forbidden themes as incest, Cozzens rejects the abnormal and the infantile. Homosexuality is treated with as little sympathy as is the childish indecency of Sam Field, the high school teacher in *The Just and the Unjust*. But in describing the normal commerce between the sexes, the novelist presents a variety of codes. At one extreme is the self-restraint expounded by the Reverend Ernest Cudlipp. When Alice Breen asks incredulously, "Do you mean that you think . . . John is being ruined because he probably wants to sleep with that nice kid?" Ernest replies, "Drunkenness and fornication are in their nature wrong and the Church condemns them." And of Geraldine Binney's disastrous affair he says, "Evil can't be done in a nice way. In violating your morals you'll certainly outrage your sensibilities."

Set against this Christian discipline is the male, animal promiscuity of Doctor Bull and some of the soldiers in

Guard of Honor. Captain Duchemin, in civilian life appropriately enough a publicity man for a chain of hotels, is a frank hedonist whose chief interest in life is the pursuit of some empty-headed Emerald or June and the hurried consummation of such meaningless affairs. To him as to Captain Wiley, the fighter pilot from Orlando, "a belly full of beer and a girl in bed were solid goods, suited to the nature of man. People who really did not want them had something wrong with them; people, a good deal more numerous, who really did want them, but refrained for various artificial reasons from getting them, struck Captain Duchemin as ludicrous."

The pagan promiscuity of Duchemin and Wiley seems all wrong to Captain Andrews, the appealing, slightly maladjusted mathematical genius. Quite apart from the lack of discrimination involved in promiscuity, he is troubled by some of the implications of sexual unfaithfulness. Once free of the bonds of reason, responsibility, and obligation, "you were free also of affection and understanding, of trust and devotion." Captain Andrews sees marital infidelity as betraying, not merely a person, but "the basic human relation, the vital understanding between human beings." This view is reiterated by Mrs. Ross, a sensible and admirable woman: "It is a matter of falsifying a relationship . . . a kind of common trust, between two people. If he is, in the very exact phrase, untrue. . . . he has made it no longer a common trust. He's made an unstable arrangement of ignorance on one side and deceit on the other."

She and Colonel Ross are talking about Captain Hicks,

and the Colonel thinks it quite possible that "a fellow like Hicks . . . might refrain for months and months from doing anything that would hurt his wife for no better reason than that he was fond of her." Captain Hicks, a little too hastily and confidently, agrees. To the embarrassingly frank questioning of Captain Wiley he answers that he hasn't "found it necessary" to be unfaithful to his wife. To himself he admits that his motive is at least in part prudential.

> Where Captain Wiley saw such a temptingly available delicacy, all Nathaniel Hicks saw was a lot of trouble. . . . Let irregularly into your life—oh, my God, the trials and tediums, the disgusts and annoyances, the quarrelings and repinings, with which she would quite justifiably plague you when, having enough, you thought of withdrawing! A short course in the dear school kept for fools would learn you that Peace, O Virtue, Peace is all thine own!

Beyond this craven respect of fear, however, Captain Hicks has "the general intention of being, or at least, the definite wish to be, faithful to his wife, whom he loved." Moved by the touching relationship between the Andrewses, he "found himself immediately thinking of his own wife, and even pluming himself a little on a continence that, after all, did not come very hard; and was . . . worth in the long run so much." It is a moment of *hubris*, for while his eyes are half-filling with tears at the thought of such devotion, a door in the hospital opens and a nurse, Lieutenant Isabella Shakespeare, enters. She is what Captain Wiley would call "a dish of a bitch," who "must have heard soulful whistles in her time," and whose "body's air of blood-warm bloom, of endocrine well-being, suggested that she often heeded them." Her manner is confident, indicating "that Lieutenant Shakespeare found all men alike and knew the way to handle them." Responding involuntarily to "those wide, melting eyes; those parted, and at such close range, moist-looking, lips; that wealth of curls from which arose a not-unpleasant odor, mixed with traces of perfume," Captain Hicks is disconcerted by a feeling not "sorting too well with those chaste reflections of a few minutes back. It might even suggest that there was a basic, objectionable truth in Lieutenant Shakespeare's experienced idea of all men, and of their usable, pandemic impulses."

The episode is a foreshadowing of the climactic scene in which Captain Hicks, moved by a mixture of compassion and desire, is actually unfaithful to his wife. The moral confusion in which, immediately after, he boards a plane for an unexpected two-week leave at home is typical of the deliberate ambiguity which throughout the novels attends Cozzens' treatment of ethical questions. Arthur Winner's mother—like Mrs. Ross, like Captain Andrews—sees things in simple terms of black and white: honesty vs. dishonesty, faithfulness vs. infidelity, loyalty vs. betrayal. The heroes of the novels, from Abner Coates and Captain Hicks to Arthur Winner and Julius Penrose, have to settle, in the conflict and confusion of values, for less simple and more unstable arrangements. Ernest Cudlipp may tell Mrs. Binney, "You have no right to put yourself in a position where you can only choose between evils, instead of between good and evil."

But the experience of most of Cozzens' characters, from Arthur Winner to Abner Coates and Colonel Ross, demonstrates that the necessity of choosing between two evils (one perhaps lesser, but still deplorable) is part of the human condition.

The heroes are painfully aware of the moral shadings necessitated by actual human predicaments. Honesty is the best—and certainly, several characters reflect, the most comfortable—policy; but the simple definition his mother gives the term, though admirable, is inapplicable to the real situation in which Arthur Winner finds himself at the end of *By Love Possessed.* Francis Ellery admires Mrs. Cunningham's candor, but he realizes that his impulsive answering candor is not an unmixed virtue. "He did not . . . lack the will to be devious; he simply lacked the skill and patience." General Beal's engaging openness of manner strikes a reader as admirable, but Captain Hicks reminds us that it is a sign of youthful uncertainty, improper in a commanding officer, who ought to relieve his subordinates "of a responsibility which it was not their business to bear" by crushing all "arguments that might aggravate uncertainty."

In reply to the rector, who argues that secretly keeping Carl Willever in the vicarage amounts to admitting that we may do what we want so long as no one sees us, Ernest Cudlipp insists, "I still think there is a legitimate difference between discretion and hypocrisy." Drawing fine moral lines of this sort is the painful, continual responsibility of the Cozzens heroes, and the reader is kept constantly aware of the moral tension by having his sympathy directed toward both alternatives. We admire the simple-minded integrity of General Beal, convinced that honor, loyalty, and duty are "solid goods" and that "everyone knew what the words meant." Sergeant Pellerino's unquestioning loyalty to the general is not only admirable in itself, it is essential to successful military operations; and General Nichols points out that one of Beal's most valuable qualities is his ability to call out this loyalty from men as different in background as the master sergeants and Colonel Ross. Yet Cozzens reminds us that this same loyalty, by protecting the brutal Carricker and the incompetent Colonel Mowbray, has been responsible for a near race-riot and the death of a number of paratroopers. We are delighted with the decency that prompts General Beal to dictate a letter of commendation for the range officer who had unwittingly demonstrated his efficiency by sharp criticism of the general's flying. But Colonel Ross notes, somewhat sourly, that this is a sentimental gesture. "For each man you decide rates a letter of commendation, there'll be fifty others who, everybody knows, rate it more; and they don't get anything."

Cozzens continually pulls the reader up short with evidence that nothing about people is simple, or easily to be judged. Before we praise or condemn an act, we must consider the alternatives. The illiterate Joel Parry hates Doctor Bull because he is convinced that Doctor Bull has killed his son. In a sense this is true: the boy had had what the doctor in his offhand way calls a belly ache, and the doctor prescribed castor oil. Actually, since the boy was suffering from appendicitis, the harsh cathartic induced peritonitis and he died. This is bad—irresponsibility if not actual malpractice. But what was Doctor Bull's alternative? It was not practicable to "send everybody he had found in forty years' practice with symptoms of a moderate belly ache over to a hospital miles away for observation." Whatever qualms the reader may have, Doctor Bull has none; but in this freedom from all sense of guilt he is atypical.

Most of Cozzens' central figures, faced with the necessity of choosing between two evils, are haunted by a sense of uncertainty and guilt after they have made the choice. Even when a course of action is clearly indicated by reason, the hero is apt to experience misgivings. Arthur Winner, for example, has mixed feelings about killing the copperhead. It is not a fair fight; the snake has no chance against a man armed with a long-handled hoe. The episode is described in terms appropriate to a cold-blooded murder: "He would return and dispose of the corpse later." And yet the reader must recognize, with Arthur Winner, that his repulsion and distaste represent a "ridiculous qualm." The children must be protected; copperheads cannot be allowed to infest the garden. Arthur Winner acts as he must, but the qualm remains. It is a token of his humanity, an evidence of the moral tension in which all men of good will must live.

The Man of Reason reflects on his deathbed that he has never been forced, by passion or circumstance, to violate his principles, and he recognizes that in this respect he has been "among the luckiest of men." But it is only on a deathbed that one can with assurance congratulate himself on such good fortune. Alfred Revere's "funny picture" of the man falling off a high building is a grim reminder that the best one can ever say is "All right—so far." How far the fall may be no one can tell, but it is a fall, and its result is all too certain. Life is a cycle, and we owe God a death. By being born, says Julius Penrose, we contract to die, and the fulfilling of the contract, whether brief or long-drawn-out, is invariably distressing. A poignant awareness of change and vicissitude, of Time transfixing the flourish set on youth and delving the parallels in Beauty's brow, runs through all Cozzens' novels. Looking with admiration at his wife, backing the station wagon in a swift, decisive arc on the gravel of the driveway, Arthur Winner feels a cold hand laid on his heart.

Those warnings of the morning had come back—Noah's craggy yet broken-down old face; the stertorous laugh of Willard Lowe's resignation; Alfred Revere's despairful calm; Colonel Minton's dazed, glazed eye. They were the successive notes, heavy tolled, of going, going, gone. They were the daily falling, falling of this life, gist of that grisly joke: *All right—so far!* They were the indirect but inescapable sad evidences of that truth, well known, well said: *Time shall rifle every youthful grace!*

This pervading sense of mortality and the steady ravages of time is heightened by frequent examples of casual but ominous accidents. Life consists of changes and adjusting to them, and many of the novels show men forcing themselves into taking crucial steps: General

Beal recovering his authority, Abner Coates deciding to marry and run for district attorney, Francis Ellery choosing duty rather than inclination, Ernest Cudlipp demonstrating his acceptance of the condition of man. But no matter how prudently and rationally he may live, man is always liable to unexpected dislocations coming from a Fate beyond his control—that is, from a chain of causes and effects outside his range of vision. Like Captain Hicks, surprised into an adultery which earlier he had explicitly rejected, Arthur Winner finds himself astoundingly committed to a course of deceit and crime, alike abhorrent to his honor and his reason, yet as unavoidable as it is unexpected.

The blow of fate, moreover, is likely to come precisely at the moment of *hubris*, when a man is priding himself on his success or well-being. George Detweiler is drowned just as he is getting the tangled affairs of the bank straightened out. The *San Pedro* begins its fatal list to port immediately after a jubilant description, as the ship prepares to sail, of "the disciplined cooperation, speed, and precision of people quick and certain about their duties." Just as the weary Doctor Shaw announces, "She'll be all right. Now it's just a matter of starting transfusions and keeping them up a while," Hope Winner dies. The Ponemah oak, carefully built up as a three-hundred-year-old symbol of vitality and permanance, is struck and blasted by lightning as unexpectedly as Arthur Winner is to be jolted out of his well-ordered virtue by the revelation of Noah's dishonesty. Man's helplessness in the face of such intimations of mortality is symbolized by the opossum, terrified into immobility by the sudden glare of headlights and crushed under Arthur Winner's car—an episode recalled when Alfred Revere reports his doctor's diagnosis.

Coming home late at night, Abner Coates notices the initials which, as a small boy, he had scratched in the wet cement of the garage floor. They represented an assertion of himself and an implicit protest against the transience of the flesh. No man should be surprised to discover that the new becomes old; but

> . . . how hard to grasp it, to know that the real today, the seen and felt today, and everything around you, and you, yourself as you stood thinking, would dissolve and pale to a figment of mind, existing, like the future you tried to think of, only in thought. While Abner stood, the old courthouse clock struck twelve. . . . Surprised to find that it was so late, Abner walked down the brick path.

That it is later than one thinks occurs frequently enough to men in middle age, and Cozzens' inescapable clocks and sundials keep the reader constantly aware of the inevitability of change, the necessity of ripening into maturity, and the end of the cycle which makes ripeness for action only a prelude to ripeness for death. A grim little story, "The Way to Go Home," illustrates the renunciations required in middle age, "a point where . . . there was nothing more to celebrate, only things to fear." Men must learn to be satisfied with dullness, "with ambitions small enough to be plausible, with pleasures kept small, quiet, unexceptionable." The hero of the story knows that life is a one-way road, "a progression, hopeless and natural. He would never meet the bunch at Johnny's again . . . but he had still a roof over his head, and he would better be careful, for soon enough he would have only earth there."

The flat hopelessness of such passages—and there are many of them throughout Cozzens' writing—is modified somewhat by the psychological realism with which they are introduced. The sense of mortality weighs most heavily on men when they are physically tired, or ill, or depleted—on Doctor Bull as he returns late at night from an evening of drink and love at Janet Cardmaker's; on Francis Ellery in his exhausted reaction to Walter's nearly fatal seizure; on Colonel Ross, feeling his years at the end of two desperately hard days; on Judge Coates convalescing from a stroke; on the ailing captain of the *San Pedro*, who exemplifies the truism that men wear out, break down.

> The drops of water wore the stone. The increment of fatigue, the featherweight's extra in every day's living, which could not be rested away, collected heaviness in the mind just as it collected acid in the tissues. The experience of seeing, of experiencing, briskly undertaken with the illusion of gain was . . . a work of destruction.

The melancholy truth remains, but men's reactions to it change as their energies flag and are restored. The morning after Doctor Bull's black thoughts he sports and wallows in the bathtub, roaring out "Adeste Fideles" in pleased anticipation of the sausage, pancakes, and coffee awaiting him below. Similarly the chief engineer of the *San Pedro*, exhilarated by "the fine steam and steel symphony of full-ahead" and the thought of the great shafts spinning "serenely on their bearings, ninety times a minute"—a symbol, like the warmth of the engine room, of vigorous life (everything all right—so far)—looks forward to dinner with a tableful of new passengers.

In addition to such restoratives as a good night's sleep, or a job successfully accomplished, man can fall back on the palliatives of philosophy or forgetfulness and the anodynes of drink and love. There are plenty of philosophies to choose from, thinks Colonel Ross, and the right one will keep you operative. "Your need would find it for you, and adapt it to you; and even support you in it." Furthermore, though everybody over fifty lives "under a definitive sentence of some kind, suspended during good behavior . . . the last, best recourse was what it always had been: you thought of something else." The middle-aged reserve officers, wearily aware at evening of their "grossened faces, thinned hair, and thickened waists," forgot "the browner horror, the brooding tempest, the crack of doom, the article of death," in the warmth of human company and whiskey. The notes of "The Last Rose of Summer," tinkling from the Man of Reason's music box, may intimate "the tears of things," but the joke of things is represented too—the little god with his bow surmounting the clock. Arthur Winner on the morning of Hope's death finds his grief mingled with fear. Against the knowledge of death's outrage, "what warmth, what wellness could avail?" One answer is given immediately: the warmth of Marjorie Penrose's bared breasts, in the gesture that is the first intimation of her passion. At the end of a day in the course of which everybody he met was odious and in which he was odious too, Colonel Ross finds similar comfort and forgetfulness offered by his wife. "'I know,' Mrs. Ross said. She moved until her head rested against his shoulder. 'Let's not go on about it.'"

The moral landscape of the novels is painted in sober grays and browns. An eye which keeps too strict a watch o'er man's mortality is apt to miss what John Cheever has called "the harsh surface beauty of life"; an ear too sensitive to the still, sad music of humanity may reject all feelings save the chastened and subdued. Like the Stoics, Cozzens seems at times to overvalue reason, renunciation, and resignation. May Tupping, in *The Last Adam*, has discovered a great truth: "If you just kept on not getting what you wanted, you would stop wanting it in any painful way. It would be all right. You would learn to like what you had." Similarly Colonel Ross, weighed down by aging and acute weariness, thinks of "the portentous truth . . . full of comfort though so melancholy, touched with despair yet supportable, that nothing, not the best you might hope, not the worst you might fear, would ever be very much, would ever be very anything. Seen in this light, all other feelings must weaken, become more temperate—really, more indifferent."

It is nevertheless not accurate to call Cozzens a Stoic; he is too much of an eclectic to be so neatly labeled. Cozzens shares, to be sure, some of the main points of the Stoic moral code: the emphasis on reason, discipline, and self-control; the acute melancholy sense of the universal flux of things, of change and vicissitude, in which he resembled Marcus Aurelius; the definition of freedom as the ability to discriminate things within our power from those not in our power. But while he agrees with the Stoics, and the Christian theologians, as to the necessity of accepting the factual situation, or the will of God, he does not share the Stoic glorification of *ataraxia*, indifference toward the external vicissitudes of life.

Marcus Aurelius has been said to exhibit a conflict between the Stoic doctrine to which he desperately clung and his own distressing observations of the disintegrating Roman world. "It is fundamentally this tension which makes the *Meditations* one of the saddest and most moving books in all of literature." Similarly, Cozzens' sense of what is reasonable and right in human conduct is constantly qualified by his observation of how men, possessed by love, actually behave; but the melancholy which runs through the novels does not come from a passive acceptance of man's limitations and mortality. Rather, it is a by-product of the experience of moral tension: Cozzens is acutely aware of the unequal conflict between what inescapably is and a healthy man's refusal to accept it with reasoned resignation.

Against disasters and the steady attrition of time, the Cozzens hero has some supports more positive than the desperate indifference of the Stoic. One of the strongest is a sense of solidarity with the past, and it is probably no accident that the novels are filled with descriptions of monuments and architectural records of another day, which serve as points of relative stability in the stream of change. Established institutions and traditions are treated with respect: the Calumet Club, the Ponemah Association, the Union League Club (links with a past somewhat nostalgically recalled), and those more universal institutions, the Church and the law. The Episcopal Church is discussed from the inside and with the sympathy of a believer in *Men and Brethren.* In *The Last Adam* and *By Love Possessed* it is portrayed more ironically, but the account of the eleven o'clock service at Christ Church, from its superb picture of the choir procession to the faintly skeptical, instantly repressed meditation of Judge Lowe, implies an affectionate regard for tradition. Tempted by Judge Lowe's hinted doubt, Arthur Winner allows himself to ponder briefly the unreason of Christian belief. He is recalled to a sense of obligation by the tightness of the morning coat he wears twice a year as usher and the "snug encasement of his neck by stiff collar and complicatedly tied tie." The costume is as symbolic as the clerical robes of the rector; though mildly uncomfortable, it is supporting and comforting, a constant reminder of one's part as a living link with the past and the traditions of one's people.

In much the same way, the law—that organization of the secular myths of justice—is in the later novels held up as a symbol of permanence and stability. The development of Cozzens' attitude toward the power of law makes an interesting progression. In *Michael Scarlett* (1925) the law, embodied in the figure of Queen Elizabeth, is depicted as the ultimate adversary—rigid, impersonal, hostile to the hot enthusiasms of youth. In the two Cuban novels the arbitrary legal order imposed by the Company is again something to be fought, and the reader is led to admire the rebellion of Lancy Micks and his daughter, and at least to sympathize with Oliver Findley, the anarchic son of perdition. The disaster that overtakes the *San Pedro* is the result of a blind acceptance of the rigid order imposed by a ship's discipline; precisely because the otherwise able officers refuse to take the law into their own hands and replace the stricken, incompetent captain, the ship is doomed. Even as late as *The Last Adam* (1933) the law—represented by the town meeting and the effort of responsible citizens to restrain Doctor Bull—is depicted in an ambivalent light, and the reader is persuaded to sympathize with Doctor Bull's triumphant trampling on due process. A change in attitude is suggested in *Castaway*, which points up the basic absurdity of anarchy: the solitary individual, like Mr. Kurtz in the jungle, goes to pieces for lack of the restraints which civilized society provides.

In the later novels, respect for the law—"all of a piece in its imposed waitings, its slow evolutions of due process, its calm impersonality of attitude"—is a major theme. The basic legal axiom that a criminal act is not to be regarded merely as an offense against a person, but must be treated as an offense against the peace and dignity of the commonwealth—that is, against the law—is implied in the morality of *Men and Brethren* and made explicit in *The Just and the Unjust* and *By Love Possessed*. A somewhat idealized picture of Pennsylvania law is presented as a model of rational order and stability. Old

Judge Coates can say, "I'm glad I spent my life in the law. . . . There are disappointments; there are things that seem stupid, or not right. But they don't matter much. It's the stronghold of what reason men ever get around to using."

Around this stronghold Cozzens builds two of his novels; the hero of a third is in civilian life a judge; and all the admirable men of the later novels possess the judicial temperament—the ability to examine dispassionately the passionate behavior of men and to reduce it to some kind of reason and rule. "That repose of law, that majestic calm of reason designed to curb all passions or enthusiasms of emotion, to put down all angers and hates of feeling," provides a sorely needed bit of solid rock to cling to in a flood of chance and change. It may turn out to be, finally, unavailing—the Ponemah oak is blasted by the thunderbolt as Judge Coates is stricken by apoplexy—but the Cozzens hero tries to preserve and conserve such points of relative stability. A significant gesture is Arthur Winner's effort to save the riven trunk of the great tree.

Traditional institutions, human company, a working philosophy, love—all these may serve as moral tonics, or as man's hourly varied anodynes. But they do not change the underlying fact that a large part of what goes on in the world is indifferent to the wishes and aspirations of the individual man. Cozzens does not follow Hardy in stressing "the dreadful eyeless face of our existence," but there are hints of naturalism in the thoughts of some of the characters. May Tupping pictures the universe as an "immense mindlessness [which] knew no reasons, had no schemes; there was no cause for it." Such speculations are complemented by occasional incidents like Virginia Banning's experience with two great Danes kept by her parents. They are never hostile, and at times they seem as friendly and reassuring as a warm spring day. No one else at the house seems glad to see Virginia, and when she returns, shaken by her stolen ride in her brother's car, the boisterous affection of the dogs makes her weep. But she knows that soon "their instinctive, reasonless jubilation at sight of her would be innocently exhausted"; they are really as indifferent to her feelings as is the starlit snow outside the garage. On her next return to the garage the dogs are bolting their dinners, too intent on their own affairs to welcome her. After Virginia's death they greet the maid who brings them food with the same boisterous, meaningless enthusiasm.

Francis Ellery is acutely conscious of the inhuman indifference of nature. After a frustrating evening in which, though near Lorna, he is unable to establish any real contact ("We sit here and yawn until all hours," says Miss Imbrie), Francis, disconsolate and coatless, steps out of the villa into a snowstorm. "Invulnerable, unanswerable, it derided him, careless of what he thought or what he did, executing its aimless joke on him, on the January flowers, on the whitening palms." A similar Hardyesque sense of the "cogent It-is, so much like hate or malice, of insentient things" comes over Francis as he realizes that his charge, Walter Cunningham, in a perfectly natural sequence of events beyond anyone's control, may die of asthma in the French ski resort. Francis Ellery's response is not stoic acceptance and resignation. "With the piling up against him of the odds or omens . . . the heart resisted, the mind struck back in anger. 'All right. Even so. Even so, God damn it, I will do something.' "

This determination to strike back in the face of odds and omens, to do something, defines the heroic temperament of the Cozzens heroes and separates them from the later Stoics with their carefully cultivated apathy. The theme is introduced in Cozzens' first novel. As the heroine with her tutor and guardian go up the Danube they pass "the ugly frame and slowly revolving wheel of a floating mill."

> "See that," said Dr. Coty, "inefficiency combined with ingenuity. It is a symbol of the mind of man."
>
> "None the less," replied Tischoifsky desperately, "it is an effort. It is better than nothing."

That making an effort is better than doing nothing is demonstrated in most of the later novels. *S.S. San Pedro* provides a negative illustration: the officers, paralyzed by the ingrained habit of obedience, have lost "the vital initiative, the intelligence to see clearly and do quickly." Although his senses assure him that there has been no outward change in the condition of the ship, the Brazilian quartermaster feels that danger has become real and imminent. He sets out to find it, and finds it in the group of officers huddled quietly in the wheelhouse, waiting. The mechanical "Yes, sir" is an omen of disaster. "Discipline, directed cooperation, ceased here to have any virtue. Habit betrayed the will and debauched the brain." When Mr. Bradell finally makes his inadequate, futile attempt to do something—to swing out the boom and jettison the deck cargo—it is too late.

Doctor George Bull knows, like any doctor, that something must be done even when nothing useful can be done; the patient must take medicine or treatment for psychological if not medical reasons. Ernest Cudlipp, as gloomily pessimistic as any Marcus Aurelius, does not permit himself the luxury of resignation; he takes the responsibility of acting swiftly to straighten out, as well as he can, the desperate tangle of lives in which he is involved. General Nichols says, "We must do it anyway." Colonel Ross heartens his flagging spirits with the maxim that "a man must stand up and do the best he can with what there is." Julius Penrose, describing how he has painfully taught himself to hobble with canes, says, "In this life we cannot do everything we might like to do, nor have for ourselves everything we might like to have. We must recognize what the law calls factual situations. . . . The becoming thing, in any given situation, is for a man to try what he can do, not just sprawl there whining."

The insistence that a man must stand up and do what he can is not supported, in most of the Cozzens novels, by religious theory or belief. Although man's work is pictured throughout the novels as the real center of his life, the Calvinist insistence on the virtuousness of carrying on one's vocation is made explicit only in *Men and*

Brethren. The parable of the talents, cited at a crucial passage, implies a moral duty to make whatever good use one can of the abilities with which he has been endowed; and the admirable men of Cozzens' novels prove themselves, in a moral sense, good stewards. For the most part, however, Cozzens seems to hold that the justification for courageous effort is intrinsic, even aesthetic. A man must live with himself, and despair, whining, or self-pity, ugly in themselves, are unbecoming to a grown man. Trying to do what can be done, facing the beast, is intrinsically admirable. Cozzens seems to have a strong feeling for the virtue which in the Renaissance was called "grace," a sense of what is fitting and seemly. It is a virtue requiring the exercise of whatever endowment of discrimination and sensibility a man may have, and it is conspicuous in the magnanimity of the "natural aristocrats" who are Cozzens' heroes. The moral imperatives that motivate the magnanimous man cannot be proved to have value. They can only be asserted, but Cozzens is eloquent in asserting them.

8

THE IMPERFECTIBILITY OF MAN

As their yacht follows the Danube through the Balkan states just before World War I, the heroine of *Confusion* makes a remark prophetic of the direction Cozzens' thought was to take in his later work. Contradicting her idealistic tutor, who believes "there will be no more wars when men are free," Cerise d'Atrée declares flatly, "I don't believe this world can ever be changed. . . . I think everything will go on pretty much as it used to." This is the first statement of a conviction which underlies all the major Cozzens novels. In contrast with romantic optimists like Whitman or Emerson, Cozzens holds that human society is not only imperfect but inherently incapable of being perfected. The Reverend Ernest Cudlipp, reflecting on the ineradicable malice of the sons of perdition, states the case against Utopian optimism:

On this trifle—it was Jeremy Taylor's wild, indeterminate, infinite appetite of man—the whole scheme—the appeal to reason, the assumption of good will, the faith in a nobler disinterestedness—by which Wilber and his friends purposed to establish the millennium, collapsed. It would be more of a credit to their intelligence if they purposed, under cover of the talk, nothing but an improvement of their own fortunes; for the new day would still find them being born Jimmy and Bill, and who but a simpleton could suppose that sweet social reasonableness would make Jimmy any less Jimmy.

But it is not only the perennial occurrence in society of men like Jimmy Jennings or Warren Winner that makes hope of the millennium delusory; even the best of men share to some degree the self-centeredness of the finite and contribute their share to life's unresolved discords. Thinking of the respected but pompous old hypocrite under whom he had read law, Colonel Ross takes occasion to review, not merely the troops passing before him, but the condition of man.

> For himself, for old Schlichter, for mankind, he could feel the same subduing mortification. There never could be a man so brave that he would not sometime, or in the end, turn part or all coward; or so wise that he was not, from beginning to end, part ass if you knew where to look; or so good that nothing at all about him was despicable. This would have to be accepted. This was one of the limits of human endeavor, one of those boundaries of the possible whose precise determining was . . . the problem. . . . It was no good acting on a supposition that men would, for your purpose, be what they did not have it in them to be.

On the point of man's imperfectibility Cozzens' thinking is very close to that of such neo-orthodox theologians as Reinhold Niebuhr. In particular he seems to share Niebuhr's distrust of a modern "liberal" Protestantism, "optimistic enough to believe . . . that the forces of reason had successfully chained all demonic powers," which "in adjusting itself to the ethos of this age . . . sacrificed its most characteristic religious and Christian heritage by destroying the sense of depth and the experience of tension. . . . Its Kingdom of God was translated to mean exactly that ideal society which modern culture hoped to realize through the evolutionary process." But "Utopianism must inevitably lead to disillusionment," since it expects "the realization of an absolute ideal in the relative temporal process" and tries "to fit the vision of perfection into the inevitable imperfections of history."

Ernest Cudlipp is the only one of Cozzens' heroes who is deeply religious in the Christian sense. Except for Julius Penrose, who has a special and personal reason for investigating Catholic dogma, the admirable men of the novels are unconcerned with the intricacies of theology. They display the moral responsibility which Niebuhr derives from an awareness of "the intolerable tension of the unqualified," but they concern themselves with "the common currency of the moral life . . . the 'nicely calculated less and more' of the relatively good and the relatively evil." Instead of contemplating and measuring the unattainable peak of the mountain, where "life cannot maintain itself," they set themselves to "the task of building roads up the mountain-side, and of coercing its wilderness into an order sufficient to sustain human life." The Cozzens heroes are primarily concerned with getting along in this world, and they appear to be, in Niebuhr's terms, "partly blind to the total dimension of life." The limitations implied may explain a reviewer's remark that the Cozzens heroes, as compared with Captain Ahab or Dmitri Karamazov, are relatively transparent, and lack the opacity of the great characters in fiction. This, however, is only another way of saying that Cozzens' heroes are not monumental, archetypal figures but recognizable, life-size men. If they are unaware of the total dimension of life and therefore "untouched by its majesties and tragedies," they are better able to "give themselves to the immediate tasks before them."

These immediate tasks, Judge Coates points out to his son, are bound to end in "deaths and disappointments and failures." As Niebuhr puts it,

> Human reason is itself imbedded in the passing flux, a tool of a finite organism, the instrument of its physical necessities, and the prisoner of the partial perspectives of a limited time and place. The consequence is that it is always capable of envisaging possibilities of order, unity, and harmony above and beyond the contingent and arbitrary realities of its physical existence; but it is not capable . . . of incarnating all the higher values which it discerns. . . . This paradoxical relation of finitude and infinity, and consequently of freedom and necessity, is the mark of the uniqueness of the human spirit in this creaturely world.

Judges Coates, however, insists on the necessity of attempting to do the impossible.

> "Nobody promises you a good time or an easy time. . . . But no bets are off. . . . The world gets up in the morning and is fed and goes to work, and in the evening it comes home and is fed again and perhaps has a little amusement and goes to sleep. To make that possible, so much has to be

done by so many people that, on the face of it, it is impossible. Well, every day we do it; and every day, come hell, come high water, we're going to have to go on doing it as well as we can."

A man must try to walk, not just lie there sprawling.

The Cozzens heroes admit their imperfection and thereby sometimes triumph over it. Julius Penrose insists that "once fact's assented to, accepted, and we stop directing our effort where effort is wasted, we usually *can* do quite a number of things, to a faint heart, impossible." He and Arthur Winner are not sustained by a religious faith like Niebuhr's; but in accepting the burden of uncertainty and contingency instead of taking the easy way of blameless, conventional rectitude, they admit "the tension between what is and what ought to be," which on the moral level is the equivalent of religion's "tension between the historical and the transcendent."

The ancient problem of reconciling determinism and free will may not be solved by Judge Dealey's suggestion that "freedom is the knowledge of necessity," but the quotation comes close to defining Cozzens' basic moral position. That men will not do what they cannot do is a truism from which both General Nichols and Martin Bunting draw some significant conclusions. One is that the wise man, the man of matured experience, will work within the limits of the possible, which give freedom its actual meaning and existence. Absolute freedom is not attainable by a finite creature, but the ideal of freedom enables men to measure the limited degree they may be able to achieve.

The necessity of making choices implies the right to make wrong choices. "Freedom just to be wise and good isn't any freedom," says Judge Coates; "a free man always has been and always will be the one to decide what he'd better do." His choices may, to be sure, lead to disaster, but perfect security is the denial of freedom and a free man must be willing to take his chances. Moreover, choices that are wrong in terms of the ideal may not be wrong in practice, as Cozzens illustrates abundantly. Perhaps the best example is the outcome of the trial in *The Just and the Unjust.* The district attorney is understandably depressed when, in defiance of the evidence and the law, the jury brings in a verdict of second-degree murder, which has the ironic effect of punishing the gangster who turned state's evidence more severely than those actually on trial. Judge Coates explains that the right of a jury to find against the evidence, even in direct defiance of the law, is a means of mediating between the inflexible demands of the theoretical ideal and the common man's sense of justice. The kidnapers on trial did not actually kill the victim; they are charged with murder only because the law holds that all participants in a felony resulting in murder are guilty of murder, whether or not they actually took part in the killing. Although the jury's decision circumvents the law, it brings about a closer approximation to justice.

Furthermore, the jury system, precisely because of its flexibility, protects the whole system of the law. Since "there isn't any known way to legislate with an allowance for right feeling," a jury is "like a cylinder head gasket. Between two things that don't give any, you have to have something that does give a little, something to seal the law to the facts." The ironic epigraph to *The Just and the Unjust* quotes Lord Hardwicke, an eminent jurist of the early eighteenth century: "Certainty is the Mother of Repose; therefore the Law aims at Certainty." Arthur Winner interprets the quotation, putting the emphasis where, despite the capital letters, it truly belongs: "In its wisdom, the law only aimed at certainty, could not, did not, really hope to get there." Similarly man only aims at perfection, never attains it—never, if he is wise, even expects to attain it. "Victory is not in reaching certainties or solving mysteries; victory is in making do with uncertainties, in supporting mysteries." Given the imperfections and contingencies of human existence, the kinds of victory attainable in life may all be "forms of defeat . . . givings-up . . . compromises."

All of Cozzens' major novels explore, by means of concrete problems, the necessity of mediating between inflexible extremes and the validity of the "supposedly terrible Jesuitical maxim" that the end justifies the means. Cozzens gives weight to the view that "the good end never . . . will justify the wrong, bad, or merely expedient means" by putting it in the mouths of some of his most admirable characters: Martin Bunting, Colonel Ross, Arthur Winner in the penultimate stages of his education. But the choices and actions of these men speak louder than their words; means, like ends, are only relatively good or bad, and it is frequently necessary, in this far from best of worlds, to choose a less desirable means in order to avoid a still more undesirable end. Once again, Niebuhr generalizes the position implied by the behavior of Cozzens' heroes.

> Short of an ascetic withdrawal from the world, every moral action takes place in a whole field of moral values and possibilities in which no absolute distinction between means and ends is possible. There are only immediate and more ultimate values. . . . The subordination of values to each other is necessary in any hierarchy of values. Freedom, for instance, is a high value. . . . Yet it is sacrificed or subordinated to the necessities of social cooperation. To what degree freedom ought to be subordinated to the requirements of social cohesion . . . is one of those problems for which there is no final answer. It will emerge perennially in human history and be solved according to the requirements, pressures, convictions, and illusions of the hour.

Circumstances, in short, do alter cases; in political affairs it is commonly necessary that "the ideal principle . . . be sacrificed to guarantee its partial realization." A sharp dichotomy between white and black may provide emotional satisfaction to the naïve and immature, but the wise man, Cozzens keeps saying, must discriminate the actual shades of gray in which all human problems present themselves. He does not deprecate principle, but considers an intemperate, blind devotion to principle almost as disruptive in society as no principle at all. Judge Coates points out that people usually do, in fact, take circumstances into consideration: "If a friend wants to borrow five dollars, most men, if they have it, will give it to him; but most men would refuse a stranger." And he convinces Abner, whose moral sensibility is offended at the prospect of taking the district attorney's office from the necessarily soiled hands of the local political boss, that his scruple is needless. The political boss may ask Abner to do him reciprocal favors ("it's a kind of modern benefit of clergy," Judge Coates says), but "it takes two to make a bargain. You know what you get and what you give."

Abner is free to set his own terms, but when he comes to formulate them, he is baffled by the impossibility of phrasing them sensibly.

> He had certainly never seen Jesse in that well-known room, little and smoke-filled, trafficking in offices, dividing booty, making deals with similar scoundrels at the cost of the just and the upright. Indeed, when you considered this familiar figure, a difficulty presented itself. How did such a man, who must by definition be disliked on sight and distrusted by everyone, win himself a position of power?

Jesse may want to have favors done for friends of his, but Bunting's reputation for integrity is testimony that illegal favors need not be granted. Actually, Jesse is shrewd enough not to ask a man to do what, by virtue of his known character, he cannot do. The kind of favor likely to be asked is illustrated in the sequel: will Abner represent at a hearing, and thereby use his reputation and prestige to aid, the superintendent of schools, against whom some citizens are ganging up? Abner has no good grounds for refusing, since he believes the superintendent to be more right than his opponents.

What it amounts to is that Jesse, though in Abner's opinion an evil, is a necessary evil. If such able men as

Bunting and Abner are to serve the public, someone has to make up the ticket and get out the vote. Judge Fred Dealey, of *By Love Possessed*, is enough older than Abner to admit both the undesirability and the necessity of the boss:

> I know somebody has to do it; and, whoever he is, very likely he has to be the least little bit of a crook—nothing serious, of course. Nobody ever catches you with your hand in the till—nothing obvious. In short, since I know who keeps me elected, hollering: stop, thief! would ill beseem me.

Judge Dealey is given to hyperbolic speech, but he is serious in admitting that the ignoble deals of the politicians are what enable him to keep his integrity spotless, his "nose nice and clean." Noah Tuttle, nostalgically defending the good old days, boasts that when Judge Lowe was district attorney, "no Mechanicsville politician would have called him up more than once!" But Arthur Winner reflects that "the pertinent question might be: Would Willard Lowe, though immaculately aloof from crooked politics, have rebuffed with righteous rudeness . . . the rector of Christ Church; the chairman of the Union League; the president of the Orcutt Potteries," if they had wished to offer advice or opinion on a case they knew about?

What is needed to answer such a question is not the innocence of the Reverend Whit Trowbridge, who cannot imagine how a politician "could stoop to consult expedience instead of principle," nor the oversimple though "natural way of viewing things in terms of yea and nay, white or black" of Arthur Winner's mother, nor the scorn of compromise displayed by Mrs. Cunningham, who, secure in the fugitive and cloistered virtue of the very rich, can afford to be as absolutely downright and honest as she appears in *Ask Me Tomorrow.* Innocence, Cozzens is saying, has its place, but it is not a sufficient qualification for the management of human affairs. Colonel Mowbray, proud of his integrity but uneasily aware of his ignorance of business and politics, has developed a protective suspicion of others' motives which causes Colonel Ross and the Air Force a good deal of trouble. When a prominent local citizen offers to provide bus service between the town and the Air Base, on a contract designed to enable him to show an operating loss and thus reduce his income tax, Colonel Mowbray gives him five minutes to get off the post, thereby insuring the hostility of the local businessmen and the newspaper publisher and putting military personnel to a good deal of inconvenience in getting to and from the base. General Beal with his boyish "unlimited integrity that accepted as the law of nature such elevated concepts as the Military Academy's Duty-Honor-Country" is morally admirable; and it is made clear at the end of the book that his type, with its innocent single-mindedness of purpose, is absolutely essential to the winning of the war. But without the direction of disillusioned publicans like General Nichols or the loyal backing of Colonel Ross, Beal would not be very effective.

Cozzens does not deny the moral virtue of the innocents, but he stresses in incident after incident the importance to society of men who discriminate more shades than white and black, and who accept the necessity of compromise. Colonel Ross's solution, far from morally ideal, to the problem of segregation on the post "might be no answer to the deep question; but it came with composure to the immediate point," and it enables the general to get on with the war. Satisfaction with such short-term gains is partly a function of age; twenty years ago, Colonel Ross reflects, he would have seen his duty, scorned other considerations, hewed to the line, and let the chips fall where they might. Now he observes sadly (for "the counsels of wisdom always and so obviously recommend the course to which an old man's lower spirits and failing forces inclined him anyway") that the "exhilaration of hewing to the line waned when you had to clean up that mess of chips."

General Nichols, with his "clear mournfulness of eye," his "stern, wakeful grasp of the nature of things," has long since given up his boyish illusions. As he now sees it, the problem is always to discover the limits of the possible, not to choose—with the delusory freedom achieved by thinking only in abstract terms—the best of all possible courses. His description of the Quebec conference, serving incidentally as a reminder of the imperfections of even great men, emphasizes the necessity of accepting something less than an ideal solution.

The object could not be simply to concert a wisest and best course. The object was to strike a bargain . . . to give a little in order to gain a lot. . . . Agreement was ordinarily resisted by mutual misrepresentations, and obtained by a balance of disguised bribes and veiled threats. Plain honest people were often disgusted when they found out that high business was regularly done in these low ways. They were also indignant; because they knew a remedy for the shameful state of affairs. Let every man be just and generous, open and honorable, brave and wise. No higgling or overreaching would then be necessary.

Actually, men and society being what they are, the course decided on at the conference was "what many people considered the third or fourth best thing, depending on how you looked at it."

Cozzens' clergymen are not more free than his lawyers and soldiers to shun evil and cling to the good. Being human, they too must often elect the expedient rather than the ideal. To be sure, the rector of Holy Innocents', Doctor Lamb, is gently ridiculed for his habit of "smoothing things over, reconciling conflicting interests, preserving decent harmony—even, his relatively few enemies declared, at any expense of principle."

He had no patience with people who demanded extreme measures or drastic stands. The making of concessions he regarded as a part of charity and a proof of good faith and will. . . . If some sacrifice of principle became, in the process, necessary, it was true that it would not unduly disturb him. As one gentleman to another, he was confident of mutual understanding with his Creator about the nature and means of forwarding, God in His great way, Doctor Lamb in his little one, the work to which they were both sincerely devoted.

Nevertheless, it is Doctor Lamb's stubborn refusal to compromise that forces Ernest once again to choose the expedient rather than the ideal. He has invited Rabbi Slesinger to speak at the Chapel on a "Faiths of Our Neighbors" program, but the rector points out that the bishop can authorize only Christian men to speak in the church and insists that Ernest withdraw the invitation. Ernest argues that the intent of Canon Twenty-three is to bar irreligious men, and he offers to take the responsibility for inviting a godly non-Christian to speak. The rector cannot allow this; Ernest's reputation has been damaged by his youthful indiscretions at St. Matthew's, and any further trouble will reflect on the parish and on Doctor Lamb.

The arrival of the renegade monk, Carl Willever, complicates the problem; the rector orders Ernest to turn him out of the vicarage to avoid possible scandal. The issue is clear: Ernest has been twice ordered to do what he feels to be wrong, and he considers resigning. Only the day before he has commented on his inability to make the compromises required in the rector's position: "It isn't that I wouldn't stand for it, it's that I couldn't. I don't know how." But he learns; the words he has used to Carl Willever are all too applicable to his own case: a greater sin than hypocrisy is presumption. Resigning would give Ernest "the satisfaction of cutting a figure," but he has no other prospects and is deep in debt. He can hardly ask his numerous creditors to join him in a gesture for conscience's sake. It is not likely, considering his age and his record in the church, that he will be called to a position of greater opportunity and responsibility; he had better follow what events have demonstrated to be his vocation, obey the rector's orders, and stay at St. Ambrose's.

It is not an easy decision. "I'm ready to temper my independence with consideration," Ernest says. "But it's still up to me to decide whether any particular obedience is sinful." This kind of moral discrimination is demanded of all the heroes, and Cozzens makes their choices the more painful by complicating the situations in which they must choose till there is no clear rule to take refuge in. They are required to endure the tension between what is and what should be, and in doing this they must frequently violate the legal and ethical axiom that no man shall be a judge in his own case. As free men, they cannot fall back on any authoritarian dogma, religious or legal; they must judge themselves and endure the uncertainties, self-doubts, and sense of guilt which are apt to follow. The injunction "Judge not, that ye be not judged" is given a positive interpretation in the Cozzens novels. It might be phrased "When you must judge, you must be willing to be judged"; the consequence is that one's conviction of right choice is apt to falter at the thought of what other people, ignorant of the circumstances, will think of the man who judges his own case.

In the final scene of *Guard of Honor* Colonel Ross, by an apparently irrelevant quotation from Juvenal, raises a question which sums up one whole side of Cozzens' moral and social thinking: *Sed quis custodiet ipsos custodes?* But who is going to guard the guardians? Though all are imperfect, men differ widely in abilities;

and leadership should be, as power usually is, concentrated in the relatively small class of able men. Ideally this should be composed of Jefferson's natural aristocrats, endowed not only with natural ability but also with the natural morality so dear to eighteenth-century theorists. But men are only human, and when economic power and social prestige accrue to such a class of leaders, power is apt to corrupt them. In a democracy, therefore, some system of checks and balances is needed, some method of protecting the guardians of the people against their natural tendency toward selfish presumption and moral complacency.

Who will guard the guardians? In the last analysis, no one. Somewhere in any system of checks and balances a stage is reached where the buck can be passed no further—where no guardian exists. At this lonely point, with moral tension at its highest, the free, mature individual must make his own decisions, unchecked but also unsupported by a reassuring father-image, superior officer, clerical hierarchy, church dogma, or body of law.

In the relations between Arthur Winner and Garret Hughes, Cozzens illustrates both the young man's need to find a moral guardian and the necessity for the mature to act as judges in their own case. Garret has given up a well-paid position in Dave Weintraub's law office to become assistant district attorney. For a year or so prior to the change Garret's fastidious nose must have been sniffing "faint whiffs of slick practice," a slight, "never exactly identified, perhaps only imagined, taint." His conscience, hypersensitive to the image of his stern, just father, will not permit him to work for a man whom he cannot serve with complete, unreserved loyalty. Weintraub has hired him because everyone knew Garret Hughes to be incorruptible and honest; because he is incorruptibly honest he has left Weintraub to work under J. Jerome Brophy in the district attorney's office. But here, too, the air sometimes seems contaminated with the faint odor of human imperfection. Since he serves as the emissary, Garret cannot help knowing that the district attorney is leaning over backward to favor Arthur Winner in the Kovacs-Detweiler case. (Fortunately for his conscience, he does not know that Winner has agreed in effect to support Brophy's bid for a judgeship. Fred Dealey *does* know it, and the fact that he is persuaded that there is no causal connection between this support and Brophy's favor must be meant to convince the reader of Arthur Winner's probity.)

When Garret delivers the message that the case against Ralph Detweiler will not be pressed, his conscience is troubled. He is satisfied that the case against Ralph is fraudulent, but he dislikes the pressure put on Mr. Kovacs to drop the charge. Furthermore, the methods employed are underhanded and irregular. Garret "could not stop feeling that without a law being broken, law was done impudent despite." In this respect he is like Abner Coates, fretting over the disparity between the theory and the practice of the law; and like Abner he seeks counsel and comfort from an older man. What will Mr. Winner—the highest authority on honorable standards of conduct

—say of this "gift-wrapped bid for favor . . . begot in guile and tendered in guile. . . . these artful, extralegal, and, as Garret himself saw them, if not definitely dishonest, perhaps dishonorable goings-on?"

Arthur Winner respects Garret's scrupulosity, but he is reminded nevertheless of the parable of the Pharisee and the publican, and he thinks that "a more temperate virtue [might] be a wiser virtue." Garret is unwilling to risk the hazard to his self-esteem involved in making his own decision; he hopefully asks a guardian to make the decision for him. Arthur Winner willingly assumes the slight burden of whatever guilt may accrue to accepting Brophy's favor. Further, he gives Garret comfortable reassurance by providing legal grounds for the conceivably dubious means used in disposing of the case. Garret is enormously relieved; once more he breathes his "uncontaminated air."

But who will guard the guardian? In accepting the burden of moral choice and resolving it in favor of an expedient justice, Arthur Winner has set in motion a chain of events leading inexorably to the more desperate choice which is the climax of the novel. Up to this point Arthur Winner, like his father, has been lucky enough never to have been forced by circumstances to do what he felt to be wrong. But in agreeing not to tell Helen Detweiler that the case against her brother is being dropped, he unwittingly deepens the despair that drives her to suicide; and the suicide, bringing to light the truth about Noah Tuttle's embezzlement, forces Arthur Winner to give up his comfortable consciousness of integrity and accept the burden of being accessory to a felony.

For Cozzens—as for his favorite writer, Jonathan Swift, and the long line of theologians preceding him—pride is the first of the deadly sins. In all the novels the self-righteous are represented in the unflattering image of the Pharisee who "prayed thus with himself, God, I thank thee, that I am not as other men are, extortioners, unjust, adulterers, or even as this publican." In her self-righteousness Mrs. Pratt resembles those heroes of Grahame Greene who are able to revel in sin because it provides an opportunity for demonstrating—by an assumption of forgiveness somewhat facilely taken for granted—their assurance of salvation through the Church. In his arrogant egocentricity Lieutenant Edsell resembles Father Carl Willever, and both characters exemplify the adage that pride goeth before a fall. Cozzens dislikes both men, but he is scrupulously fair in presenting their virtues and in explaining, and thus to some extent justifying, the psychological causes of their faults.

Edsell, an uncomfortably accurate portrait of a type of fellow-traveling intellectual common in America in the late thirties, is sufficiently unpleasant to have become a kind of rallying point for critics who disapprove of Cozzens' political views. The complete antithesis of General Beal, Edsell feels loyalty only to the Cause, which he defends in stereotyped catch phrases, and never to people as individual human beings. One of his earliest recorded acts is to incorporate into a story published in a national magazine a satirical, recognizable, extremely unflattering portrait of his section chief. "What were you to think of a fellow free and friendly to your face, who, all the while, was working away at something that, at elaborate length, in the permanence of print, would hold you up to the ridicule of a large audience?" What, for that matter, is one to think of a champion of Negro rights who uses individual Negroes as though they were insentient pawns in a game to advance his own bigoted notion of their ultimate best interests? His scorn of short-term, partial solutions is of course part of the political line he is following, but his love of trouble for its own sake is, as Cozzens later points out, a part of his personality. He never really knows what is going on (his information is partial or distorted and his inferences usually erroneous), but he plots and connives with a malignant energy motivated not so much by devotion to a cause as by compulsive, deep-seated resentments.

Although he is rude on principle and approves of what he calls Lieutenant Turck's "nasty disposition, which is the first thing you need if you're going to stand up to these sons of bitches," he is rude also because he enjoys contention; he thrives on opposition and feeds his scornful vanity on the petty triumphs of shocking and outraging his companions. Cozzens sums up Edsell's qualities in an analysis of his face in repose.

Left to itself, it still expressed those mixed, sometimes antagonistic sentiments which it was most often called on to express—suspicion mingled with contempt; derision never wholly free of resentment; impulsiveness hampered by calculation; vanity unsettled by doubt.

Left to itself, not roused to fight, not exercised with scheming, Lieutenant Edsell's face expressed also despondency and defeat. While he brooded, faraway, he acknowledged some considerable reverse he must have suffered in his long standing quarrel with the state of things, some new disappointment added to that sum of disappointments whose galling recurrence were no doubt his real casus belli. It was the face of the unresigned man of sorrows, angrily acquainted with grief—the well-known sorehead.

The explanation, though shrewd, does not make a reader like Edsell any better, but it serves as an introduction to his good qualities, and Cozzens takes pains to point these out. He really is an unusually capable writer; his section chief admits it and Nathaniel Hicks, somewhat more experienced in judging writers, considers getting him to do a major article on AFORAD. Edsell has earned his commission at OCS, instead of receiving it on a silver platter, like most of his colleagues. The dignity with which he defends himself against the charges of the regular army officers who have him up on the carpet is impressive. His liberal principles, whether or not the product of an inner wound, look very good when contrasted—as Cozzens pointedly does contrast them—with the cold stupidity of Lieutenant Colonel Howden, the Counter-Intelligence officer. Howden believes that all radicals are crazy and argues, in the true McCarthy vein, that the scanty evidence of disaffection he is able to uncover just goes to prove how dangerously secret the whole radical conspiracy is. A grim prototype of the secret police, he smiles only when the provost marshal, boasting of the marksmanship of his men, says that Lieutenant Kashkin could put a slug through any part of a man's leg at fifty yards. Compared with the sinister Howden, Edsell is relatively likable; and Colonel Ross admits that, of all the officers involved in the problem of Negro rights on the post, Edsell and his rich-boy friend are "the two, obnoxious, only champions of the dignity of man."

Nevertheless, the whole picture of Edsell is strongly unfavorable, and the reason is his arrogant, presumptuous certainty that he knows all the answers—his self-righteous, doctrinaire pride. With such pharisees, Cozzens contrasts men like the publican who, "standing afar off, would not lift up so much as his eyes unto heaven, but smote upon his breast, saying, God be merciful to me a sinner." Not all publicans go up into the temple to pray, but whether they do or not, they bear a burden; they do the unsavory, unpopular jobs which need to be done in society, but which the self-righteous prefer not to soil their hands with. Jesse Gearhart, the Republican county chairman and local political boss in *The Just and the Unjust*, gives young Abner Coates a lesson in decent humility.

The qualities in Abner which irritate his friends and his sweetheart are perilously close to those of the pharisee. Abner is a little too proud of his integrity, a little stiff-necked in his attitude toward politicians, almost complacent in the assumption that, his virtues being well known, the rewards—from jobs to fiancée—should be tendered him as of right. Running for office on the

Republican ticket involves being indebted to Jesse, the local boss, and Abner's disapproval of Jesse's control of patronage and offices in the county is mingled with "resentment at a power, without regular authority or justification in law, that allowed Jesse to interpose between Abner and Abner's long-standing aims and (he might as well say it) deserts, the impertinency of Jesse's pleasure or displeasure." His father and Bunting both help Abner in the painful task of bending his pride to the realities of the political situation, and by the end of the trial he has agreed to run, even though his acceptance involves him at once in "deals" with the publican.

Jesse Gearhart is portrayed, on the whole, with sympathy. His pale, tired eyes and gray face showed that "politics was hard on a man. It was a waiting game, with all that meant in delays and postponements, in negotiations never quite finished, in nursing plans, in working things little by little. There was never any rest; and the rewards, as far as Abner knew, were neither very great nor very certain." Year after year Jesse goes through the tiresome, difficult business of getting the best available men on the ticket and doing what is necessary to put them into office and keep them there. If this involves a veiled threat to the publisher of the local newspaper, who is writing editorials against the superintendent of schools (one of Jesse's men), Jesse does not hesitate to defend his own: ". . . the *Examiner's* was not the only shop where the county printing could be done; and unless Maynard wanted to lose seven or eight thousand dollars worth of business, perhaps he ought to be careful." This is politics, to be sure, and no one likes politicians. But, as Judge Coates says, "If you want to get away from them, you'll have to get away from human society. There wouldn't be any society without them." Jesse has disciplined himself to the virtues requisite in his position: patience, realistic judgment, slowness to take offense, and a self-control which "was as good as a saint's." If his standard of what is honorable is considerably more flexible than Abner's, at least, like the publican in the temple, Jesse makes no pretense to virtues he does not possess.

Between the pride which, according to Judge Coates, "does a good deal to make us fit for human company" and the pride that leads the Pharisee to thank God that he is not as other men, the precise line is hard to draw. Cozzens, however, is continually trying to draw it. His heroes generally exemplify the mean between a necessary self-respect and a decent humility, and Julius Penrose is an interesting example of precarious balance between the high self-estimation of the magnanimous man and the humility learned in a long struggle to overcome his paralysis. The exceptionally gifted Captain Andrews may be overmodest about his abilities, and Doctor George Bull is a little inclined in the opposite direction. The best example of the golden mean in this respect is District Attorney Martin Bunting of *The Just and the Unjust.*

Bunting has the quiet assurance of competence, but he is not too proud to take moral responsibility for the dirty jobs that go with his office. The most extreme example

—so extreme that few readers may be willing to go along with Cozzens' implied condoning of it—is Bunting's acceptance of third-degree methods in securing evidence. Everyone knows, from the confession of the leader of the gang, that the wretched Howell is guilty as charged, and the FBI knows what kind of evidence is needed to make a case stick. Still, nobody, neither Abner nor the jury nor the judge, likes the coercion, involving actual torture, needed to insure a successful prosecution. Bunting, however, points out that some degree of coercion is always involved in police methods, and he cites the case of Sam Field, the high school teacher who molested girls.

> We had to work on him. We say he confessed of his own free will. It isn't true. We broke him down. Of course, all we had to do was just talk to Field and keep after him; but how far would you get just talking to Howell? In principle there isn't a nickel's worth of difference.

Abner still doesn't like it, but he would have to agree that raw force, embodied in police officers and prisons, underlies and supports the ideal structure of the law. It is only the pharisees, striving to preserve their "uncontaminated air," who dodge the moral tension involved in the deliberate exercise of force by ignoring it or delegating it to the publicans.

The ultimate degree of force, capital punishment, Cozzens rejects. A long discussion of it near the end of *The Just and the Unjust* is deliberately left inconclusive, although Judge Vredenburgh's disapproval is clear. The hint of Cozzens' attitude implicit in the judge's remarks is made unmistakable in a review of Arthur Koestler's *Reflections on Hanging* which Cozzens wrote for the *Harvard Law Review.* He subscribes to the argument that capital punishment is no deterrent to crime, that it brutalizes the society that applies it, and that it is irreversible, allowing no chance for later correction or compromise. Capital punishment, in short, is an absolute, and a distrust of absolutes is natural to anyone convinced of the fallibility of man.

Cozzens is continually trying to make some compromise between the demands of human dignity, which comes from a sense of freedom, and the humility which ought to grow out of an awareness of man's limitations. The seemingly pointless incident in which Ann Winner surprises her father and stepmother on "the dim disordered bed" leads up to an interview next day when Ann speaks with scornful indignation to her father, now "sedately clothed as though he always wore clothes," as though he were not possessed by the universal human passions. Angry at being forbidden to go to a disreputable roadhouse and still smarting from the remembrance of the "man's brute big body" the night before, Ann demands, "Would I be ruined if a Fallen Woman was in the same room with me? What am I? So pure and holy I'm too good for her? All of us are just human, I guess."

Her father, agreeing that we are all just human and should never imagine otherwise, underlines a basic moral axiom. Despite his alert sensitivity to the range of differences, Cozzens constantly reminds us that all men are alike in sharing the human predicament. Typhoid strikes indiscriminately the poor and the rich; all men are in some sense possessed by love; competent and incompetent share alike the hazards of war, the law's delays and penalties, the weaknesses of the flesh. We are all just human; the glaring headlights of Fate dazzle into stony helplessness both Negro and white man, and privileged and underprivileged are equal in respect of their mortality.

The point that even the best and greatest are only mortal men ("though you sit on the highest throne in the world, you sit there on your own tail"), is driven home by a device possibly borrowed from one of Cozzen's favorite authors, Jonathan Swift. It is the constant reminder that men, as well as dreaming and creating, must also feed and excrete. More people go to the bathroom oftener in Cozzens' books than in the least inhibited of contemporary novels. Like some of the early Fathers of the Church, Cozzens is fond of reminding the reader that as "a concomitant of any human assembly . . . the end-product does pile up." Colonel Ross makes the remark in answer to General Nichols' joking reference to the shortage of toilet paper at the high-level Quebec conference, at which "some very important people were tearing up newspaper. . . . Nobody knows whether it was enemy agents, or whether they just didn't realize how much it takes to keep up with a conference." The scatological note is matched by many similar allusions throughout the novels—the milk bottle which serves the paralyzed Joe Tupping in *The Last Adam*; the concern of Mr. Lecky in *Castaway* to build his fortress around the ninth-floor lavatory; the pungent urinals in the basement of Saint Ambrose's Chapel House; the constantly swinging door of the attorneys' lavatory in Childerstown courthouse.

As well as being pervasive, the allusions are sometimes pointed. Lieutenant Edsell's first brush with the authorities in *Guard of Honor* comes from his taking a leak in the bushes at a bus stop. Lieutenant Amanda Turck, who is impelled by her psychic wound to a fanatical cleanliness and to continual self-deprecation, interrupts the story of her unhappy marriage to go to the bathroom. "I manage to sound as though I wished I never needed to, don't I. I suppose that is the truth; and it's not a good sign." It certainly is not a good sign, for it is closely related to her refusal to admit the human need for sexual love—a refusal which has led to her unhappy marriage and which leads to her abortive affair with Captain Hicks. Abner Coates deflates the defense attorney who emerges from the lavatory quoting "Onward, Christian soldiers" by saying, "If you're marching as to war, you'd better button your fly, hadn't you?" The humiliation of Mrs. Pratt, badly shaken by successive encounters with a poisonous snake and an armed, angry man, is rounded out when she has to go to the bathroom, reality's "surely unkindest prank of all."

A reminder of their physical necessities may disconcert the simple-minded, but Colonel Ross provides a saving bit of common sense,

> . . . the important truism that men are men, whether public or private. A public man had a front, a face; and then,

perforce, he had a back, a backside, and in the nature of things it was so ordered that the one was associated with high professions and pronouncements and the other with that euphemistically denoted end-product. They were both always there. Which you saw best would depend on where you stood; but if you let yourself imagine that the one (no matter which) invalidated or made nugatory the other, that was the measure of your simplicity.

The imperfection of even great men is pointed up by a contrast between Churchill and Roosevelt—the one, with "brandy-soured stomach and throatful of cigar-flavored phlegm," grumpy in the knowledge of his country's declining power and prestige; the other, the cocky, confident "champion of the Four Freedoms . . . in cruel fact, not free to leave his chair; he could not do it unless somebody helped him."

Paralysis, it may be worth noting, is a recurrent image in Cozzens' novels—from the moral and psychological paralysis of the ailing Captain Clendening to the physical paralysis of Joe Tupping in *The Last Adam*, Judge Coates in *The Just and the Unjust*, and Walter Cunningham in *Ask Me Tomorrow*. Of the novelist's two most fully developed heroes, Colonel Ross is gloomily anticipating the stroke which will incapacitate if it does not actually kill him, and Julius Penrose's crippling paralysis is kept constantly in the reader's mind by the references to his canes; if he is not using them in his painful efforts to walk, he is pointing with them or sighting along them.

Julius' superficial response to the handicap of being crippled is a fierce pride, manifested in his mockingly affected speech. But, as Arthur Winner notes, the defensive pride that sustains Julius in his perpetual struggle with pain and immobility serves also to conceal from possibly pitying eyes a sincere humility which he shares with the other Cozzens heroes. This humility does not involve total surrender or blind self-abasement; it is intelligent and discriminating—an informed, realistic estimate of one's limited capacities and relatively minor place in the scheme of things. Among the pharisees, from Mrs. Banning to Mrs. Pratt, false humility goes hand in hand with a moral complacency not shared by the self-confessed sinner. May Tupping in *The Last Adam* notes "the quality of mercy, the openness to human appeal, so much readier always in sinners than in the saints," when the Clark sisters, whose frankly recounted sexual lapses have always shocked her, display an unexpected understanding and willingness for self-sacrifice when she is in trouble.

May Tupping herself, though only in the theological sense a sinner, has been taught by misfortune to forego both the moral complacency of Mrs. Banning and the helpless despair of her neighbor, Mrs. Talbot; and she has developed a truly humble heart. In the course of the debate on the best methods of ousting Doctor Bull from office, the only two men who have moral scruples against ruining the doctor's career are the two whose daughters have contracted typhoid as a result of Doctor Bull's negligence. Julius Penrose, with characteristic self-deprecation, may deny that "afflictions improve character, enlarge the understanding, or teach you charitable thoughts," but all his behavior in the novel proves the contrary. His sharp tongue and self-mocking affectation of speech serve as a cover for a kindliness which his cool intelligence preserves from becoming sentimental. There are, to be sure, equally good examples of men who are embittered, or even corrupted, by misfortune and frustration. But it remains true, on the whole, that in the world of Cozzens' novels humility is a basic virtue.

Humility, moreover, seems to be a prerequisite to another virtue, a sympathetic good will toward one's fellow man. To appreciate the absence of malice in the Cozzens characters, and in Cozzens' attitude toward them, both admirable and unadmirable, it is illuminating to contrast him with John O'Hara, a novelist who writes about the same class of people in the same kind of small eastern town. O'Hara's communities are filled with people whose motives are mean or selfish and who frequently display a wanton cruelty almost completely absent from the later Cozzens novels. In his attitude toward his characters, moreover, O'Hara is obnoxiously knowing, as though he were determined to prove that he is not taken in by any kind of pious pretension. Cozzens' characters are sometimes warped or weak, but except for the special case of the sons of perdition, they are seldom malicious. Lieutenant Colonel Carricker and Warren Winner seem almost monstrous in the Cozzens world, and the shock effect of an occasional incident like Carricker's rejection of the friendly advances of Captain Manny Solomon—the kind of cruelty that is routine in O'Hara—shows how far such malevolence departs from the Cozzens norm.

Instead of condemning people, Cozzens tries to understand them; his just discrimination of the motives for human behavior comes close to the moral realism which Lionel Trilling attributes to Henry James. Trilling compares James to a father who, loving and understanding all his children, has no need to disguise from himself their differences and faults, and whose affection for them is not altered by his perception of their imperfections. "The discriminations and modifications of such a man would be enormous, yet the moral realism they would constitute would not arise from an analytical intelligence as we usually conceive it but from love." Moral realism, making us question ourselves and the motives behind even our good impulses, is an antidote to moral indignation. "The moral passions are even more willful and imperious and impatient than the self-seeking passions," and moral realism is needed to control that "paradox of our natures [which] leads us, when once we have made our fellow men the objects of our enlightened interest, to go on to make them the objects of our pity, then of our wisdom, ultimately of our coercion."

In the sense of a discriminating love which recognizes and accepts without condemnation the flaws in imperfect man, moral realism approaches the theological conception of *agape*, which Anders Nygren distinguishes from *eros*. All forms of love directed toward the inherently desirable, beautiful, or good, from sensual infatuation to the Platonic love of the ideal, are classified as *eros*. Love as *agape* is distinguished by being "spontaneous and 'unmotivated' "; it does not look for, or depend on, worthiness in the object of love. Rather, *agape* is creative in that it gives value to things worthless in themselves; and it implies the imperfection of man, since if man were good, (*i.e.*, lovable), love for man would not be spontaneous and unmotivated. To the Christian theologian *agape* is an image of God's love for man, and it is derived from the Sermon on the Mount.

> Love your enemies, bless them that curse you . . . that ye may be the children of your Father which is in heaven: for he maketh his sun to rise on the evil and on the good, and sendeth rain on the just and on the unjust. For if ye love them which love you, what reward have ye? do not even the publicans the same?

And not only the publicans. Most of Cozzens' characters, like most men, are motivated by *eros*: they turn toward certain people or a certain way of life because it is inherently desirable. The highest morality of love as *eros* is embodied in the statement that virtue is its own reward: seeking the beautiful or the good is in itself satisfying. *Agape*, going beyond such basically selfish considerations, implies a saintliness rarely achieved. The Reverend Mr. Johnston of *Men and Brethren* comes closest to it among the Cozzens characters, and it is ironic that in his social and personal relations he should be so maladjusted and immature. Nevertheless, as Ernest Cudlipp notes, he is "altogether without guile," and

> . . . it would be possible to imagine Mr. Johnston, simply and naturally in his nervous, diffident way, performing the sublime moral feat of distinguishing between the hatred of abomination and the hatred of enmity. With purest benevo-

lence, he could probably manage to hate quietly any bad deed; yet love, as he was bound to love all his fellow men, the doer.

Mr. Johnston is a kind of saint, and accordingly he fits very poorly into the competitive world in which Ernest Cudlipp and the other Cozzens heroes struggle. He represents a moral ideal at which men may aim, but which, even though they bestow all their goods to feed the poor and give their bodies to be burned, they should not presumptuously expect by their own imperfect merits to attain.

Nevertheless, despite their common failure to achieve the highest kind of moral perfection, Cozzens' heroes usually show evidence of progress. One of the best examples is Arthur Winner. At the beginning of *By Love Possessed* he comes close to moral complacency, and those readers who have condemned him as a prig have some grounds for their dislike. In the early stages of the Detweiler case he shows, to be sure, a humane understanding of the weaknesses that have brought Ralph and Joanie Moore to their unhappy predicament: Joanie's desperate gamble for affection and security, Ralph's sexual drive diverted into the easiest channel because of his lack of initiative and discrimination. But there is no warmth of fellow feeling in Arthur Winner's attitude. Noting Ralph's acute distress under questioning, he remains detached and clinical, comprehending without being sympathetic. He feels only "a discomfort of pity"; it's like "stepping on a worm." Later, under the persistent, insidious questioning of Mrs. Pratt, Winner recognizes how Ralph, "found out, sitting in paralysis," must have felt. "The burden of pretense, when you saw pretense to be vain, was grievous. The sheer wearisomeness of a long lie weighed on you." His own long lie, carefully repressed from consciousness for six years, is being brought out in the open by an odd type of Grand Inquisitor. But although his acute discomfort and shame make him welcome any relief from his "penance of Mrs. Pratt," he feels a trace of sympathy when she is put to flight,

> . . . that same sympathy which . . . must regret all defeats of human hope—the sillier the hope, the sadder, in a sense, the dashing. The sadness was of the vain attempt, the sadness that turned irony's edge. . . . The test the true believer had just flunked was only that often-flunked test of little things—*what, could ye not watch with me one hour?* . . . To taunt Mrs. Pratt with her weakness . . . would be the bootless business of taunting her with her humanity.

This touch of fellow feeling nevertheless has about it a hint of condescension; Arthur Winner, secure though shaken in the cool privacy of his mind, feels himself to be still self-sufficient. He does not recognize his need for and dependence on other people until he is stricken by the twin blows of Helen Detweiler's suicide and the discovery of Noah Tuttle's fraud. Then, "in a stunned sense of solitariness, as though the early Sunday afternoon world around him . . . had dissolved, had withdrawn in space, leaving him on a point of rock, the last living man," he says aloud, "I am a man alone." And as if in response, the door latch clicks and Julius Penrose, "with a deliberate practiced plying of his canes," enters to comfort, advise, and aid his friend.

The conversation that follows constitutes a summary of Cozzens' moral views: the conflict between passion and reason in man's heart, the difficult necessity of adapting to the obduracy of fact, the need to compromise without completely abandoning principle, the moral imperative to try to do something with what there is. In addition Julius demonstrates that man, even though falling considerably short of saintly perfection, is capable of a disinterested love. In his comments on Helen Detweiler he shows that, like the Reverend Mr. Johnston, he can distinguish between the bad deed and the redeemable doer of the evil. He *feels* that Helen was good and virtuous, though he *thinks* that her act was bad. More important, he demonstrates that his love for a friend is not contingent on the friend's virtues. Julius has known of, and forgiven Arthur Winner for, the affair with Marjorie, and he is grateful that Arthur has tried to conceal a knowledge which would presumably hurt the crippled husband. Julius's love for his friend is not, like the Christian *agape*, completely spontaneous and unmotivated; Arthur Winner has many good qualities to elicit *eros*, and Julius is no saint. But his feeling goes far beyond ordinary friendship: he loves his friend, not in spite of his faults, but *with* his faults.

Unsmiling, compassionate still, still steady, Julius's gaze, the speaking clear dark eyes, rested on him, as though without use of words to say: Yes, I know that you have been afraid I would find out. But you had nothing to fear. Don't you see, I've known all along. Our pact is: As I am, you accept me; as you are, I accept you.

The effect on Arthur Winner is a surge of joy, "shame's sudden remission, a breathing-deep of the amazed, enlightened heart." This final step in his moral education strengthens him to bear his new burden of duplicity, and Julius channels this fresh source of energy by asking Arthur's aid in the immediate business before them: ordering Noah Tuttle's tangled accounts.

Arthur Winner is not alone in receiving a lesson in love. The heroes of the other novels are shown taking steps in a progress toward greater sympathy for their imperfect fellow men. Ernest Cudlipp, who had originally regarded the ministry as an opportunity for self-expression, arrives in *Men and Brethren* at a relatively selfless dedication to his calling. Abner Coates, at first a little complacent in the consciousness of his virtue, takes a step toward the commitment and involvement in the lives of others required of an adult. Francis Ellery of *Ask Me Tomorrow* moves from the hypersensitive pride of the young and talented toward the discriminations of moral realism. In *Guard of Honor* Nathaniel Hicks discovers, among other things, the vulnerability of the morally complacent, and General Beal's boyish notions of loyalty are tested by actual problems and strengthened by the example of Colonel Ross's disinterested good will.

Moreover, the novels in chronological order show a parallel growth of moral warmth and depth in the author. The clinical tone of the early novels reflects an ironic detachment similar to the troubled aloofness of Francis Ellery. In the course of thirty years Cozzens' objectivity, though it remains unsentimentally, realistically alert to men's differences and failings, has been sweetened by the compassion for imperfect man which is the message and the mark of all great literature. Albert Camus, in his acceptance of the Nobel prize, speaks of the necessity for a writer to recapture "the feeling of a living community which will justify him." His words describe the course of Cozzens' literary career.

To me art is not a solitary delight. It is a means of stirring the greatest number of men by providing them with a privileged image of our common joys and woes. Hence it forces the artist not to isolate himself; it subjects him to the humblest and most universal truth. And the man who, as often happens, chose the path of art because he was aware of his difference soon learns that he can nourish his art, and his difference, solely by admitting his resemblance to all.

NOTES

The following abbreviations are used for the novels of James Gould Cozzens:

AMT	*Ask Me Tomorrow*
BLP	*By Love Possessed*
Cast	*Castaway*
Conf	*Confusion*
CP	*Cock Pit*
GofH	*Guard of Honor*
J&U	*The Just and the Unjust*
LA	*The Last Adam*
M&B	*Men and Brethren*
MS	*Michael Scarlett*
SofP	*The Son of Perdition*
SSSP	*S.S. San Pedro*

References to quotations and works mentioned in the text are given below after page numbers in the book.

CHAPTER I *The Novelist*

PAGE 6 Irving Howe, *Politics and the Novel*, New York, 1957, pp. 20, 19; John Lydenberg, *Critique*, Winter, 1958, p. 6.

7 BLP, 353.

8 BLP, 395.

PAGE 9 Eric McKittrick, *The American Scholar*, Winter, 1957-58, p. 53; Francis Fergusson, *Perspectives USA*, Winter, 1954, p. 36; Richard Chase, *The American Novel and Its Tradition*, New York: Doubleday Anchor Books, 1957, pp. 4, 2.

10 Stephen Spender, *New York Times Book Review*, July 20, 1958, p. 12; BLP, 565, 545.

11 M&B, 12; BLP, 547; *The Art of the Novel, Critical Prefaces by Henry James*, New York, 1934, p. 12.

12 Harvey Breit, Introduction to *Absalom, Absalom*, Modern Library, 1951, pp. x, xi; Richard Ellmann, *The Reporter*, October 3, 1957, p. 44.

13 GofH, 21; J&U, 140; Lionel Trilling, *The Liberal Imagination*, New York, 1950, p. 87.

14 E. H. Cady, *The Gentleman in America*, Syracuse, New York, 1949; Aristotle, *The Nichomachean Ethics*, trans. R. W. Browne, London, 1914, IV, 3.

15 J&U, 433.

16 *The Selected Letters of John Keats*, ed. Lionel Trilling, New York, 1951, p. 92.

17 BLP, 3; Stanley Edgar Hyman, *New Mexico Quarterly*, Winter, 1949, p. 487, 497; Richard M. Ludwig, *Princeton University Library Chronicle*, Autumn, 1957, p. 4.

18 Ludwig, p. 5; Conf, 95.

19 BLP, 368; David R. Weimer, *Critique*, Winter, 1958, p. 36.

CHAPTER II *The Early Novels*

PAGE 24 Zechariah Chaffee, Jr., *The Harvard Law Review*, March, 1943.

26 Ludwig, 10.

27 Conf, 55.

32 CP, 82.

33 SofP, 226, 194, 230.

34 SofP, 235.

PAGE 36 *The Saturday Evening Post*, February 15, 1936.
37 LA, 301.
39 Cast, 10.
40 Cast, 178.
41 Cast, 181, 178.
42 Cast, 117.
45 Cast, 141.

CHAPTER III *Style and Structure*

PAGE 49 Malcolm Cowley, *New York Times Book Review*, August 25, 1957, p. 1.
50 Dwight Macdonald, *Commentary*, January, 1958, p. 36, 42; BLP, 461.
52 BLP, 503; M&B, 43f.
53 "The Bear," *Go Down, Moses*, New York, 1942, p. 194.
54 S. H. Butcher, *Aristotle's Theory of Poetry and Fine Art*, New York, 1951, *Poetics*, XXII, 1.
55 GofH, 532; M&B, 44.
56 BLP, 397.
57 BLP, 201.
58 GofH, 601, 171, 600, 171; BLP, 563.
59 BLP, 227; Ludwig, 9.
61 AMT, 180; BLP, 564, 547, 338-39, 250, 401.
62 BLP, 410, 4, 366.
64 *King Henry VI, Part III*, Act II, v; *Coriolanus*, I, iv; *The Tempest*, IV, i; BLP, 117.
65 *Julius Caesar*, IV, iii.
66 Joseph Warren Beach, *The Twentieth Century Novel*, New York, 1932, p. 182.
67 Ludwig, 6-7.
68 GofH, 334, 599; AMT, 181; Howe, *The New Republic*, January 20, 1958, p. 16.
70 Mark Schorer, *New York Herald Tribune Book Review*, October 10, 1948, p. 4.
74 GofH, 415, 484.

PAGE 75 GofH, 503, 598, 630.
76 GofH, 630, 631.

CHAPTER IV *Techniques*

PAGE 79 Ian Watt, *The Rise of the Novel*, Berkeley, 1957, p. 21; *Poetics*, VI, 15; XXIV, 4; VII, 2; X, 3.
80 LA, 144; BLP, 13, 288.
81 BLP, 118.
83 Beach, 148.
84 LA, 26; SSSP, 100; BLP, 509; SSSP, 136; BLP, 119.
85 BLP, 119, 506, 366; AMT, 127.
86 AMT, 131; BLP, 516.
87 GofH, 547f.
88 GofH, 594; BLP, 204.
89 Hyman, 493; M&B, 22; AMT, 29, 188; J&U, 247.
90 BLP, 368; M&B, 176f., 15, 172.
92 Ludwig, 5.
93 LA, 39, 77.
94 Ludwig, Plate I, facing p. 8; AMT, 148, 149, 148.
95 LA, 34; J&U, 98; GofH, 318.
96 BLP, 495; SofP, 120; BLP, 9, 570.
97 Schorer, 4.
98 SSSP, 24, 9, 5.
99 SSSP, 127; Acts 9:1; M&B, 258f.
100 BLP, 55.
102 LA, 235; BLP, 493, 495.
103 BLP, 493; Ludwig, 7; AMT, 91; BLP, 439, 445.
104 GofH, 491, 258, 261; BLP, 66.
105 GofH, 494, 495, 497; BLP, 380, 382.
107 BLP, 506, 503, 507.
108 BLP, 526.
111 *The Saturday Evening Post*, August 15, 1936.
112 LA, 156; GofH, 442.
113 GofH, 93; BLP, 397, 416, 397.
114 BLP, 415, 386, 416, 420, 419, 414.
115 Ludwig, 7.

CHAPTER V *The Range of Human Differences*

PAGE 120 John W. Ward, *The American Scholar*, Winter, 1957-1958, p. 99.
122 Bacon, "Of Youth and Age."
123 BLP, 6; CP, 21; AMT, 202.
124 M&B, 83, 9, 84, 141; BLP, 156; M&B, 108.
125 AMT, 204, 235, 114.
126 GofH, 397, 396.
127 J&U, 239; GofH, 95; J&U, 365.
128 J&U, 327, 360, 404.
129 (Appearance: CP, 15; M&B, 55; AMT, 30, 157; GofH, 55; BLP, 124, 291, 422.) J&U, 180, 350, 423; M&B, 170.
130 M&B, 249; BLP, 230; LA, 74.
131 GofH, 235, 284, 274, 167.
133 *The Saturday Evening Post*, May 23, 1936; December 26, 1931; GofH, 54-56.
134 LA, 38, 32; AMT, 284; GofH, 174.
135 GofH, 174, 454, 215; AMT, 22, 23.
136 AMT, 21; BLP, 233; M&B, 40; BLP, 492.
137 BLP, 130; AMT, 31; BLP, 487, 372; AMT, 21.
138 BLP, 293; M&B, 80; J&U, 268.
139 M&B, 58; GofH, 42.
140 GofH, 54f.; AMT, 331, 332.
141 *Collier's*, March 3, 1934; AMT, 256, 306; M&B, 234; GofH, 607.
142 BLP, 286; GofH, 598.
143 BLP, 334.
145 J&U, 156, 163; BLP, 518; J&U, 162; GofH, 147.
146 M&B, 55.
147 J&U, 74.
148 J&U, 75.
149 M&B, 193, 275; M&B, 182.
150 M&B, 182f., 92, 93.
151 J&U, 164; LA, 74, 216.
152 LA, 74; *The Saturday Evening Post*, May 23, 1936.

PAGE 153 LA, 261; M&B, 192.
154 M&B, 191; J&U, 295; BLP, 168; AMT, 158.
155 LA, 118; BLP, 466, 422, 424.
156 BLP, 422, 66.
157 BLP, 68; M&B, 268; BLP, 111.
158 BLP, 64; M&B, 68, 199, 24.
159 BLP, 226; J&U, 131.
160 Gunnar Myrdal, *An American Dilemma*, New York, 1944, I, xliii.
161 Myrdal, I, xliv; I, 97; GofH, 122, 129.
162 J&U, 37; GofH, 98.
163 GofH, 70; SSSP, 82, 83.
164 *New York Times*, November 15, 1928; May 30, 1929; July 6, 1929.
165 BLP, 360; GofH, 415; Myrdal, I, xlvii.
166 GofH, 345, 251.
167 GofH, 311; BLP, 68; GofH, 327; BLP, 202.
168 BLP, 201, 517, 518; GofH, 33.
169 GofH, 166, 233.
170 GofH, 233, 434, 440.
171 GofH, 440; Warren: *Segregation, The Inner Conflict in the South*, New York, 1956.

CHAPTER VI *"Men and Brethren, What Shall We Do?"*

PAGE 175 Ludwig, 10.
176 BLP, 351, 350, 351.
177 BLP, 519; SofP, 166; CP, 59.
178 BLP, 233, 228.
179 Ludwig, 10; BLP, 231, 232; J&U, 109; BLP, 347; M&B, 197.
180 BLP, 229, 228, 229.
181 BLP, 388; M&B, 73; Conf, 241; "Judas Iscariot," *The Collected Writings of Thomas De Quincey*, London, 1890, VIII, 177-206.
182 M&B, 45.

PAGE 183 John Calvin, *Institutes of the Christian Religion*, III, 10, 5; III, 10, 16; III, 10, 6; Max Weber, *The Protestant Ethic and the Spirit of Capitalism*, New York, 1930, p. 115; GofH, 120.

184 M&B, 237; George Garrett, *Critique*, Winter, 1958, p. 42; Howe, 16; *Institutes*, III, 10, 5; BLP, 352.

185 M&B, 55, 282.

186 Acts 2: 36-37.

187 M&B, 210.

188 M&B, 28, 236.

189 M&B, 259, 240.

190 M&B, 240, 259.

191 M&B, 261, 262.

192 *Doctrine in the Church of England: The Report of the Commission on Christian Doctrine Appointed by the Archbishops of Canterbury and York in 1922*, London, 1938, p. 47.

193 M&B, 280, 244.

194 LA, 300; GofH, 525.

195 GofH, 535, 536; BLP, 118.

196 BLP, 120; LA, 11; GofH, 398.

197 GofH, 399; MS, 26; LA, 249.

198 M&B, 57; "Articles of Religion," *The Book of Common Prayer*, Article 17.

199 *Doctrine*, 221.

200 M&B, 139, 140.

201 SofP, 284, 193, 144, 304; *Paradise Lost*, I, 70-72; John 17:12.

202 Conf, 257; SofP, 303; *The Saturday Evening Post*, January 16, 1937.

203 BLP, 321.

204 BLP, 330, 331.

205 BLP, 338; M&B, 175, 249.

206 M&B, 250.

CHAPTER VII *Self-Division's Cause*

PAGE 209 M&B, 263, 10, 89, 266, 8.
210 M&B, 257, 272; *Doctrine*, 224.
211 M&B, 210; *Doctrine*, 42.
212 Julius misquotes from "Chorus Sacerdotum," *Mustapha*, ed. G. Bullough, London, 1939, II, 136; M&B, 250; GofH, 51.
213 BLP, 203, 66, 204.
214 J&U, 97; AMT, 297.
216 LA, 194, 138, 235; AMT, 74, 75.
217 AMT, 297, 230, 231.
218 AMT, 230; BLP, 386; LA, 301; BLP, 236; GofH, 216, 300.
219 GofH, 566; BLP, 174.
220 BLP, 446, 445, 555, 376.
221 GofH, 534; M&B, 36.
222 M&B, 34, 35, 59.
223 GofH, 134, 360, 282.
224 GofH, 282, 263, 264, 360, 362.
225 GofH, 362, 363; M&B, 65.
226 AMT, 115; GofH, 68; M&B, 220.
227 GofH, 67, 501
228 LA, 23; BLP, 419, 557.
229 BLP, 358, 369.
230 SSSP, 6; BLP, 114.
231 J&U, 424; *The Saturday Evening Post*, December 26, 1931.
232 GofH, 533; SSSP, 30.
233 SSSP, 31; GofH, 534, 198, 122; BLP, 9, 403.
234 GofH, 285; LA, 16; GofH, 573.
235 Whitney J. Oates, *The Stoic and Epicurean Philosophers*, New York, 1940, p. xxiv.
236 BLP, 519.
237 BLP, 140.
238 J&U, 109; BLP, 190, 40.
239 LA, 202, 71; AMT, 203, 205, 273.

PAGE 240 AMT, 321; Conf, 96; SSSP, 98.
241 GofH, 396, 534; BLP, 556, 557.

CHAPTER VIII *The Imperfectibility of Man*

PAGE 245 Conf, 92, 93; M&B, 250.
246 GofH, 532.
247 Reinhold Niebuhr, *An Interpretation of Christian Ethics*, New York, 1935, p. 16, 15, 19, 69, 103, 104.
248 *Time*, September 2, 1957, p. 74; J&U, 434; Niebuhr, 66f.; J&U, 434.
249 BLP, 556; Niebuhr, 8, 9.
250 J&U, 428, 427.
251 BLP, 566; 569; Niebuhr, 194; J&U, 67.
252 Niebuhr, 194f., 197; J&U, 242.
253 J&U, 242, 243, 299.
254 BLP, 446, 192, 193, 346, 6.
255 GofH, 67.
256 GofH, 415, 51, 396, 395.
257 GofH, 395; M&B, 93.
258 M&B, 17, 230.
259 M&B, 230.
260 BLP, 478.
261 BLP, 472.
262 BLP, 473, 482.
263 Luke 18:11.
264 GofH, 179, 305, 491.
266 GofH, 535.
267 J&U, 140, 190, 359.
268 J&U, 242, 193, 433.
269 J&U, 281.
270 *Harvard Law Review*, May, 1958, pp. 1377-1381; BLP, 490.
271 GofH, 394, 390.
272 GofH, 602; J&U, 307; BLP, 428; GofH, 393.
273 GofH, 394.
274 LA, 231; BLP, 214.

PAGE 276 Lionel Trilling, *The Liberal Imagination*, New York, 1950, p. 88, 221; Anders Nygren, *Agape and Eros*, London, 1953, p. 75.

277 Matthew 5:44-46; M&B, 166, 192.

278 BLP, 165, 400.

279 BLP, 400, 415, 427, 542.

280 BLP, 543, 563.

282 Albert Camus, *The Atlantic Monthly*, May, 1958, p. 33.

SELECTED BIBLIOGRAPHY

Novels

Confusion, Boston, B. J. Brimmer Co., 1924
Michael Scarlett, New York, Albert & Charles Boni, 1925
Cock Pit, New York, William Morrow & Co., 1928
The Son of Perdition, New York, William Morrow & Company, 1929
S.S. San Pedro, New York, Harcourt, Brace and Company, 1931
First printed in *Scribner's Magazine*, August, 1930
The Last Adam, New York, Harcourt, Brace and Company, 1933
Castaway, New York, Random House, 1934
Men and Brethren, New York, Harcourt, Brace and Company, 1936
Ask Me Tomorrow, New York, Harcourt, Brace and Company, 1940
The Just and the Unjust, New York, Harcourt, Brace and Company, 1943
Guard of Honor, New York, Harcourt, Brace and Company, 1948
By Love Possessed, New York, Harcourt, Brace and Company, 1957

Selected Reviews of the Cozzens Novels

CONFUSION

(Anon.,) *New York Times Book Review*, April 27, 1924, p. 14

Carter, John, *New York Evening Post Literary Review*, May 10, 1924, p. 739

MICHAEL SCARLETT

(Anon.,) *New York Times Book Review*, November 15, 1925, p. 8

COCK PIT

(Anon.,) *New York Times Book Review*, October 7, 1928, pp. 28, 31

THE SON OF PERDITION

McFee, William, *New York Herald Tribune Books*, September 1, 1929, p. 2

Poore, C. G., *New York Times Book Review*, October 6, 1929, p. 7

S. S. SAN PEDRO

McFee, William, *The Saturday Review of Literature*, September 12, 1931, pp. 117, 118

Southron, Jane Spence, *New York Times Book Review*, September 6, 1931, p. 7

Warner, Arthur, *New York Herald Tribune Books*, August 30, 1931, p. 12

THE LAST ADAM

Chamberlain, John, *New York Times Book Review*, January 8, 1933, pp. 6, 14

Paterson, Isabel, *New York Herald Tribune Books*, January 8, 1933, p. 6

CASTAWAY

Benét, William Rose, *The Saturday Review of Literature*, November 17, 1934, pp. 285, 289

Tilden, David C., *New York Herald Tribune Books*, December 16, 1934, pp. 15, 16

MEN AND BRETHREN

Blackmur, R. P., *The Southern Review*, Spring, 1936, pp. 895-897

Connolly, Cyril, *New Statesman and Nation*, March 14, 1936, p. 421

Davis, Elmer, *The Saturday Review of Literature*, January 4, 1936, p. 5

Hurley, Albert S., *Christian Century*, February 5, 1936, p. 228

Kingsland, Dorothea, *New York Times Book Review*, January 19, 1936, p. 6

Kronenberger, Louis, *The Nation*, January 15, 1936, p. 79

Schorer, Mark, *The New Republic*, January 15, 1936, p. 289

ASK ME TOMORROW

Daniels, Jonathan, *The Saturday Review of Literature*, June 29, 1940, p. 11

Feld, Rose, *New York Herald Tribune Books*, June 16, 1940, p. 2

Hawkins, Desmond, *New Statesman and Nation*, November 2, 1940, p. 450

THE JUST AND THE UNJUST

Chafee, Zechariah, Jr., *Harvard Law Review*, March, 1943, pp. 838-836

Gorman, Herbert, *New York Times Book Review*, July 26, 1942, pp. 1, 18

Hays, Arthur Garfield, *The New Republic*, August 17, 1942, p. 205

Hergesheimer, Joseph, *The Saturday Review of Literature*, July 25, 1942, p. 5

Sylvester, Harry, *The Commonweal*, July 31, 1942, pp. 354-355

GUARD OF HONOR

Gill, Brendan, *The New Yorker*, October 9, 1948, pp. 126-128

Schorer, Mark, *New York Herald Tribune Book Review*, October 10, 1948, p. 4

Woodburn, John, *The Saturday Review of Literature*, October 2, 1948, pp. 15, 16

BY LOVE POSSESSED

De Mott, Benjamin, *The Hudson Review*, Winter, 1957-58, pp. 622-626

Cowley, Malcolm, *New York Times Book Review*, August 25, 1957, pp. 1, 18

Gill, Brendan, *The New Yorker*, August 24, 1957, pp. 106-109

Harding, D. W., *The Spectator* (London), April 18, 1958, p. 491

Hicks, Granville, *New Leader*, September 2, 1957, pp. 17, 18

Nemerov, Howard, *The Nation*, November 2, 1957, pp. 306-308

Stern, Richard G., *Kenyon Review*, Winter, 1958, pp. 140-144

West, Jessamyn, *New York Herald Tribune Book Review*, August 25, 1957, p. 1

Selected Critical Articles (in chronological order)

Van Gelder, Robert, "James Gould Cozzens at Work," *New York Times Book Review*, June 23, 1940, p. 14

Hyman, Stanley Edgar, "James Gould Cozzens and the Art of the Possible," *New Mexico Quarterly*, Winter, 1949, pp. 476-498

DeVoto, Bernard, "The Easy Chair," *Harper's Magazine*, February, 1949, pp. 72-73

Hicks, Granville, "The Reputation of James Gould Cozzens," *College English*, January, 1950, pp. 177-183

Bracher, Frederick, "Of Youth and Age: James Gould Cozzens," *The Pacific Spectator*, Winter, 1951, pp. 48-62

Fergusson, Francis, "Three Novels," *Perspectives USA*, Winter, 1954, pp. 35-39

Coxe, Louis O., "The Complex World of James Gould Cozzens," *American Literature*, May, 1955, pp. 157-171

Eisinger, Chester E., "The American War Novel: An Affirming Flame," *The Pacific Spectator*, Summer, 1955, pp. 281-285

Fischer, John, "The Editor's Easy Chair: Nomination for a Nobel Prize," *Harper's Magazine*, September, 1957, pp. 14-15, 18, 20

Ellmann, Richard, "The American Aristocracy of James Gould Cozzens," *The Reporter*, October 3, 1957, pp. 42-44

Ludwig, Richard M., "A Reading of the James Gould Cozzens Manuscripts," *Princeton University Library Chronicle*, Autumn, 1957, pp. 1-14

Lydenberg, John, "Cozzens and the Critics," *College English*, December, 1957, pp. 99-104

Ward, John W., "James Gould Cozzens and the Condition of Modern Man," *The American Scholar*, Winter, 1957-58, pp. 92-99

Macdonald, Dwight, "By Cozzens Possessed," *Commentary*, January, 1958, pp. 36-47

Howe, Irving, "James Gould Cozzens: Novelist of the Republic," *The New Republic*, January 20, 1958, pp. 15-19

Watts, Harold H., "James Gould Cozzens and the Genteel Tradition," *Colorado Quarterly*, Winter, 1958, pp. 257-273

Bracher, Frederick, "James Gould Cozzens: Humanist," *Critique*, Winter, 1958, pp. 10-29

Garrett, George, "*By Love Possessed:* The Pattern and the Hero," *Critique*, Winter, 1958, pp. 41-48

Lydenberg, John, "Cozzens and the Conservatives," *Critique*, Winter, 1958, pp. 3-9

Weimer, David R., "The Breath of Chaos in *The Just and the Unjust*," *Critique*, Winter, 1958, pp. 30-40

Frederick, John T., "Love by Adverse Possession: The Case of Mr. Cozzens," *College English*, April, 1958, pp. 313-316

Bibliography

Meriwether, James B., "A James Gould Cozzens Check List," *Critique*, Winter, 1958, pp. 57-63

INDEX